Prodigious Son

A Memoir of Miracles

Ralph "Corky" Matson

Registration No. TXU-2-097-527

ISBN 978-1-09830-887-2 (print)
ISBN 978-1-09830-888-9 (eBook)

With deepest appreciation and gratitude,
I dedicate this book to my saintly mother, Mary Matson,
and to the soul mates, whose unconditional love and support
has sustained me from the very beginning, to this moment.

Table of Contents

Introduction

THIS IS AN INTRODUCTION to explain why at 71 years old, I am prompted, even compelled, certainly pushed, from inside and out, to record some of the events of my life. In certain ways, on the surface, my life has just been an ordinary life. I was born into very ordinary circumstances; I was raised very ordinarily, and in many ways, I lived a very ordinary life. But interspersed in my ordinariness, I also have lived many great adventures, experiences, highs and lows, joys, and tragedies. I've truly swum from the depths to the heights. I've spent a good portion of my adult life in exploring and trying to understand human beings, nature, the outer world, the world of manifestation. I've also spent a great amount of my life's hours on this planet, exploring the inner realms of my consciousness. In certain ways, I would describe myself as an avid inner-space explorer and an interested, although more random, outer-space explorer. I feel that in the content of this book, there may be for some readers, moments of understanding. Not just for understanding what I've experienced in my life, but understanding bits, or pieces of their own lives, their own puzzles. There may be for some readers, a reflection, a mirror, so to speak, of some of the human conditions or situations that I found myself in that the reader may have found themselves in. Perhaps the reader may glean some greater insight or greater understanding into not just what I experienced or they experienced, but part of the human condition and sometimes the human plight of all of the billions of us on this planet. I believe that since my early adulthood a crucially important of my life from that time on was engaged in an attempt to know myself and to understand what made me tick, what made me think, what made me act, what made me respond to life the way I did. In my early adulthood, like many, I was very lost, very confused, out in the world on my own, not very well prepared. Perhaps very well prepared for survival, but not to live life, enjoy life, to experience the potential bounty and joys of life. In my early adulthood, I felt very vacant and very aware that, throughout all that had happened in my early childhood, my formative years, my school years, and my early years out into the world on my own, there was so much missing. There was so much that hadn't been shown to me or taught to me, or hadn't made itself clear from the depths of my own consciousness, nor from any source in the outer world.

To the reader, I would only say this: though each and every person walking this planet could say, "I could do the same thing," it seems incumbent on me, that at this time in my life I am not to just think that all of my life is worth sharing with the world, but instead I believe that for some people, somewhere, in some way, there may be some gift, some ray of hope, some ray of light in this work. There may be some solution to a mystery; there may be some moment of understanding, where prior to that moment, there was only confusion or quandary. So I will share my life, my experiences, my observations, my perceptions. I'm going to do this in a different format than most people would share their lives. From the time I was able to read, I became a very avid, almost obsessive, reader of biographies. In second grade, in my school library, the librarian put a book in my hand and said, "You might like to read this. It's the story of a great man. His name is Abraham Lincoln. Read this book." Even though I understood few of the words, or what was the inner meaning of the biography, I was amazed to be involved in another person's life in that manner. So now, I am in a position where I am going to write an autobiography. And I've chosen a different way of presenting it. After years of pondering, "Where would I start?" I had a dream, about 4 years ago, and in the dream, I was clearly told, "Tell your life story from the beginning by decades." So I'm going to, in the first chapter, tell what happened, not from the birth of this man, in 1943, but I'm actually going to start with my knowledge of the conception between my mother and father, because that's where this story actually starts.

I want to make it clear to the reader that regardless of how I've presented the introduction to this point, it is not my intention, nor my need, in any way, shape, or form, to convince anyone of the veracity or the truth or the perfection of the stories and events that I am going to lay forward. Though I intend from the depths of my heart to present only the truth, I can only present my perception of what I believe to be factual reality in all of the events that I will bring about. I have no need to convince anyone or change anyone's beliefs in relation especially to what might look like other-worldly events or spiritual experiences

This is the beginning of the story of Ralph "Corky" Matson. Delivered by him with the clearest memory, focus, and intent.

'40s

The "Corker"

I'LL START WITH THE VERY BEGINNING, 1943—MY BIRTHING. Before I give any of the very interesting stories of my birthing, I'd like to tell the readers what actually led up to the events of the day of my birth. It all started when my mother and father got married in their late 20s.

My mother and father were both 18 or 19 years old, living in Chicago, and very much in love. My mother became pregnant immediately and had 2 daughters. My father didn't like that in any way, shape, or form. He had told my mother that he would like a son, first of all. After my twin sisters were born, my father again emphasized to my mother, very powerfully, he expected a son on her next pregnancy. A few years later, she became pregnant and gave him a third daughter, much to his consternation. Again after the third daughter he said, "You better get it clear, I want a son."

So my mother became pregnant again and gave him his 4th daughter. My mother later gave me the details of how upset he was at each of these births. He had been present at all of them, waiting for the arrival of his son and been gravely disappointed each time. At the birth of his 4th daughter, he apparently went into some sort of a rage and told my mother, "I'm not interested in a son anymore. I don't want anything to do with anymore of your pregnancies. I refuse to get involved with anymore children we might make."

Not too long after that, she informed him, "Ralph, I'm pregnant again, and I think this time it'll be a boy!"

My father said, "I don't care what it is. I want nothing to do with it. I've already washed my hands."

That brings us to March 10, 1943, the day I was born. At this point I had been in my mother's womb for 10 months. She described herself to me as being absolutely gigantic. She lived in a 4th-floor tenement walk-up at the time, and after the 9th month, the doctor informed her that there was no way she could go down the stairs in the condition that she was in. He told her that the birth was to be done at home, and he would send an intern and a midwife when the baby decided to come.

On that day, my father left the house and went on a very long, extended drunk. My mother welcomed the intern and the midwife, both men. And it is this point in the story that we can explain where the name "Corky" comes from.

My mother had my aunt with her and nobody else. The midwife was an amateur magician. He told my mother and my aunt, "Until this baby comes out, I'll show you my magic tricks." He did one after another after another. He amazed them with great tricks. He reached down into his bag and said, "This is the last one I have left. I call it my 'Corker.'" At that moment, I interrupted the trick and shot out of my mother.

At the birthing time, my mother's bed was old and squishy and beat up. The intern said, "There's no way we can deliver this child on this bed." So they found an ironing board and laid my mother down on an ironing board. One of the things I can claim is that I'm the only person I've ever known in my life that was born on an ironing board.

When I came out, I came out very quickly, and when the doctor was filling out the birth certificate, he asked my mother, "What will you call this boy?"

She said, "Ralph Vincent Matson Jr."

He said, "Will you call him Jr.?"

"No."

"Will you call him Ralphie?"

My aunt said, "Noo."

"Well, what are you going to call him then?"

"We'll call him Corky," said my aunt, "since he interrupted your Corker."

So essentially, I've been Corky from the very time of birth.

The next day, my father came home. My mother said proudly and happily, "Ralph, I finally got you a boy!"

He was still drunk and hungover and said, "I don't care what you got me. I don't want anything to do with him."

That was the beginning of what was, for my father and me, a very, very hard relationship. He essentially ignored me while I was growing up. He literally would pay no attention to me whatsoever, and to my 4 sisters, he would give small amounts of attention. But he would never address me, talk to me, or touch me. I don't recall him touching me until I was 3 years old and he had to get out a plum seed that was lodged in my throat.

But my father was a product of his past also. He was born to a man that was reputed to be a very domineering, insensitive, unloving father. When my dad was 13, my father's father actually sold my dad to a mining group that was passing through Kansas. My grandfather sold my father to these men, who took him in a truck up to far northern Canada and made him the camp slave for 5 years. My dad was seduced and abandoned in the worst way. At 18, he snapped and went on a violent rampage. My mother gave me the details, as he had given them to her. He tore through the camp and, in his words, "rendered unconscious every last man in the camp." For 6 or 8 hours, he sought out men and beat them until they were completely unconscious—16 or 18 men.

He then left the camp and walked from far northern Canada to the American border, where he jumped on a freight train that dropped him off at the stockyards, with all the cows in Chicago. A few months later he met my mother, fell in love, and they made babies.

So my dad, in the way he treated me, wasn't cruel in the regard that he was overtly mean to me. He was noncommunicative. He wasn't a mean father; he was no father. We never had a conversation until I was 15 years old. That was the first time that we ever exchanged more than a few words with each other. My mom, meanwhile, protected me from his anger. Basically, it's not an exaggeration to say that my father hated me before I was even born; he hated me after I was born, and almost to his last day that was our relationship. He hated me, and I, as much as possible, hid from his hatred.

I made myself invisible as a young boy. I figured out staying out of his way was the best thing for me, so I did that. But he never went out of his way to hurt me or to do anything mean to me. There was the incident when I was 3 years old and was choking on a plum seed, my sisters went into the house and woke him up. He came out of the house, very angry, yelling at them for waking him up. He saw me in the backyard, lying on the ground. My sister was yelling, "Daddy, he's turned purple, he's purple!!!" My father picked me up by the wrist, held me up as high as he could above his head, and smashed me in the middle of my back with his fist with such force that this plum seed shot out of my mouth and traveled probably 50 or 60 feet where it hit a metal garage door with a loud clanking sound. That is the first, maybe second, time that I remember my father touching me.

On the other hand, my mother protected me. My mother gave me all the love that I needed to maintain sanity. He never gave me anything. She made up for it all. My mother ended up having 7 kids: 5 girls, myself, and my kid brother Mike. Basically, my mother lived a life of trying to be mother and father for 7 kids. That was the beginning of my growing up.

At 5 years old I had had a period of about 2 years that were sort of idyllic for me. My mother was not yet working, all my sisters were in grade school, and my younger brother and sister weren't born yet. And I had days, five days/week where it would just be my mother and I all day long. Those were, in my memory, the only happy, fulfilling times of my entire childhood. Those days my mother would be baking and cooking, and I'd just hang out with her in the kitchen. All of that came to an end when I was 5 years old, when the most dreaded thing in my early childhood came to pass. And that was my sisters haranguing me and saying, "You're not going to stay home with mom much longer. You're going to have to go to school too." And it burst a giant bubble of happiness that I once had. And school for me was no fun—ever. From 5 years old, until the day I quit school at 16, school was nothing to me but a misery and drudgery. But I made my marks, I did what I had to do, and I survived my school era.

Tough Times

STARTING IN GRADE SCHOOL, I really looked up to my sisters as leaders. I didn't get any of that from my father, and my mother was essentially busy taking care of everybody. But some of my sisters were not real nice kids. The best way I can remember it is that it seemed like meanness was absorbed by my sisters from my father. My father was an extremely cold, tough, bitter, mean, angry man. My sisters started absorbing that when I was a little boy. And I could see it grow. I don't believe any of my 5 sisters had any kind of real love for my father. I don't think he ever loved any of his 7 kids at any point for any reason. But my sisters started really showing a lot of potential cruelty and meanness, from the time I was 2, 3, 4, and 5 years old. But it played out more and more as they got older. My sisters were known in the grade school that we went to, as a group of wild, tough kids that no one tangled with. No boy in my entire school would dare mess with my sisters. They got real, real tough by my early teens.

9

So it manifested in my life that anger and bitterness and actual mean-spirited behavior among us kids grew. I got a good portion of it because I was on the bottom of the totem pole. I can't say that my sisters ever wanted to be the people that they were turning out to be. They were in a trap. Meanness begat more meanness, and cruelty begat more cruelty. I saw my sisters fight among themselves at times with bitter savagery. Even to the point of taking butcher knives and slicing at each other. My sisters, most of them, had a penchant for cruelty to nature. They seemed to vent a lot of their bitterness to creatures of nature and animals. I especially remember all the terrible things they taught me to do to all growing things. How to destroy flowers, how to destroy caterpillars that were in their cocoons, and more and more things that I don't care to go into at this point.

But it was a very, very sad scenario along with the poverty and the hardship. Along with the sickness and disease that all the kids had. There were no doctors; we didn't have a toothbrush in the house until I was 10 or 12 years old and one of my sisters had bought herself a toothbrush. We were neglected and deprived, but the stability of our world was always with my mother. My mother always knew how to do the right thing at the right time. She knew how to lift everybody and protect everybody. She was truly an amazing woman who had been dealt a terrible, terrible hand of cards. She told me when I was a little boy, "I only have one hope in the world, and that's for all 7 of my children to grow up and be good people." And in actuality, that's about how it turned out. By the time each one of us hit adulthood, we maintained, or found, some level of sanity. We never were a tight-knit group. We weren't touchy-feely; we didn't talk "love" talk. But under my mother's continuous powerful influence, we survived and were essentially good human beings.

In our youth, neither I, nor any of my siblings, were ever involved with any trouble with the law. We never broke serious laws; we never violated decent moral behavior. Essentially, we all landed on 2 feet, even though the making of all of our childhoods could have turned out crazies, psychopaths, schizophrenics—only my mother's powerful love kept everybody sane. Especially through the late years of the '40s.

One of the things that my early childhood presented to my siblings and I that was very hard to accept was the creatures that lived in our lives. For instance, the 5 kids in my family (my little brother and sister not born yet) would perpetually get head lice—bugs—in our hair. We'd get them from other poor kids. At that time, for a whole class to have head lice was not unusual. The school would regularly give a date and require that all parents treat their kids' hair on the same day with a product named Bornate, sold in Walgreens. Bornate is a very violent poison, which kills all the head lice when the head is soaked in it.

So this was a very regular occurrence. Head lice could become extremely dangerous to a highly infested head. One sister in particular would have the lice dig into her skull. There would be big holes, the size of a quarter, and there would be red open flesh, and the lice would dig in. The lice fed on blood, just like mosquitoes.

So we grew up with head lice. Bedbugs too. A bedbug is a creature that, again, lives off of human blood. So if you were in a building that had bedbugs, they spread through every floor of the building and through every apartment. They traveled through the walls. They would end up in the mattresses, and that's where they would find people sleeping. From there they could suck their blood out in such a gentle manner that you hardly ever knew what was happening. But if you lifted up the corner of an old mattress and found 100 bedbugs and started squashing them, there was blood everywhere, human blood. So we lived with bedbugs. And we would wake up in the middle of the night and pick bedbugs off our bodies that were feeding on us. This was very hard.

The other adversarial relationship was my father's personal war with rats. We lived on Sheffield Avenue, next to an open sewer. It was underground, under the street, but it was very wide, and it was for sewage. The wall to the sewer was the wall to our bathroom. And the rats would eat through the concrete and come into the house. My father had every kind of trap there was. Traps weren't made big enough for sewer rats. Some rats that came into the house were as big as cats. So what evolved out of this is that my father had a very big club. At any given night of any week, in the middle of the night, he would hear one of the sewer rats come in the kitchen, he would get his club, the lights would go on, and there would be a war. And finally, my father would beat the rats to death. I saw him kill rats that weighed 20 to 30 pounds. Finally, my dad brought sheet metal, Brillo pads, and scouring pads from where he worked and just put pounds and pounds of that stuff down in the holes. And then he nailed sheet metal over the holes into the walls. And that was the end of the rats after about 5 years of rats terrorizing the whole family. I remember my sisters up on the bed, my mother screaming, and my father running around in his boxer shorts, clubbing giant rats. He had to hit them 50 times before they'd finally die.

So that was a difficult part of early childhood that I don't think is allowed to happen anyplace in this country anymore. I don't think things like that really happen here anymore.

In my childhood, the common denominators, from five years old on, were always hunger, cold and sickness. And it really got worse every year until I was eleven or twelve. We never had enough food, never had warm clothes. I never had a pair of boots in my childhood. I never had a pair of gloves, but a few winters I did have a hat. In my grade school, we were probably the poorest family. It was very challenging as I grew up. It was hard to survive. The only thing that kept all the kids going, and in truth, kept my father going, was my mother's pure and unconditional love that she showed to everybody in her life, all of the time.

'50s

School

By THE TIME I REACHED 7 YEARS OLD IN 1950, the hardships of life considerably deepened. The nightmare for me of grade school and, at that time, of bullies was not fun at all. In the 1st, 2nd, and 3rd grades, I seemed to have attracted the major bullies in the school. It was pretty terrible leaving the house in the morning and trying to find new ways to get to school to avoid the bullies. They basically always took everything I had, if I had a few pennies, or marbles or baseball cards; they'd take anything. Bullies were such a big part of my early life that I grew not to like bullies at all in my entire adult life; bullies are my least favorite people.

So going into that period, there were also increasing hardships at home. My mother gave birth to my little brother, and then she had to go to work for the first time. My father wasn't making nearly enough money to support the family. And he drank more money than he contributed to his family each week. So my mother went to work, and that left me under the thumb of one of my sisters, who became a very cruel, tyrannical control freak. I never understood her in those days—why she felt such hatred, and why she was so mean to me. I won't give a lot of details about that. But it was way out the realm of normal little brother and little sister bickering. This was very serious, bordering on hate-filled behavior that I had to deal with every day. Coming home from school was darkness for me. Because my sister was responsible for all the housework that had to be done, she enjoyed making me do it. So I scrubbed the floors on my hands and knees as a little boy. I did all of the dishes; essentially all of the dirty work she'd have me do.

My mother would go to work at 3 in the afternoon, right before we got home from school, and for the rest of the night, neither parent was ever there. They would come home at 2 or 3 in the morning. So home life, as our poverty deepened, got harder and harder. There was less food; there was continuous hunger for all us kids. Basically, we got into survival modes that have actually, in my life, served me quite well in the regard that things were so hard and so difficult to survive in that I grew a great compassion for other peoples' suffering. As I grew up in that environment, I more and more appreciated any situation that was harmonious and peaceful, without fighting and ugly behavior. I grew to really enjoy and relish a peaceful state of mind, a peaceful room, a peaceful building.

There was one time in this period when I was 8 or 9 years old. My mother took me aside one day and said, "Son, I have a very important favor to ask of you. It won't be easy, but I really need your help."

I was very helpful all the time to my mom, so I immediately said, "I'll do anything."

She said, "I need you to grow up fast. I need you to not have a childhood. I need you to help me keep this family together. Your sisters don't help me much, and your father is no help whatsoever. And I need somebody to help me. So I would like you to put aside your childhood and become more of the man of the family than even your father is."

That had a tremendous impact on me—that talk. I not only agreed to it, but I loved being in that position. From that point on, she and I had an understanding that anything she needed, I would do. Any chore, any work, it didn't matter what it was. I would be glad to do it and felt great that I was the person that was really helping her survive. Because it was apparent to me from 2 or 3 years old that my mother had the short end of the stick in this whole family. That she had the hardest position, hardest job, hardest work, the hardest everything.

That was a big event for me that played through for the rest of our lives. Even well into adulthood, she often called upon me first of her 7 kids, no matter what she needed. She would reach out to me, and I would play the role of the important person for whatever it was she needed to survive. I became her helper, her partner and her confidant, but I believe that we were all special and equal to her.

Struggle for Food

THOSE SAME YEARS, I was very weak (I seem to remember that whole period of time from the time I was 4 or 5 years old on till I was out of school as one long sickness after another). I was a very sickly, skinny, scrawny little kid. During that that period, what was going on at home or at school, both of which were nightmares for me, none of that ever helped me in any way to resist sickness or illness. So I was the scrawny sick kid in our family, and that seemed to go on and on. In those years, from the beginning of the '50s until the end of the '50s, we kids at home, surviving, we got into some really bad habits to survive. One night when we had no food, (it was common for us not to have dinner because there would not be a piece of bread in our house or a potato, or a can of anything) one of my sisters started - I don't know why she started it - but she came in the front room, and she had a can of kitchen cleanser, and the whole top of it was all wet.

She said, "You gotta try this. This is great."

I said, "What are you doing?"

She shook the can up a little, and it got the white powder on the top, and she licked it right off. Then one of my other sisters at the same time admitted that she had been eating my father's shoe polish. She had been taking the top of my father's Shinola can, and she would lick the shoe polish. Shortly after that revelation, of them doing both of these bizarre little food trips, I got an idea to see what oil tasted like. I would go in the back of our oil stove, and I would take out the screen, and I would stick a coffee cup down in the well, and I would get it half full of oil. I remember the first time I tried it; I took a little sip. It didn't taste bad; it was oily, and it went down my throat. But I drank probably a half cup of it and had the most marvelous experience; I had no more hunger for the rest of the night. The oil, I guess, had coated my stomach and I slept easier that night and I woke up less hungry. So all of us engaged in these "eatings" of the only things in the house which were not locked up or hidden away. What we all did was put something in our stomachs to quiet down the hunger, quiet down the continuous nagging, gnawing feeling, which for a good portion of my childhood I felt every day.

In the early '50s, when he was 3 or 4 years old, my little brother had been watching the older ones eating all the inedible food in the house, and he did something terrible. This is a night I'll never forget because it was high tension and high trauma. It was about 7 in the evening, and we had had no food, no dinner. All of a sudden, my brother started screaming wildly at the top of his lungs. One of my sisters and I raced into the room, and he was up on the table and had opened a can of Crystal Drano, drain cleaner. He had a tablespoon in his hand and was screaming horrifically. He had just taken a whole tablespoon of these crystals and put it in his mouth and swallowed it. And now it was burning his entire GI tract. My one sister screamed at me to run down to the fire department. We didn't have a phone or anything, but one block down there was a fire department.

She said, "Go down and tell the firemen! Tell the firemen that Mike ate Drano!"

I ran down Sheffield Ave to the firehouse, almost a block away. I barged in; they were sitting around playing cards, and I screamed, "My brother's just eaten Drano! My brother's just eaten Drano!!"

So one of them grabbed me, picked me up, and ran back to the house while the fire engine got there. They took him to Children's Memorial Hospital. My mother was working at a restaurant at the time, and one of the neighbors went down and informed her about Mike. She left work and got home before the firemen took Mike out of the house. They told her that he would not likely live through the night. At Children's, they pumped his stomach, but the damage was so horrific that he spent the next 6 months in a bed in Children's while they fought to keep him alive. After 6 months, they finally brought him home. I remember hearing my mother tell my father that one of the doctors said that either he would die very early, by 10 or 12 years old, or he would have such a powerful immune system that he would have amazing health. Well! That's the way it turned out with my brother. Because after that experience, in my entire memory, I don't remember 1 day of sickness from him, all the way through his entire adult life. He could eat any amount of poison, any kind of garbage; he could drink an entire quart of whisky and wash it down it with 2 six-packs. He never had a hangover in his life, never vomited once. Never had a headache. He said he never even knew what headaches were about when people talked about them. He was incredibly powerful, healthy, and strong. He became a living legend in Chicago as a street warrior. But the night he ate the Drano and was taken to the hospital, none of us kids ever thought we would see him again.

Those were some of the events that crystalized those years of being able to handle very harsh, very unnatural, unhealthy living conditions and get through and survive. Up until '55, all the things I just mentioned were a daily living reality.

Then, at one point, around '56, when I graduated from grade school, I started working a lot. I had already done that from the time I was 5 or 6 years old. I always could figure out how to make money, and then I'd take the money back home to my mother. When I graduated grade school that summer, I took a full-time job, and then I worked for the rest of my teen years after school and on weekends with regular paying jobs. I almost always gave my whole paycheck to my mother. When I finished grade school, I remember thinking that the worst thing that could happen to me is that I would be trapped in high school for 4 years. I knew the state law said I could quit the day I turned 16. I couldn't wait to get to 16. I never thought of finishing high school, never ever.

At that time, I was a pretty good athlete; I had a very successful little league career and then a very good pony league career. Then in the late '50s when I had to choose a high school, I chose Lane Tech, because it was the only school in Chicago where major league baseball scouts would regularly go. It was the best baseball school in the city. So I decided to go there in hopes of someday being a baseball player; but the day I turned 16, I quit high school, took a full-time job, and made it a lot easier in those years for my mother to survive. Even at my age, I can still say that maybe the worst mistake I ever made in my life was choosing to go to Lane Tech. Going to Lane Tech from where I lived required that every morning I walk to a bus stop take a bus, get on the L-train, get off the L- train, and take another bus to get to school. It would take as long as 1 ½ hours. So I would be leaving when it was still dark out, when every other kid in the neighborhood in high school was still in bed sleeping. Meanwhile, Lane Tech was a boy's technical school. So I had put myself in a building with 5,600 boys. I had put myself in Lane Tech instead of Waller High School, which was 1 block from my house and full of girls. And that summer was the summer I became interested in girls. So I didn't get to go to Waller High School and have all the romance that all my buddies had. I was stuck with 5,600 boys every day, in a situation where I was never going to be seen by a major league scout because I was doomed to quit by my 3rd year and could not join the baseball team.

So that's just a funny mistake that I've never forgotten.

First Job

THE '50S WERE PROBABLY THE HARDEST YEARS OF MY LIFE. The hardest survival years, the hardest on me emotionally, physically. Same thing on the siblings; none of them had any emotional breaks. We had nothing. We were a family of 2 parents and 7 kids, who basically had nothing. We saw all our neighbors and relatives give kids Christmas presents and birthday presents, but we never had any of that.

So when the '50s came to an end, this was a very good time for me because I was 16. I was able to quit high school the day I turned 16, March 10th, 1959. My mom had a giant argument with me. She wanted me to be the first one of her kids to get a high school diploma. But I told her that working to make money and take pressure off of her and help us live was more important than any diploma. So finally she agreed to let me quit school when I was 16.

And she told me something I'll never forget. She said, "Son, in the end, anything in the world that you want to learn, you can read about. Go get books; go take classes; go find people that teach about it. Anything you need to learn, you go and teach yourself or find someone to teach you."

I took that to heart and lived that out for the rest of my life.

Let me go back to explain about my first job. All around our neighborhood, there were big apartment buildings and they had garages. Next door to us they had a garage big enough for four cars, with a ramp out of the alley, so you drove up. It was just made out of wood. Two Japanese brothers in 1946, rented this garage, and all of their customers spoke Japanese. We're only a year from the end of the war and here's two young Japanese mechanics; every white face within miles hated them. But I was just three or four years old. So they moved in and started working; when the weather was warm they'd come in at like seven in the morning. And I'd come in and

I'd get up on the walkway near the garage and get up close so I could see and hear them. I was mesmerized by them. Mainly because they were speaking Japanese all of the time. They knew I was there, but I was like invisible, so they didn't care. So I started doing that every day. I started to figure out what they were doing; they were fixing cars. They had these crawler things that they'd lay on and scoot under the car. One of them would always go at lunch time, drive some place, and come back with food. So one day he goes, the other guy doesn't realize he's gone. The one guy under the car is yelling for what I knew was a big mallet hammer. And I just hopped over the railing, went up the rest of the stairs, went over. I knew what the mallet was, and I was just barely able to pick it up, and I struggled to walk it over to the car and dropped it. His hand went out and he grabbed it. And he must have seen my legs or something because he scooted out from underneath and said something like, "You go away!!"

The next day I came, the same thing happened. But he had told the brother. The brother thought it was incredible that I would do that. So they invited me into the garage and they started telling me, showing me wrenches, and telling me what they were in Japanese. And I didn't know what they were in English, so I didn't have any point of reference. So they both would be under the car and one of them would yell Japanese at me and I'd bring them a monkey wrench or rags or something.

That first Friday after I started helping them out, they called me over and one of the guys went in his pocket and took out the shiniest 50 cent piece that I had ever seen. He put it in my hand and patted me on the head. I ran next door and found my mother and she went bananas. For the next year, every Friday, I got a 50-cent piece. That was from ages three to four. And then, some of the hate filled neighbors torched the guys' garage at night when they weren't there. When my father found out that I worked for them, he was furious, he was going to go beat the life out of both of them. My mother stopped him and said, "You leave them alone! They're doing something for your kid that you don't do. They're showing him how to make money honorably. You stay away from them." And there was never another word said about it.

Hard Jobs Tough Choices

THE DAY I TURNED 13, I made a deal with my mom. I had already been working after school and during summers. The day I turned 13, I said, "Mom I want to give you a birthday present." She said, "Son, it's *your* birthday." And I said, "No I want to give YOU a present." And she said, "Ok what?"

I said, "From this day on, you don't have to pay a penny out of your pocket for anything in my life. I'll buy all my own clothes, pay all my own school way, pay all my transportation. Any school supplies I need, any shoes, etc. From this day on, you have one kid that you don't have to worry about haranguing you for money." And I did that, I never took a dollar from her after that.

The day I quit school, I worked for a company downtown. It was called the Union News Company, and they ran all the little stores in the train depots, and in the big office buildings. I had worked for them since I was 13 years old. So the day I got out of high school, they gave me a full-time job as an assistant supervisor, putting me and another man in charge of 17 retail outlets all around the loop in downtown Chicago. And we would continuously go to each one and check their books and their paperwork; we did inventory; we would make sure that the money that the company was making was being deposited in the banks, etc. So I went from high school to wearing suits and ties, the first time I had ever put on a suit in my life (except for my grade school graduation). Essentially, I became a pretty sharp young businessman working for this company. But I only worked for them until I was near 17. This was right at the end of the '50s.

There was a hotel downtown called the Blackstone, a big famous theatre and hotel. There was a cigar stand that sold cigars, cigarettes, candy, and newspapers in the lobby of the hotel. The woman that I had known for many years, who had run that concession, had gotten into stealing. My partner was a hardcore 50-year-old Jewish very mean businessman. And I was a 16-year-old, wet-behind-the-ears kid. So we went into her store and did an inventory one day. When we figured out all of the paperwork, she was short several thousand dollars. So we pretty much knew she was stealing. So I took her aside and talked to her and said, "If you're stealing money, you might as well tell us."

She said, "I am. I'm stealing 40 to 50 dollars per week because my husband is crippled, and we can't pay the bills anymore."

So I pleaded her case to our boss in New York, and he flew out to Chicago, and he sat down with me and my partner. My partner wanted her fired immediately and prosecuted. And I didn't want her fired or prosecuted. So the man from New York, who was a VP, he said to my partner, "Sol, you've been working for us for 25 years."

He turned to me and said, "Ralph, you've only been with us since you were 13, so I have to go with Sol, and she'll be fired, and we'll prosecute."

And I stood up right away and said, "I quit."

They were both shocked and this man said, "Wait a minute, you have the biggest future of any man in this whole city."

I said, "I'll have no part in this, if you're gonna hurt this old woman just because she's stealing money from a couple packs of cigarettes."

He said, "No, but she *can't* do that."

And I said, "Okay then fire her, but you can't hurt a woman in her position with the law. This money means nothing to this company. They have 1,900 stores. This means nothing."

And the VP said, "Okay the prosecution is out of the question. Ralph is right. Letting her go is going to hurt her enough, and we don't need to prosecute."

So the next day when I went to work, Sol got in my face real hard, telling me I was a punk and I didn't know anything and I interfered with him and I made him look bad in front of the VP.

And I just turned to him and said, "Sol, go fuck yourself."

And that was my last day at that job. But they had told me that by the day I was 25, they wanted me to run all of the outlets they had in Chicago. And I walked away from that in a heartbeat. No trouble at all. Because I knew this old businessman was so angry with me, he was going to make my life miserable. I was 16 and I didn't have to take it. And I found a job in a factory the very next day.

When I was 18, I had been working in a little factory on Irving Park. I think I made $1.60 an hour, something like that. My sister had a boyfriend who was a superintendent at the Electromotive Division of General Motors, and they made giant train engines.

One day she said to me, "If you want, if you don't mind traveling all the way out of the city and working the midnight shift, I can get you a job at General Motors."

I said, "How much does it pay?"

She said, "$3.20/hr."

I said, "Oh my God! That's twice what I make now!"

So I took that job, and I was a workaholic. By then my sickness stuff had pretty much gone. I was very strong. I was wiry and strong. I took a job under a roof with 10,000 men working under it, putting out six giant locomotive engines per day. I was probably the youngest person of the 10,000, but I had a maniacal work ethic. I could work through breaks, through bathroom time, through lunch. I so wanted to impress my sister's boyfriend, who stuck his neck out and got me the job that I became like a tool for the foremen, general foremen, and superintendents. Whenever in our area there was a job that needed to be done very fast, or they needed a lot of extra parts, they would single me out and take me to the machine. A normal worker in a day would make 90 parts, I would make 120.

So I got a reputation in 1 year where I was essentially not liked by any of the hundreds of men that worked right around me. And I was loved by all the foremen and general foremen. They would have me come in on Sundays, Christmas, and on Easter, when there was not 1 man working in the whole factory. They would put me on a machine and tell me for 16 hours to go wild, "make as many pieces as you can."

The union had quotas of how much a man had to do in 8 hours on a machine. I could double all of the quotas. So I became a very controversial kid. The next oldest to me were men in their late 20s, and then 30s, 40s, and so on. They all wanted to be foremen their whole lives. When they started there, their lives were aimed at working for 20 years and then getting a foreman job and cruising for the rest of their life.

So one day, I'm 19, my sister's boyfriend calls me into the office. There was another superintendent, the head of all 10,000 workers, sitting there. And they knocked my socks off. They said, "We want to make you a foreman."

At that time, General Motors had a solid set of rules. In order to be a foreman you had to have 20 years with GM. In order to be a foreman, you had to have a college diploma. In order to be a foreman, you had to be at least 30, somewhere around there. I was sitting there, 19, and they were telling me they wanted me to be a foreman.

I said to my sister's boyfriend, "Art, this can't be. I know all the rules!"

He said, "We're flying to Detroit tomorrow and meeting with a vice president there, who we think we can convince to break the rules of General Motors to make an exception and make you a foreman."

I was absolutely stunned. I went back to work, and the older guys were saying, "What'd they call you into the office for? What'd they want with ya?"

I didn't open my mouth. I wouldn't tell them anything. When I went home that night, I slept very fitfully, and I thought of what would happen if I were put in charge of one area—they called it a "bay." There were 50 bays; each had about 200 men in it. I thought, "These guys already hate me because I work hard, and I don't pay attention to their rules. What are they gonna do if I'm made their boss??"

I just laid there, and thought. When I went in the next day, I gave them 7 days' notice. They were freaked out. Freaked out. The 2 guys were in Detroit right then, setting it up for me. And when they got back from Detroit, they brought this VP with them. He sat me down for a half hour, telling me how my future would be locked up in GM—by the time I was 40, I would be a VP. I would have a life like no one could believe.

I listened to every word of it, and when they asked me to respond, I said, "I already responded. I gave my notice yesterday. I will not be put in a position, at 19 years old, of telling 50-year-old men what to do. They hate me enough now. It would be horrible."

So the next day, my sister's boyfriend came in. And he had a note, a letter, on GM letterhead. He said, "They just called from Detroit and insisted that I have this typed out and given to you."

I took it and opened it up, and it said,

"To whom it may concern,

This man, Ralph Matson, is to be given employment, upon his request, at any General Motors facilities in the world. No questions, no considerations. He is to be given work immediately upon presentation of this letter."

And it was signed by the president of GM.

I showed it to my mom, and she said, "Son, this is great!"

I said, "Ah, it doesn't mean anything."

I threw it away 2 days later.

In the very beginning of working at GM, there was a machine that ran 3 shifts. The guy who taught me how to run the machine was 58 years old and had been running the machine for 30 years. The man on the second shift was about 48 years old, and he had been running the machine over 20 years. I came in at midnight shift, and if they did 88 pieces during the day and 90 at night, I'd do 120. And the guy in the middle, he told me one day, he said, "You are the dumbest fuck I've ever seen in my life. You are so fuckin' stupid. You're siding with this company against all of us. You're making us look bad."

And I told him, "You go fuck yourself. I came here to work. They're paying me good money. I work. I don't give a shit what you think about my work."

But in that atmosphere, I knew that first night when they made me the offer, someone might kill my ass.

When I left GM, I knew I'd never consider even for 1 minute working in that environment again. It was like servants and masters. All these guys that were foremen and general foremen…they made a lot of money, but they ran these 200 guys with bullwhips; and they had to be nasty, and they had to be threatening. I wasn't going to do that to anybody. I was like, "They're fuckin nuts."

They blew it with me, the minute they made me that offer. I might have worked there for 20 years just on the machines! This was the end of factory work for me.

So basically the 50's ended with me working full time, being very able to help my mother. I got my first car and with it, my first independence. I got a sense that things were changing and maybe life would get a little bit easier or a little bit better. I had basically been a very unhappy, angry, introverted young man. I was very pragmatic and anchored in my work patterns. I had a sense change was coming, but no real idea of how true my senses were. As the fifties bowed out, the sixties began unfolding experiences and life changes I had never imagined or fantasized would be my realities.

'60s

Porch

IN THE EARLY SUMMER OF 1960, we lived in a 3rd-floor apartment building. It was my mother, my younger brother and sister, and I. The older girls had all gone off and gotten married. I'd gotten home from work one day, and was helping my mom with dinner. My mother said, "Son, go outside and get your brother and sister for dinner."

So I went out on the back porch of the 3rd floor, and I told my sister, who was playing with a pigeon, "Come on in, it's time to eat!" She didn't pay any attention to me. Well, I had been cutting up vegetables, and I had a knife in my hand; so to get her attention, I pretended to try to hit the pigeon with the knife.

I said, "You better go inside, or I'll cut your buddy."

She laughed at me, so I swung the knife, with no intention to hit the pigeon. As I swung the knife, the pigeon took off, and so I leaned my body out at it. I hit the wooden railing with my hip. The railing was rotted at both ends, and all of a sudden, I was out in midair—instant karma!

Everything that happened from that point on was slow motion. I first realized that the railing had given way and I was actually in free fall. But it was absolute slow motion. Even as I think now, I remember so much detail, I could fill pages. As I started to fall down feet first, knife still in hand. I looked down, and directly below me was a 7-foot-high, 4x4 wooden stake in concrete that the women in the building hung clothes from. I was going right down, with my crotch aiming straight toward the spiked stake.

And then things got very strange and slower. Suddenly my life started replaying. It replayed with my eyes open, right in front of me, backward. Starting with that moment, I shot back in time to the day before, month before, year before. I went all the way back to being born, and then that mental film stopped, and I looked down. I had fallen only halfway down the 3 floors. And I started leaning backward slightly. To get my balance, I started swinging both of my arms forward in a circle. I righted my body and looked down, and the stake post was still right underneath me.

I remember thinking, "This is the end."

I closed my eyes and braced myself to be impaled. At that moment, it felt like a hand cupped my whole butt and pushed me straight forward. I landed on both of my feet, in this dirt backyard, about 6 feet away from the pole—6 feet farther into the yard than the trajectory of my fall. I landed on both feet. I remember feeling the crunching of my whole body. I think I went down into a squat position, and then my legs boomeranged like a spring, and I did a complete somersault and landed flat on my back in the yard.

My first realization was looking up at the sky between buildings and watching the railing. It had broken off and hung for a second or two on some rusty nails. So I lay there, and I watched the railing continue the end of its fall, and it smashed right across my head and midsection, pinning me to the ground.

It seems funny now, almost like some kind of cartoon. So I'm lying there, pinned down by this heavy, old wooden railing, flat on my back. Looked up in the sky and saw the big gaping hole of my 3rd-floor porch. My kid sister was standing right on the edge, holding her hands over her mouth. And all of a sudden, my mother came into view, screaming at the top of her lungs, "Oh my God! My son! My son!"

I saw her turn and head for the stairway. In a split second, I saw her clearly in my mind's eye, tumbling down the stairs, head first. And I thought, "Oh my God, she's going to fall down the stairs trying to get to me."

In the strongest move I could muster, I put my hand under the edge of this heavy railing lying across my body and flung it off of me. I sprung to my feet and dashed for the stairway, and I heard my mother screaming and screaming. As I tore up the first floor and then turned to head up the second floor, she was turning to come down that stairway. I ran to her as she tripped on the stairs and literally caught her right in midair, with my arms pushing her back and pinning her down on the stairs. It was a spiritual experience, as well as an absolute disaster for my body. I just lay there, holding her. We held each other; she was crying and screaming. I had her pinned on the stairs. I knew she was safe.

When we got up and started heading upstairs, she said, "I've gotta get you to a hospital. I've gotta get you to a hospital!!"

I said, "No, no, there's nothing wrong with me."

We argued a bit about it as we went upstairs. Basically I told my body, "You can't be hurt because it'll hurt her."

So I went to bed that night. I refused to go to the hospital. All the neighbors saw this; there were probably 20 people out on their porches when it happened. But at that time there were no cell phones and no 911; no one interfered in peoples' business. So nothing essentially came of it that night.

The next morning, my ankles, my lower back, my upper back, and my neck were all killing me. I tried to hide it, but my mother saw right through me. She insisted that we go to the hospital. At the hospital, they X-rayed my back. The doctor said, "There's nothing wrong with his back except his scoliosis."

My mom said, "He doesn't have scoliosis."

The doc said, "You might not have noticed, but from birth, your son has had an extreme exaggerated scoliosis."

My mom said, "Let's get out of here."

My ankles were both bad; I was limping. But we both knew that if I could limp, I just had sprained ankles. Even 3 months later, my back never got better. It got worse every day. I lived with it, went to work every day in the factory.

A friend of my mother had told her about the best orthopedic back man in Chicago. I'll never forget him; his name was Dr. Redden. We had an appointment with him. He took a ballpoint pen, had me take my shirt off, and marked the tips of my vertebrae. He showed my mother—it was a big S.

The doc said, "Your son just has the bad scoliosis that he was born with."

My mom said, "My son's back was perfectly straight."

He said, "You must be wrong."

She said, "Don't tell me I'm wrong. I birthed him. He fell from a porch 3 months ago."

He said, "No, this couldn't be from a porch fall."

So he sat us down and told me, "You'll have to wear lifts in your shoes for the rest of your life. You'll wear a spinal brace and support for the rest of your life. You can never lift anything heavy again. Never over 40 pounds. Lifting could snap your spine. Don't ever get in a fight; if you do, you could be crippled or dead. And as far as I'm concerned, I have to advise you against lovemaking with women."

My mother looked at me, looked at him, grabbed her purse, and said, "Son, let's get the hell out of here. This guy is going to really cripple you."

So I had a long time of dealing with my spinal and body problems. Eventually I figured out how to live with everything. But that was an experience that really, in certain ways, showed me that there must be some sort of higher power. I knew about the God stuff from Bibles and all that. But this one was personal. I *knew* I was going to be impaled by that stake, and then all of a sudden I was out in the middle of that yard. That was a beginning for me of realizing that something was watching over me, or something would help me if I needed it. I didn't pray or thank God or anything like that. I didn't have that kind of spiritual awareness, but that was a powerful experience that showed me beyond any question that miraculous things could happen. Because being alive after falling into that yard was actually pretty miraculous.

Father's Death

THIS IS THE SECOND MAJOR EVENT OF 1960, after my very perilous journey down into my yard from my porch. I actually wrote this out on the morning of 2/2/15, at 4:23 a.m. I woke up from a sound sleep, and I was directed to write it exactly like this. This event happened on October 7, 1960; that's the day my father passed. I call this "My Father's Last Days."

The following is verbatim what I wrote:

For the last hour or so I have been flooded in a dream state of remembrances and realizations of the last 36 hours of his life. Perhaps the last pieces of the puzzle of our ever-so-strange karmic bond, agreement, and completion between my father and me. The pieces that I, in this moment of clarity, now understand are as follows:

I must go back 1 year to when he entered Augustana Hospital to live his last year, slowly dying in a cancer ward. The doctors had given him 1 year to live if he did not stop drinking. On that day, he not only didn't stop, but he increased his whiskey intake dramatically. From the day he entered the hospital to the day he passed, it totaled 366 days. To the best of my memory, I did not miss going to his room, with each of us in abject silence for the whole visit, for even one of those days. I went every single day. I now understand those 366 days; though at the time, I only knew in my young 17-year-old mind that I must go and see him every day.

In my 17 years as his son, he never ever showed any desire to talk to me or to communicate as a father to a son. From the very beginning he clearly communicated his anger, hatred, disdain, and even his disgust at my presence in his life and on this Earth. This is how it was when he entered the hospital with few small breaks since my mother threw him out a few years earlier, when I was about 14. These were short small moments of hope for some end to the ongoing war between us since before my birth. In these few times, he let me come to the bar he worked at, sit at the end, drink Cokes for a while and then send me home. But no real talk or dialogue.

Now to the end of his life. I was at work at the Great Lakes Tool and Manufacturing Shop on Irving Park Road, when I was told by my foreman, Eddie Stuckland, to get to the hospital because my dad was in a coma and dying. I drove like a wild man through the streets of Chicago and entered his room to find my father unconscious and in an oxygen tent, with my mom and a few of my sisters standing around. Mom told me that he would die any minute. I went to his bedside, took his right hand in mine, pulled up a chair, and began crying freely. The tears would only stop briefly in the next 36 hours, when I let go of his hand. In that time, I refused to leave his side, refused food or water, and just stared at him and cried (many years later, a wise spiritual woman said to me, "Son, you were not crying your tears. You were crying his tears," upon hearing the story. I now know the truth of her insight). For almost 36 hours straight, I cried and did not let go of his hand— no bathroom, no food, no interruptions. My mother tried a few times to get me to leave his side but mostly just left me alone.

In the middle of the second day, the doctor told my mom that I was having a nervous breakdown. He brought in 2 armed security guards to take me out. I became somewhat crazed, and I jumped up and let go of my father's hand. I told the bigger guard—closest to me—that I would throw him out the window if he came near me. We were on the 6th or 7th floor at the time. And I knew that I could easily throw this man through the window. He saw the fire and the fury that I was feeling, and he left the room, telling the doctor, "You're not paying me enough money to go near that kid." That ended that situation; the other guard left, and the doctor told my mother, "I'm not responsible." And he left.

My mom and older sisters came in for visits, but they were like images in the background, and I was barely aware of anybody's presence. The only reality was me holding his hand and the continuous flow of tears, until about 1 a.m. the next morning. My mom and I were alone at that time with him.

She was behind me, looking out the window, when all of a sudden a very loud voice in my head screamed, "**He will not die until he is baptized!**" I was shocked and didn't know what to do. I then told my mom what the voice had said. She rushed over to me and said, "What do you think it means?" For a few minutes, we discussed this strange event, and she told me, "We should get a priest and see if it could be done."

I ran downstairs; I didn't take the elevator, I ran down the stairs to the lobby to a pay phone. I called the local church at St. Vincent DePaul. Got a nun in the rectory and made her wake up a priest I knew at the time. He came to the phone and listened to my whole story, and then he told me it was not possible for him to baptize my father as my father was in a coma and was an atheist. He said he was very sorry and hung up the phone. I went back to my father's room, told my mom, took his hand in mine, and began crying again.

Within a few minutes, I again heard the deep male voice loudly proclaim, "**He will not die until he is baptized.**" I was so startled, I turned to my mom and told her about the voice's statement again. She immediately said, "Son, you know more priests. Go call one and try to get one to come here." Again I ran down to the lobby, and I called Father Brennan at St. Alphonsus's Church, who had given me catechism instructions. Again an angry nun was finally convinced to wake up the priest. He came to the phone, and I repeated the story of my father's condition and situation. And then I repeated proclamation of the voices in my head. He sadly repeated what the other priests' voices had said. He could not baptize an atheist unless that person made a full confession and requested baptism.

Then he paused for a moment and said. "Answer this question honestly." I told him I would. He said, "If your father woke up for one minute and you asked him if he would accept baptism, would he say yes or no?"

I, without a second's hesitation, said, "He would say yes."

He then very quickly said, "Son, I cannot baptize your father, but you can."

I was stunned, and I quickly said to him, "I can't do that. I don't know how. I don't know anything about that."

He said, "Yes, you can. I give you authority and will give you the exact instructions."

In a literal daze, but with a strange awareness and energy coursing within me, I listened and did as he told me. I ran back up to his room, got a nurse, and explained what I was going to do and what I needed from her. I had to have clean cloths, oil, water, salt, cotton, etc. As we waited for the nurse to bring the tools for the baptism ritual, my mother encouraged me, telling me that this was definitely the right thing and that I could do it. When the nurse returned, she stood on the opposite side of the bed, with the objects on a tray. My mom stood next to me on my right. I began by blessing all of the contents on the tray. Then it was almost like a blur to me; it was as though someone took over from me and performed every step of the entire ritual, perfectly and flawlessly. When it ended, I put the last of the tools on the nurse's tray. She turned and left the room without ever having made a sound. I pulled the chair back over to the bed, sat down, and with my mother's hand on my shoulder, I took my father's hand in mine and again began crying. It was only a matter of a few seconds, not minutes, but seconds, and he left his body. The oxygen suddenly ran freely. His labored, deep breathing stopped, and we both knew that he was gone and it was over.

My tears stopped instantly, and my first thought was "I do not ever want to cry again" (I would regret that powerful emotional vow for many years to come).

Mom and I shortly left the hospital at about 3:00 a.m. on Saturday, October 8, 1960. We walked home in silence, each of us in our own world. I was somewhat dumbstruck by the amazing events of the last few hours and the last few days, dimly aware that some enormous, long struggle between my father and I was over. I felt a clarity and a freedom that I did not understand or could have verbalized. But somehow I knew that both he and I were free of some great burden. My mom, I believe, silently said goodbye to the love of her life, the father of her children, and their (his and her) true long love. She also, that night, made a hard vow that she told me. She said that she would never be with another man for the rest of her life. She lived with that vow until her last day.

At my father's funeral, all the people who came to visit him were his old bar friends and the tough men of Chicago. My family all showed up. I went through the whole funeral and 3 or 4 days of the wake and funeral in a detached way, almost happy. In fact, I walked through the funeral home for days with a deck of cards, showing people card tricks.

One of my sisters said to me, "How can you show card tricks at Daddy's funeral? You should be crying."

I remember saying to her, "Oh no, I shed my tears already."

About 2 to 3 weeks after, my mother asked me if I would go to the hospital with her. She had gotten a letter to come in and see the administrator of the hospital. So I went over there with her; we went in his office and sat down. He told her that he knew we had no insurance of any kind whatsoever.

He said there was a sizeable bill that has to be paid. He said to us, "I know you have no money, so I want to give you some papers to sign, and we'll have various agencies pay for your husband's stay."

My mother immediately, very abruptly, said, "No you won't! This is my husband. He is my responsibility. I'll pay the bill."

The administrator said, "It's not possible for you to pay it."

The bill for 366 days was 17,000 dollars. But in 1960, to a woman in my mother's position it was truly impossible to pay it.

He said, "No, the county and the state will pay the bill. Just sign the papers."

She said, "I will not sign anything. I will pay this bill myself."

I tried to talk to her and said, "Mom, let them pay it. We don't have that kind of mon—"

She said, "Son, you stay out of this one."

She pointed right at the administrator's face and said, "I will pay every penny. I will pay when I can. I will pay at least a payment every week."

This man was shocked. He said, "Mrs. Matson, you don't have to go through this. We'll take this burden from you."

She said, "No. No one takes my husband's burden from me."

And that was the end of it. She refused, absolutely refused, not to pay the bill.

So what she did, at that time, was start sending the hospital about $5/week. Or sometimes $3.75. She made a payment every single week. Little teeny amounts of money.

I know that within a month of her death, she made the last payment of her hospital bill, which was about 15 to 20 years later. She paid every penny of that bill.

I remember her telling me one day, "I've sent the last payment in. I'm straight with Augustana now. His bill is paid."

John's Bargain Stores

IN **1961,** I became some sort of a workaholic junkie. It was like a fulfillment for me to walk into a factory or store and do their bidding, do the best job. I could outwork anybody. I was totally focused; I was a machine. It became my whole life. I had girlfriends on the side; I had street buddies, but my main focus was on jobs.

I worked the GM job until I was about 20. I realized that in the GM years, I had to drive an hour or more every day to and from work. So when I quit GM, I decided to get something closer to my home. I found a job as a management trainee for a New York Company called John's Bargain Stores. They were rapidly opening stores in the Chicago area.

I was supposed to train for 3 months. In less than 1 month, they gave me my first store. If I remember right, it was the 38th-ranked store in the Chicago area for sales. There were about 50 stores in Chicago. For a new manager to get a store at that level was sort of eye-popping.

The store was on Milwaukee Ave and Diversey. And I just threw myself into that job. I did it with such a passion. I wasn't necessarily smart or creative, but I was focused and determined. So I would put in longer hours than any manager. I would work harder. After some few months, I was told I was going to be given a promotion.

I said, "Okay, where do I go?"

They said, "We're going to give you a real troubled store, in a real troubled area of Chicago. At Pulaski and Madison Ave. At the heart of a deeply troubled black area of Chicago." They said, "We're a little nervous about putting a young white man in a store that will have 98% black customers. Do you think you can handle it?"

I didn't even think about it. I said, "Of course. What are you talking about?"

They gave me this store at Madison and Pulaski. It was something I never want to go through again. At that time, the racial divide of Chicago was at a peak. The hatred between blacks and whites was the strongest of any time in my lifetime. Of the maybe 50 retail stores and businesses in the area, I was the only white manager. Every company, every store had black employees only.

But I took the job. I hired some young black girls as cashiers and store workers. And just like all the others, I just dug into it. And I performed like a champion. I knew that very few people could have even tackled this job. The job was very dangerous. At least once a week, I would get a call from a gang, and they'd tell me, "Okay, tonight we're taking you down."

The way we had the money structured was that at the end of every night I had to do the books, put the money together in a bank deposit bag, walk it out to my car, get in my car, and drive about 20 blocks away, deeper into the very dangerous south side of Chicago. Then I had to get out of my car at a bank and go and pull the door at the side of the bank and drop the money in.

So these phone calls would say, "We didn't get you last week, but we're gonna get ya. We're gonna kill ya. We're gonna take the money." And I lived with that.

And then I remember I got a call from the company, and they told me, "We're going to give you an assistant manager." I had just my little skinny white ass and 2 young high school black girls running this very lucrative business. So they told me they'd give me an assistant manager because the store was doing so well.

I said, "Okay, I'd love that. Give me the biggest, tallest, toughest, black kid you can find."

They said, "Oh no, no, no. We're giving you a young Polish kid."

I said, "Don't give me no young Polish kid. I don't want no kid in here, and I don't want no Polish kid in here."

The next week, a 120-pound Polish kid—not streetwise, not smart—walked in. I called the company and said, "You didn't do me any favor. It was easier just to have to watch my back, but now I have to watch his because he has no idea how to deal with any sort of tough people in any way."

I had a half day off 2 weeks later. I had Sundays off when a different manager would come and watch my store on Sunday. But the company was generous enough to give me this Monday morning off as well. So I planned to do some things I had to do. So the kid had to open the store, and I had instructed him in absolute clarity 100 times, "If someone is trying to steal something, you let them have it, get out of their way, and let them go."

So at about 11 in the morning, this big burly black girl came in and started stuffing her purse with ladies' panties. He saw it, and he thought he knew how to handle it. He ran to the front door and locked the front door.

She came down the aisle at him and said, "Open that door."

He said, "No. I'm going to call the police, and you're going to be arrested."

She told him, "I'm gonna to tell you one more time to open that door."

Both of my young cashiers were screaming at him to open the door because they knew who this woman was. He wouldn't open the door. She pulled a straight razor out of her purse, came at him, threatened him with it, and told him, "I'll give you 5 seconds to open that door."

He wouldn't move; he had the key in his hand; she made a move to grab it, and he pushed her away. She swung the straight razor at him from down at her hips in an upward direction. He jumped back with his arms open wide, and she cut him all the way through his armpit. The knife went deep into his armpit and cut him right to the bone. She took the key out of his hand, opened the door, and left him in a bloody mess.

I got there at noon. Police were everywhere, and the ambulance had already taken him to the hospital. He never used that arm for the rest of his life. She had cut all of the ligaments, all of the nerves. They saved his life, but his arm was just hanging.

This was a tough, tough neighborhood; this was a tough job. That day, I went out on the street and bought myself a .38 snub nose. From then on, every morning when I opened the door, I would stick the gun in my back pocket and leave the handle hanging out so that everybody would see the gun butt hanging out of my back pocket. My mother was crushed; she was so frightened, so scared. We would talk about it regularly, and she begged me to get out of there. I told her, "Mom, you know me. I ain't quitting nothing because somebody is threatening me."

I stayed there for several more months, and then the company called me up one day and said they wanted to give me the second best store in all of Chicago. I said, "Okay, great! Give it to me."

My new store was at Maxwell and Halsted, one of the most famous areas in Chicago for being able to buy anything in the universe. At that time, a predominantly black area and again extremely crime ridden. They felt this store was so dangerous, they closed it at 6:00 p.m. All their other stores in the United States, 6,000 or more stores, all closed at 9:00 p.m. This was the only store in the chain that was so dangerous that they decided all the employees needed to be out of the area by nightfall.

At the suggestion of a prior store manager of that store, I went out the first or second day into the neighborhood to find a street kid to work for me. So I saw a group of 8 or 10 tough-looking black kids across the street in a vacant lot, just milling around. As soon as they saw me standing there and looking at them, they started talking; they were ready to come over and do a number on me.

So 3 or 4 of them started across the street, and I shouted out, "I want your leader. I want your toughest guy, your leader."

He was standing at the back of the pack, and he yelled something, came out, walked out into the street, told his guys to go back to the sidewalk. He walked over to me and stopped about 10 feet away.

He said, "I'm the leader. I'm the toughest guy in the neighborhood. What do you want?"

I said, "I want to hire you."

He said, "What are you talkin' about?"

I said, "I'm the new manager of John's Bargain Store, and I want to hire you."

He said, "I ain't putting no shit on no counters for nobody."

I said, "No, no, no. I want to hire you to protect me."

He said, "What exactly are you asking me?"

I said, "I'm going to buy you a 10-foot ladder and put it by the front door. I want you to come in every day. I'll pay you in cash. You sit on that ladder with an 8-lb ball-peen hammer in your hand and just watch me, wherever I'm at in the store."

He said, "You're kidding me!"

I said, "No, no, no. You don't have to do anything else. If you want anything from the store, as long as you don't get crazy, you just take it out. You just walk away with it."

I hired Bobby. Bobby saved my life at least twice, undoubtedly. There was one incident with a Native American heroin addict, known in the neighborhood by everybody. When the store owners saw him on the streets, they would close their doors and lock up until he was out of the neighborhood. He was a bitter, powerful, strong, ugly, angry man.

So I'm in the back of the store one day, and I'm getting a box of something to restock the shelves. I come out, and there's the big heroin addict standing right in the middle of the store. I look up, and I see Bobby pointing at him from behind him; he's still up on the ladder. I knew who this guy was. So I walk down the aisle toward him. As I walked toward him, he went in his coat—he wore camouflage jackets—he went in his coat and pulled out a bowie knife.

I said to him, "Whatever it is you want, just pick it up, take it, and go"

He said, "I want to kill somebody."

I said, "No. That's not acceptable, but whatever it is you want to steal, just go right ahead. Nobody will bother you."

He said, "What about your tough guy on the ladder?"

I said, "He's only here to protect me. He ain't bothering you. You don't have to worry."

He said, "I think you're the one I want."

He started toward me with that knife. Well, Bobby came off the ladder flying. He didn't hit the ground ever. He jumped off the ladder onto a table of clothes, bounced off that table across an aisle, onto another table of clothes. As this thug got within about 3 feet of me, with me backing up rapidly, Bobby put the ball-peen hammer on the back of his head. He went down.

I said to Bobby, "That was good, Bobby. You're quick."

He said, "You're paying me!"

I said, "What do you want to do with this guy?"

He said, "Help me drag him out in the alley, out the back door."

We dragged him out there, and Bobby started whistling. He could whistle real loud. In a matter of seconds, 8 or 10 of his street guys were flying down the alley.

He said, "You go back in now."

I said, "What are you going to do?"

He said, "You don't have to worry about what I'm gonna do. You just go back in because there's a mess in there. You go in. I'll take care of the Indian, and he won't bother you again."

I never spoke a word to him about it, never saw that guy again, and never had any idea of what Bobby did with him. That one really made me think, "This has got to end. I'm in a firing line where sooner or later somebody is going to hit me."

So from the first store that I had on Diversey, I knew that working for this company was dangerous. Because there were never guards; there was never backup. There was never male help. In my first store, the company's policy was if someone is stealing, let him have it. They can only steal about $5 to $10 of junk. Don't confront them. The first time I confronted a shoplifter in my first store, it was a young kid about my age. I saw him sticking pairs on Chino pants that we had on sale—$2 per pair for pants that you could wear for 25 years. He was stuffing the pants in his black leather coat. As he made a break for the door, I went after him. Cardinal rule that you are not supposed to do.

He went out to the street, and I chased him out into the street. He saw me following him, and he ran. I ran after him. He ducked into the first alley, and I tore into the alley behind him. About 10 feet into the mouth of the alley, he was standing there; the pants had all fallen onto the ground, and he had a .38 snub nose in his hand. He started shaking and screaming, "I'll kill you! I'll kill you!"

I stopped dead in my tracks and I said, "No, no, no. I'm sorry. You take what you've got. You're okay, don't worry."

The kid reached down, scooped up all the pants, and stuck them under his coat. And then he turned, but he didn't want to take his eyes off me, so he turned and ran. But he didn't have his bearings right. So while he was looking back at me with the gun over his shoulder, he ran smack-dab into a telephone pole. He smashed himself. I heard the gun clattering onto the concrete, and I said to myself, "Oh! NOW he's mine."

I jumped for him and I got right near him. He scrambled and grabbed a hold of that gun, and as I went down to get him, he had the gun right on my face, right on my face. His hand was quivering and shaking, and he was screaming, "Now I'm gonna kill ya! Now I'm gonna kill ya."

I said, "No, I wasn't going to do anything. I just wanted to see if you were okay!"

Somehow it must have tangled his computer. He didn't know what to do. I quickly backed out the alley. He again scooped up the pants and said, "If you come after me again, you will die."

I said, "I will not come after you again." And I let him go.

That was my first store, and my first encounter with how dangerous it was to work at this company.

At that point I'm down on Maxwell Street, Bobby has already saved my bacon, and I thought, "Okay, it's now time to pull the plug."

New Beginnings

I CALLED UP MY DISTRICT MANAGER whose name was Joe Martins; he was the head of all the Chicago stores. He was a Puerto Rican man, tougher than nails. Big, strong, 225 pounds—grew up in Spanish Harlem. This guy was one of the toughest men I ever met in my entire life. I called him up and said, "Joe, I think I'm done. I think I'm gonna quit."

Over the prior year, we had become very good friends. He was 10 years older than I, but we were both street rats. He liked me, and I liked him, so he tried to talk me out of it.

I said, "Joe, just call New York and tell 'em I'm done. "

So he called me up the next day and said, "New York doesn't want to lose you. So they're going to offer you to get out of Maxwell St. And they are going to give you the number one store in the city, at State and Madison, downtown in the loop. It's safe. It's the only store in the whole chain that has an armed guard all day, and you're not going to have any trouble."

I had told my mom the night before that I was quitting. She had called my uncle John, who was a partner with 5 other men who were about to open a Rush St. bar. She begged my uncle. She said, "My son is willing to let go of that department store outfit. Please call him and offer him a job."

This was my mother's youngest brother.

The next day, I got a call from my uncle. He says, "Why don't you let me teach you how to tend bar. You'll be out of all that craziness. You'll be in nightlife, and you'll make twice the money you make now."

I agreed.

So when my friend Joe Martins called and offered me the best store in the city, I told him, "Joe, it's just too late. I've made a decision to be a Rush St. bartender."

And I left John's Bargain Stores. A month later, I was down on Rush St. I'd just turned 21. The whole world changed for me.

This was a dramatic change from when I was 17 and 18, when I was working full-time in factories and business places. All of a sudden, I was thrust into the middle of Chicago's nightlife and the best up-and-coming bar in the Rush St. area. It was terribly exciting. I was dealing with people I had never dealt with before. All of a sudden I was in contact with an absolutely unbelievable flow of young women. I was the nephew of one of the owners. My life changed dramatically. It went from hard-work craziness and danger to party time all the time.

I still had my workaholic stuff in me, and I very, very quickly became an absolutely excellent bartender. My uncle was an old-time pro bartender in Chicago, a classic old pro. He worked very slowly and methodically, a perfectionist. He taught me how to be that way; only I did it at triple his speed. At one point a few years later, one of the Rush St. bar owners told me that I was the fastest bartender on Rush St. There were hundreds of bars in the Rush St. area. I was proud beyond belief.

That was my focus. I was faster than everyone I worked with. I never spilled anything. I see bar people now spilling liquor all over. I was impeccable. There was never a person at the bar who needed to light a cigarette. If I had 20 people at the bar and 6 waitresses, anybody in my periphery who was going into their purse or taking a cigarette out, I'd stop everything I was doing, run 20 feet, have a lighter out, light their cigarette, and go back to doing my stuff. I was crazy.

But the people that I met in those years on Rush St. were just amazing. I met every kind of cross section of people. I met all of the burglars, the criminals, the mafia leaders, the hookers, the pimps. All the professional athletes in Chicago hung out on Rush St. At one point, Mike Ditka said that I was his absolute favorite bartender on Rush St. I knew Bears players, Cubs players, Bulls players, Hawks players. I just had my world blow wide open. I did this Rush St. thing with a passion.

The downside of it was that I became a serious drinker. The main owner of this group was a crazy Englishman alcoholic. He demanded that his bartenders were able to drink. By the end of my first year on Rush St., I was drinking a minimum of 1 quart of VO myself. Absolute minimum. I spent about 4 years on Rush St. In that time, I worked at a basement bar that could put 1,200 people in it. Pretty much, most of the years I was there, at least 5 nights a week, we were packed. We had the biggest thing going on Rush St. We were the first ones to bring in rock bands to play. The name of the bar was the Spirit of '76. We were the first ones to sell 50 cent glasses of beer. People would line up from our entrance, a block down the street going down Division and a block going the other way down Dearborn. From 2 directions, people would line up for a block. This was pretty much 5 nights a week, except for Sunday and Monday, we were packed.

I had money flowing through my hands that I never even imagined. I had a fancy car. At one point I had a beautiful Cadillac convertible. And

I had a 4-door black Cadillac Fleetwood sedan that I parked in a lot upstairs. I never even used them. I never left the Rush St. area. So I did Rush St. and I did Rush St. right. In 4 years, I went from being one of probably 1,600 to 2,000 bartenders—a face in the crowd, to one of the most well-known bartenders on Rush St. All the owners on the street liked me. Many bars I would walk in, I couldn't even take money out of my pocket; the owners would insist I drink on the house as soon as they saw me. And I knew all these owners. It was a great life. The alcohol, I seemed to be able to handle without any bad effects. I could actually talk for a long time about Rush St., but I think I'll bring it to a close now.

I do want to mention 2 powerful events. In 1963, when JFK was assassinated, people will often say, "Do you remember where you were?" Well, I remember that day. I remember being crushed with sadness and despair. It was like I lost my best friend, mentor, best everything in the universe, when he was killed. And some years later, I was on Rush St. It was my night off. I remember I was walking past a bar. It was a warm summer night. I looked in the bar, and there was some commotion on the television. And everyone in the bar was frozen. So I walked in the front door, and I heard the words immediately: "Bobby Kennedy has been assassinated."

It brought me instantly into a place that ended up, some hours later, in a rather profound spiritual experience. As soon as I heard the news, I left the place and went back to my apartment. I had an apartment down the street from the Spirit of '76 by myself. I went and got in my reclining chair and started first praying, then meditating. Then I had an idea that I should really try to go deep inside of myself. So I did that, and about an hour later, sitting in the chair, I had my first out-of-body experience.

What happened was that I literally left my body, floated above the easy chair, looked at myself, and realized I was out of my body. I understood what astral projection was; I had experienced it before. I immediately desired to go where Bobby Kennedy was. And in one split second, I went from my house on Rush St. to where I was zooming in like a jet plane on Los Angeles.

It was dark. I could see the whole city's panorama. I was slowing down rapidly in midair. And I saw 2 figures up in the air. I would say like a mile over the city. I slowed down rapidly and began approaching, sort of floating, these 2 figures suspended in the air. The 2 figures were Bobby and John F. Kennedy. John was kneeling in midair and Bobby was laid out, with his head in his brother's lap. And John had both of his hands on Bobby's head. He turned back over his shoulder and saw me approaching, and he shook his head "No." And I immediately stopped in midair. He telepathically told me, "Thank you, but we don't need your help. Everything is done." And in one second, I was back in my reclining chair in my house.

The next morning I made some phone calls to people I knew at the *Chicago Sun-Times*. To try to get the mailing address of Ethel Kennedy. While I waited for a call to get the address, I sat down to write her a letter, a long letter, explaining the experience that I had had the night before. I closed the letter up and put a stamp on it, and eventually the phone rang. A friend who worked for a columnist called Irv Kupcinet gave me Ethel Kennedy's mailing address in Washington. I mailed the letter that day. After 2 days, I came in the house in the morning and opened my mailbox, and there was a card from Ethel Kennedy. It had no postage or stamp on it. However, it got in my mailbox; some person had put it there. It wasn't a personal message; it didn't respond to anything that I had said about my astral projection. It was a card with Bobby Kennedy's favorite spiritual sayings on it, and it was signed in her handwriting. "Thank you, Ethel Kennedy." I still have that card.

First Psychedelic Experience

Aᴛ ᴛʜɪꜱ ᴘᴏɪɴᴛ, I need to explain a most important part of my life. The biggest change point of my life. It was when I was 23, and I was on Rush St. I was working the bars now for a few years. I was very involved with bar life, nightlife, nightclubs, bar people, waitresses, bartenders, owners. It just enveloped every moment of my life essentially.

Then one day, at the end of a shift, one of the employees of the Spirit of '76—her name was Mary—she asked if I could come over to her house with the idea of smoking some Panamanian Red pot with her and her husband. I did a little bit of pot smoking but mostly drinking in those days. But I accepted the invitation and when I got over to their house, we got high.

Mary said to me, "The real reason we asked you here today is that we want to offer something to you."

I was a little suspicious about what they were going to offer me. And Mary said, "Have you ever heard of LSD?"

"Yea, it's that stuff you take that makes you go bonkers."

She and her husband laughed and said, "We feel that LSD would be very helpful to you."

So we talked about it for quite a while.

I was questioning what they were saying. They were essentially telling me that they felt that I was somewhat blocked or stuck in the past or in old habits. I was only 23. I didn't really know what they were talking about. But that they felt that this drug would open up my life. Expand my understanding. They were using a lot of phrases that I really didn't comprehend. They were both very intellectually advanced from where I was. The husband was an existentialist, and Mary was an astrologer and a spiritually astute woman.

They were both about 10 years older than me. Anyways, I told them that I would think about it.

The next day, I went downtown to the big bookstore, Krock and Brentano's. I asked if there were any books on LSD. I was told that there was only one that had recently come in. So I bought it. It was a pocketbook. I don't remember the author or the name, but I read it in just a few days. And what I got from it, essentially, was that this drug was being used since the mid-'50s around the world by psychiatrists and psychologists and that it had the ability to break old patterns and give people much deeper and greater understanding of themselves. It intrigued me, everything I read. At that time, the drug was not against the law, and there was nothing negative or scary in the whole book. So I told Mary and Dan, "Yes, I'll accept this gift."

So it was probably a week later on a night that we all had off. I went to their house, and they gave me a sugar cube, in which there was supposedly one drop. I think they said it was 250 mg of a pure LSD 25, manufactured by the Sandoz chemical company in Zurich, Switzerland, which was the company that first synthesized LSD. So I was getting the pure product from the best source in the world.

They told me they would stay with me the whole time and guide me. Basically, I took the sugar cube and let it dissolve. I didn't make any notes at the time, but I began feeling feelings that I don't ever remember having had before. I remember feeling somewhat euphoric, somewhat alive inside of my body in a way that I don't ever remember. I felt different waves of happiness that I had never felt in my entire life. Feelings of bliss, feelings of joy. And they weren't overwhelming. I was not incapacitated in any way. I was able to function, to get up and walk. My guides, essentially, just left me alone and watched me. A whole awakening ensued inside of me. I had visionary, not hallucination, but visionary flashes and recalls of earlier times in my life. I had a sense of profound understanding of joy and happiness and these feelings of elation. I had a sense of understanding that they were natural, that they were supposed to be experienced, that they were part of who I really was, which I had never encountered up to that point. A little while later, they took me for a walk. We walked down a quiet side street a couple blocks. And then they took me into another house, where they introduced me to a couple who became lifelong friends of mine. In that house, I sought out a room where I was just by myself. I sat against a wall, and I had tremendous memories of parts of my childhood, all the way back to one particular time at 3 years old, which was excruciatingly traumatic while I lived it at 3. And I essentially saw that period of time and those events that were so painful for me when I experienced them, but then I also had a tremendous understanding and overview that, in truth, at that time, I was not really being traumatized. It was a misunderstanding in my young mind and body. And as I sat there, it all replayed... it replayed in such vivid detail that I was literally experiencing it, not just remembering it, and what I saw was that I had misinterpreted. I hadn't understood. My conscious mind at 3 years old was not grasping what was actually happening. And the outcome, which was a lot of fear and trauma, wasn't actually present, wasn't actually happening. So I sat there, and I rationalized in my conscious mind that a whole traumatic part of my childhood was actually a distortion and a fabrication of the truth of those days and those events. I sat there, and I felt just a tremendous flood of release and relief from the burden of carrying what I thought was terrible experiences. I just watched them all evaporate. I watched them literally disappear. It probably went on for 15 minutes or something like that, and when that period ended, I felt incredibly clean and free and unburdened. So much more happened that night, but I so clearly remember that when the drug wore off and I went back home, the sun was coming up and I went to bed. I remember lying in bed and feeling that the overall experience had been not just beneficial, but life changing. I felt, before I fell asleep, that my life would never be the same. I felt unburdened, unblocked. I felt free, and I felt happy to my core. As I lay there, ready to drift off, I remember thinking there not only is a God, but I now know that God is a reality because I've just been touched by God. And I felt there will never be a time in my life where I ever have to doubt the existence of God, or where I will have to be afraid of death.

The next day, I went to work, and I felt like I had had my brain put through a washing machine and then cleaned and polished. I felt lighter, more fluid. I could already feel the beginning of old patterns from birth, and I could feel them beginning to dissipate. I could feel fears that I carried my whole childhood and into my adult life beginning to just literally melt away. So for several days, although no one seemed to notice, I continued on this strange path of feeling like I had a new life. My body felt different. My mind was certainly profoundly different. I guess what I was really feeling was my first deep and conscious connection to my own spirit, or my own soul. So that was the beginning of what, in the next 10 or 20 years, would be a number of different psychedelic experiences. Some I'll mention later, where they're appropriate. That couple that had singled me out, they didn't make a habit of this. I never heard of them doing this again in the 20 or 30 years that I knew them after that. They had just been profoundly led to give me that opportunity. For certain that opportunity began my spiritual inquiry, my inner investigation of who I really was, what I was, what my life was about. With a little sugar cube, they, literally, put me on a path of self-exploration, self-investigation, and self-analysis that was never to end for the rest of my days, right to this day for sure. So I'll just mention further that the effects of that first LSD trip were like flipping a page from one chapter of my life to another. From my first 23 years, most of it very difficult, very dark, to the rest of my life to this very day, of broadening awareness and new revelations, and at that same period, I began to have an insatiable hunger and desire to know about spiritual realities. I never had any interest in the Catholic Church, even though at 13 I became baptized and part of the church. I saw through the hypocrisy and the dogma. By 18 or 19 I gave up on church-going and church BS as I saw it.

So all of a sudden I had a tremendous drive to search out and find out what was happening on spiritual levels. A short while after this experience a friend of mine, a bartender I worked with, came over to my house one day and handed me a book.

He said, "I have a feeling you'd be interested in this." I looked at the book, and it was called *The Tibetan Book of the Dead.*

I said to him, "Why would I be interested in this? I have no interest in this."

He said, "Stick your nose in it."

I read that book, and then shortly after, another friend gave me a book called *ESP and How to Make it Work for You* by Harold Sherman.

I grabbed that book and devoured it and actually began a 2-3 year-period where I started having what Harold Sherman would call ESP or extra sensory perceptions. I started meditating and having various actual spiritual experiences that were what scientists merely called paranormal experiences or extra sensory experiences. But those couple years after my initial trip, the whole world of spiritual investigation exploded to me, exploded wide open. In that period, I became a voracious reader. And I found that I could comprehend everything I could read. None of it was a mystery. None of it was too hard to understand or to incorporate into my conscious mind. In my early years of all the reading and the meditating I started doing, I had many paranormal experiences: I had telekinesis, I had telepathy, I had profound precognition. I was having visions of events that were going to happen. I started having prophetic dreams. In that period I started having dreams about horse races that were going to run the next day. I essentially began to feel that the whole spiritual world was a vast landscape that as per my desire, my will, my choice I could investigate at any level. And interspersed in those years were more psychedelic journeys. I tried different types of psychedelics. I found many of them to be not pure and not really beneficial. I tried mushrooms and I tried peyote, but when I was able to find a good form of LSD, every single experience I had was a powerful, worthwhile, beneficial experience. I had no negative side effects. I had no scary flashbacks. There was nothing negative about using psychedelics to explore deeper into my own beingness and out in the cosmos.

This was probably the single most major turning point in my life. That first LSD trip undoubtedly in my entire life was the most important event. I cannot even imagine if I had not had that experience, what my life would have been. Instinctively, I feel like I would have been off the planet by 30 or 40 years old. So the inclusion in my life of a drug synthesized by a man named Albert Hoffman in Zurich, Switzerland, profoundly changed my life from one of repetitious, self-destructive, unproductive thinking and acting to a rabid investigation and change of course and this deep desire to know all things spiritual. To understand the workings of my mind. To understand how my body functioned. And with it came, for the first time in my life, a way of being connected to others that I had never felt, a way of being connected to the human race as I had never felt. So this was the beginning; this was a powerful turning point. And it all happened by taking a little sugar cube in my hand and putting it in my mouth. It changed my life, changed everything related to my entire reality. Later I'll talk more about some of the people I met that were known in the psychedelic world like Timothy Leary and Richard Alpert. Jokingly, I said to myself at that time that I wasn't sure I could trust anybody who had not had LSD. I started feeling like there were 2 kinds of people on the planet: those who knew and those who knew not. Anyone who hadn't done a psychedelic was in the "knew not" category.

The Dawn of a Spiritual Life

I'LL GO INTO A LITTLE MORE DETAIL about those first 2 or 3 years after the first LSD trip. I still worked on Rush St. as a bartender. I still socialized and did a lot of alcohol. Everything was status quo on the outside, in the work world. When I walked out of my house, I would go back to living this sort of exciting, street bartender, street nightlife, bar club person. I lived in a very small studio apartment with 2 cats, and when I got home, I would delve into my books. My best friend was Joe Martins, who had been my district manager at John's Bargain stores. After I left that company, Joe and I stayed close, and I brought Joe into the psychedelic world. I guided him on his first trip. We became as 2 intrepid explorers. We worked together investigating and trying to understand the whole spiritual world. The "Alter World," as we called it.

So when I encountered *ESP and How to Make it Work for You*, Harold Sherman was considered to be the preeminent expert and most knowledgeable source about things like telepathy. He engaged in things like tremendous telepathic exploration with a man at the South Pole.

In his book, Sherman explained how to have these experiences, how to do mental configurations, meditations, to open yourself up to those higher realms. So some of them happened quite by accident- others by planning, meditation and discipline.

For instance, I was lying on the floor, doing a meditation one morning, at about 11:00 a.m. I didn't go to work until about 2 in the afternoon. I was doing a meditation, and I was pondering telekinesis—moving objects with the mind. In one of my earliest trips I had had a vision of the word "telekinesis." I didn't know at the time what it meant but found out that it meant the ability to move an object with your mind. So I'm lying on the floor, and I opened my eyes; the meditation had just come to an end, and the room was pretty bright. I was lying next to a big old console television. Hanging off of the edge of the television, dangling down 3 or 4 inches, was a necklace that I had bought to give to a girl I knew. It was a big gaudy necklace with different colored quartz stones. Anyways, part of it was hanging over the edge of the television. I just very casually, with no intent and no energy expenditure, I casually thought, "I wonder if I could move that necklace." And instantly, the necklace flew off of the television and landed on the carpet next to me. It was literally profoundly shocking because it was nothing more than a simple random thought. But I had apparently put my consciousness through the meditation into a place of power. I had, without realizing it, revved up my paranormal abilities. And I lay there for several minutes with the realization that, yes in fact, telekinesis is possible because I had just done it.

There was maybe a year after the first time I had done it. I had another real powerful experience of it. I was at a friend's house; we were doing a meditation, and he had a strobe candle. A strobe candle is a candle that has a very thick wick. It is almost like a solid hard core to the candle. Strobe candles were made to be used outside of temples or lamaseries in the Tibetan Himalayas. They were made in such a way that they could not be blown out. Winds of 100 mph could not blow out a strobe candle.

My friend had a strobe candle sitting across the room. The other significant thing about a strobe candle is that it pulsates very powerfully. If you're sitting and looking at it, the flame flashes very strongly. Like heartbeats.

So we were sitting and meditating, and with my eyes closed, I could still see the flashing, the strobing, the pulsing of the candle. And it became annoying to me. I thought again very randomly without conscious intent, "I wish I could put that out." Instantly, the candle went out. Just instantly. My friend, sitting in front of me said, "Why did you do that?"

I said, "I don't know. It was bothering me."

He said, "I like them, so don't do it again."

Well, as we both sat there and the reality sunk into us, the only way you could put a strobe candle out was to stick the wick into a container of sand. As we both realized that I had just done that from across the room, we almost became giddy. My friend realized what had happened, and he said, "Corky, do you realize what you just did?"

I said, "Yea, I think I do."

The interesting thing about all the ESP phenomena was that each one that I accomplished or experienced, I never had a desire to reproduce again. I didn't seem to need in any way to be able to develop that ability or to use that ability as a skill or as a tool. I never had the thought of being able to do psychic tricks in front of other people. It was as though my personal progression through this paranormal world was that I was being shown that these were realities by my own experience of them, and then they became no longer important. As soon as I knew they were realities, I had no desire or feeling to develop the ability to reproduce them at will.

Another experience that I had happened one night when I was meditating at home. It was a night off and I came out of a meditation, and I had a strong, powerful feeling of wanting to see a friend of mine who worked at the Spirit of '76. I was sitting in a lighted room. There was a lamp on, and I sat up on the floor, and I turned my head in the direction of where the bar was that I worked at. And out of nowhere, just suddenly I could see through the wall of my apartment and through the wall of the next apartment and out into the street; it was Division St. that I lived on. The bar was on Division, 2 blocks down. I progressed at a rapid speed from seeing through my wall, through my building, down the street, to the building that the bar was in, down through the ground through the wall, and there was the friend of mine, standing behind a cash register, ringing up some liquor sales. As I sat there and stared at her, I realized that this wasn't any type of illusion or fantasy. I had no drugs in me. I was actually able to have a type of X-ray vision. I watched her for a minute or two until I saw her engage with a couple of people, exchanging words. I couldn't hear their words though; there was no auditory input, only visual. Then I just closed my eyes and broke it off. And the next day when I saw her, I asked her about a few of the things I had seen and a few of the people that she was talking to.

She said, "Yea, they came in. How did you know? I didn't see you here."

I told her of my experience, and she was quite amazed. That X-ray experience later reoccurred once when I was on an LSD trip. I looked up through my ceiling and out through my building and out into the stars and rapidly accelerated up past the moon, and then I became so taken aback by it that I just stopped the experience. The X-ray ability turned into an astral projection.

Astral projection or having the spirit leave the body—I had a number of those experiences. The first one again was quite by accident, where I found myself in a meditation floating above my body. I had 2 friends in the room with me, and they were trying to talk to me. I floated around in the room; I would look over in a corner and wonder what it would be like to be in that corner, and I would instantly be in the other corner. I kind of experimented and bounced around the ceiling. And then I saw that my friends were getting concerned. They were trying to wake me up, and I realized they were afraid that something was wrong with me. So I desired to go back into my body and went right back into my body instantly.

I opened my eyes and asked them, "What's all the commotion about?"

They said, "You weren't breathing! You weren't talking!"

I just laughed.

I had a number of astral projection experiences. And then there was also a telepathic connection with my friend Joe and myself. I was able to telepath with him from different rooms. The way the telepathy worked was very interesting. The way that it happened again, I didn't intend it, it wasn't a plan, and I didn't know what I was doing. I was in a back bedroom of this house we were at; we were actually in the Bronx in New York, on vacation. I was in the back bedroom, and I wanted to talk to Joe. But he was in another room with his family. I didn't want to intrude on them, so I started feeling, not thinking, but feeling that I wanted to talk to him. And a strange thing happened. I started to feel a pulsation running through my brain. It was like a quivering pulsation. It had a sound like, "BRRRRRRRGGHHHHH BBRRRRRGHHH." It was sort of strange, a vibration, an actual physical experience of a pulsation going from the back of my brain through the front and then from the front to the back. I had maybe 10 or 12 of those. While I was feeling that pulsation or vibration, I was feeling, "Joe, come here! Joe, come here!" And then I sort of got tired of it. I changed my mind-set and started thinking about something else. About a minute later, the door to the room I was in burst open, and my friend rushed in and said, "I'm here! I'm here!"

I said, "Oh, could you feel me or hear me calling?"

He said, "Yea, plain as day. You kept calling me, but I was in a conversation with my mother and wife, and I couldn't just walk away. And I broke loose as quick as I could. - I could feel you. I could hear you in my mind saying, 'Come here.'"

That was my first real, real clear telepathy experience that again, more or less, happened without any desire to make it happen, without any thoughts of "I'm going to do this experiment" or anything like that. All these different paranormal things seemed to build up in my desire body. I had desire to know if they were real. If these potentials could actually be experienced by me. And then at some point down the line—a week later, a month later, or a year later—they would actually find a moment in time where everything was in harmony to just spontaneously have that experience. So those were some of the very beginning and very obvious experiences that I had, which were all a result of reading Harold Sherman's book.

When I began having them, when I had the first few, I wrote to Harold Sherman—his address was listed in the back of his book. I wrote a long letter to him, telling him what was beginning to happen. Then a week later, I received a handwritten letter, and he was most encouraging. He was excited for me. He essentially said that I was breaking ground into realms that the majority of the human race would never know or never experience. He encouraged me to continue my investigations and to keep him informed. And then as different experiences came to me, I would write to him again, and he would write back. He answered every letter I ever wrote to him.

Mostly all he would do was encourage me. Encourage me to keep meditating, to use spiritual protection, to use his techniques to expand and develop these abilities. But unlike him, I didn't feel any desire—as I said before—I never felt the desire to really develop these abilities or be able to do these things at will. There was one more experience that happened that wasn't covered by his book or his experiences, but it was a profound experience. And to this day, I have an intuitive understanding that I was shown something of immense proportion, immense importance to understand as an underlying reality and truth.

I was lying on my living-room floor next to my TV, and I had just finished doing the meditation outlined in his book, which would essentially put a person in a receptive place, whereby universal forces could show that person whatever they wanted that person to see. Right now, I would say it was my high self that brought on this experience, but Harold never used the expression "high self." He called all the higher energies, "universal energies." So I was lying down, doing his meditation. I finished with it and knew it was getting time for me to go to work; I was already dressed in my bartender uniform. So, I lay there and let myself come back from the meditation; I opened my eyes, and my body was gone. Instead of seeing my body, I saw what I could best describe as my light body. All I saw from my eyes down was brilliant luminous white light. Shiny, pulsating, strong white light. I actually lay there with my eyes open, looking at the place where my physical body should have been, and it was just brilliant light. At one point, and this was pretty common when new experiences first came to me, I began to be concerned. I closed my eyes right away, and I wondered if I had just done something wrong and wouldn't be able to see my body again. So I opened my eyes again and still brilliant white light. I was looking down at what metaphysicians or New Age people would say was my "light body." It again was just nothing but brilliant light. So I again closed my eyes, this time even more concerned. In my mind I said, "I want to see my body." I wanted my body back. But this time when I opened my eyes, I was looking at my clothes and my shoes, and my body was back. I sat up right away and thought,

"What was that one?" Because prior to that moment, I had never encountered any kind of information about the light body. I think in the *Tibetan Book of the Dead*, they talked about when leaving the body, possibly being in a body clothed in white. It actually was many years later that I ran across various writings from this theosophical society when Madam Blavatsky and Annie Besant explained in great detail what the light body was and that everyone had a light body. They said that when you left the physical body, you would be in your light body. And that if you attained a high spiritual realization or experience, you would be in your light body, as I was in that moment. That was one that came out of nowhere, not expected, and then afterward, not understood. It was quite a while before I fully comprehended what that experience actually was.

Horses and Dreams

IT WAS THIS EXACT SAME PERIOD OF TIME where I had been introduced to thoroughbred racing and thoroughbred gambling. I was probably 18 or 19. I occasionally went out to racetracks. I had a mentor who knew how to handicap. I used to run bets for him. And then when I got on Rush St. and started working the bars, I had no interest in it. I never went to the track anymore.

But right at this point and as a direct result of doing the Sherman's meditation— again spontaneously, without desire, without forethought, without plan, without intent—one night I had a dream of seeing a horse. In the dream I recognized a racetrack; it was Sportsman's Park. And I saw a horse coming down the stretch, and I heard the announcer's voice yelling about the horse's name. The horse's name was Real Fast. The announcer was saying, "It's Real Fast by 5 lengths." And then when the horse went past the finish line, all of a sudden I saw a picture of the tote board, and it had the horse's number up first. The payoff was $17.40.

So I woke up and remembered it. I didn't know what to make of it. But I went to breakfast where I usually did—at the drugstore lunch counter above the Spirit of '76. I sat down in a booth that was reserved for the owner of the drugstore. His name was Bob Hefley. From behind the counter, he saw me sitting there. He would usually come out, order a cup of coffee, and sit with me and talk while I had breakfast.

So I'm eating my eggs, and I said, "Ya know, Bob, I had the weirdest dream last night." And he said, "What was that?" I said, "I dreamt of a horse race." He said, "Oh yea? Tell me about it." So I gave him the entire detail.

He didn't say a word. He got up out of the booth and walked up out of the drugstore. Out in front of the drugstore was one of those old-time little paper newsstands. He went out there and got a little green sheet, which was a listing of the horses running that day at Sportsman's Park. So he came in a few minutes later and sat down.

He said, "You got $20?"

I said, "Sure."

He said, "Give me $20."

I said, "What for?"

He said, "Don't ask me what for. Give me $20."

So I took out a 20 and handed it to him, and he said, "Okay." He said, "I have to go back to work." And he went back behind the counter. I didn't know what the $20 was for. I hadn't put two and two together.

The next morning, I woke up and did my routine, went and sat down in his booth, and ordered my eggs. He saw me. He got his cup of coffee, and he sat down. He went in his pocket and pulled out a wad of bills and threw them on the table in front of me. I looked at them all. It was all $20 bills.

I said, "Bob, what's that?"

He said, "That's your share of the winnings."

"What winnings?"

"Your horse dream!"

"What do you mean my horse dream?"

He said, "Real Fast ran in the 7th race yesterday. It won and paid $17.40. That's $174."

I asked Bob, "You bet my $20 on that horse?"

"Yea."

"How much did you bet?"

"$200," he said.

You could have knocked me over with a straw. I was like more than shocked. I had just had an event happen in my life that had never happened before. It was a premonition dream. And it played out exactly as I had seen it in my dream.

He said, "If you have any more dreams, let me know."

So maybe a week later or a little more, I had another dream, very similar—saw the horse, heard the name, the tote board showed $8.20. So I went in, sat down, and ordered my eggs. Bob came over. I said, "I had another dream." He said, "Let's hear it!"

I told him the dream. He went out to the newspaper stand, came back in, and said, "Give me $20."

Again the whole day I never thought about it for 1 minute. The next day I come in, he throws down $82. I said, "You're kidding me!"

He says, "Nope, paid $82, and there's your money."

I said, "And you bet?"

He said, "I bet $200."

That was the 2nd of 6 dreams. Each one became a little bit less clear, a little bit less detailed. I think by the 4th one, I didn't see the tote board anymore. I had an extremely strange detachment from the moment I had the dream and knew I was going over to the drugstore and knew I'd be betting $20. I never felt like upping my bet even after the 3rd horse had won, and it was pretty apparent that this was actually some incredible entry into the world of premonition. I didn't change the pattern; he didn't either. Each time, we played it out exactly the same.

After the 6th one, I never had another one in that period of my life again. After they stopped, he said to me, "Son, haven't you had any dreams lately?"

I don't know exactly what caused them to start, and I don't know in that period what caused them to end. But after I left Rush St., the dreams came back. I had football dreams. I had basketball dreams. For the first 10 or 15 years of having these premonition dreams of sporting events or horse races, each time they seemed to get harder and harder to interpret. In the beginning, they were like free gifts, factual exact premonition. As they went on, they went from seeing races to no longer seeing any races, but seeing images or symbols. It was like my challenge was to interpret what I saw into finding what track the horse was running at. In the beginning it was all local Chicago tracks. Later, I dreamt about New York and Florida tracks; it was always spontaneous. There was only a short period where I could actually request a dream at night before going to sleep. A few times, I would actually request a horse dream and then have that happen that night. And then have the horse run the next day, or very shortly after and win. So, premonition began with me through these horse dreams.

There were later times in my life, even to this day, where spontaneously I have a premonition and I know that what I'm feeling often is about some negative event on the horizon that I'm being shown and given an option to change or to avoid. One such event happened later in my life. I had a very close friend who ran an after-hours nightclub on Rush St.

He we would open the bar at 3:00 a.m. And then after 4 a.m., nothing but night people would come in there after all the other bars on Rush St.

closed. So he would have bar owners, and hookers and pimps and athletes. An amazing array of different people. He did all of this illegally, and it worked quite well for him. He made a large amount of money. He offered me a job to work there at night. I didn't take him up, even though at the time I was out of work and really needed money, but I didn't do it. I knew that an operation like that couldn't just go on undetected for long. He had picked another friend of ours to be his partner. Billy and Jack were the 2 guys that ran this bar. They would run it from 3:00 a.m. to 7:00 a.m. and then close it up. They made quite a profit. So one night, I had this dream that they were being busted—the doors broke down, police were flooding into the place, and the dream was funny to me because it had one type of every cop. It had a state trooper with a big round hat. It had a Chicago policeman, it had a plainclothes detective, it had a park ranger—every kind of police. And in the dream, they were searching this place for cocaine, which I knew was part of the after-hour attraction of this bar. He would supply cocaine and alcohol. So I woke up from that dream at about 11:00 a.m. And I immediately jumped into my car and drove over to where Billy and Jack were.

I pounded on the door, pounded again. I heard them grumbling and yelling and stirring. Billy opened the door and said, "You know we're sleeping. What the hell are you doing?" I said, "I've got to tell you this dream."

So I went inside. They both sat down, and I told them the whole dream. Billy said, "So what in the hell am I supposed to do with your dream?" And I said, "You're supposed to pay attention to it."

"Pay attention to your dream? You've gotta be crazy. Get outta here. I'm going back to bed." Jack said, "Billy, wait a minute, maybe we should listen." Billy said, "You're nuts." And he threw me out.

Two nights later, I have the same dream; only this time it's more detailed, and this time the police bring in a woman. She shows them where the cocaine is hidden and then they are handcuffed and taken out in handcuffs. I got in my car again, drove over, pounded on the door, and woke them both up. Billy was furious with me, just absolutely furious, screaming at me.

We went in, and I sat down and told him this version of the dream. Billy said the same thing, "Corky, you're crazy."

Jack said, "No, Billy, if he had this dream twice, it's gotta be something we should pay attention to."

Billy said, "No, I ain't paying attention to it. It's all his BS."

So later I found out, Jack quit. Jack told Billy, "I'm out. I'm finished."

Billy said to Jack, "Okay, your call."

About a week later, Billy was going up the stairs to the building where the bar was. It was sort of an old brick building. He was going up the stairs; his arms were full with a case of liquor and hidden was a big bag of cocaine. As he's going up the stairs, people come out of everywhere, out of the gangway, out of the front door, out of the police cars, and they grab him, take him upstairs, go to his stash place in the bar, find more cocaine, and they arrest him.

Billy was very fortunate that his mother had very high political connections, and his mother was able to buy off the arrest and had the record of the arrest completely wiped out for a lot of money. He never had to go to court. The record was expunged, and he got out of it. But in the process of the police cutting him loose and clearing the record, they told him that he had been turned in by a hooker whom he had thrown out of his bar a couple weeks earlier. And that was the woman that I saw in the second dream, who had pointed out where his stash was hidden. So the dream turned out to be a reality.

Jack thanked me profusely after that because he had no political contacts and no money. And had he been with Billy, he would have inevitably had to go to prison and suffer the whole deal. But that was the type of premonition that would come at intervals, and to this day, I have what I would call mini premonitions, which will tell me about somebody's illness or some kind of accident or some event that is just on the horizon. The premonitions were very much a part of Harold Sherman's whole book, and we would talk about them in our letters back and forth. He felt one of the great gifts of ESP was the premonitions. To be able to see, especially, negative or dangerous events. If a person was shown them and they trusted and believed in the process in their own consciousness, then they could avoid bad experiences. For me, with the horse dreams, they were more or less the opposite; they were opportunities for me to actually make money. From the time they started, probably for at least 40 years, I would occasionally, spontaneously, be given another gift through dreams. In the later years, they would often coincide with me being in some financial trouble. If I was in a real troubled money squeeze, it was not uncommon for me to have a premonition dream about a horse race. I would go and bet it the next day and win enough money to pay rent and to get out from under bills. So it actually became a way of manifesting abundance that just showed me that in a certain way, the universe had my back, if I would pay attention and trust the process!

Synchronisity and Symbology

O**N A SLIGHTLY RELATED NOTE,** one of the abilities that I attribute to my early Harold Sherman ESP work was not exactly in the category of an extra sensory ability, but it was still very helpful. I started to be able to relate symbols in life or the world and put together symbolic messages or events and was able to make money off of them. I'll give a few examples.

The following may be the first time that I really saw that if I paid attention there was money to be made just from what was going on around me. Some might call these events synchronicities.

I was in Florida, getting on a plane to fly back to Chicago, and a niece of mine said, "Uncle, here, read this, you might be interested in it."

It was sort of a conspiracy-type newsletter that a man wrote and put out on a mimeograph machine. He called himself Ducky. And so I read this 6- or 8-page mimeograph deal on the plane. I didn't understand a lot of it. It was about things that at that time I had no interest in. But at the end of the letter, he would answer letters from his subscribers. All of them would say something like, "Dear Ducky, what does it mean that the Federal Government…?"

I got off the plane in Chicago and went to my house. The next morning, I got up, and one of my roommates had gotten a *Sun-Times* and was just finishing it when I got up. I said, "Chuck, let me see the paper. I want to see who is running at Arlington today."

So I'm reading through the entries, and I got to the 8th race, and about 4 or 5 picks down was a horse named "Dear Ducky." And I cracked up, and my roommates were saying, "What's going on?"

And I told them. I took the newsletter out and showed them. "Look, they address their letters 'Dear Ducky!' And here is Dear Ducky running this afternoon."

So one of my roommates said, "Well, what are you gonna do?"

I laughed and said, "You know what I'm gonna do!"

I only had about $80 to my name. I went out to Arlington and bet $80 to win on the horse; it won by about 10 lengths. I got back about $600 or $700.

But I thought after that experience, "Wait a minute. What is this? What just happened? My niece gives me a newsletter, I get to Chicago, there a horse running with the name of the guy. I gotta pay more attention."

Not long after, I was back behind the bar; I was working at a Rush St. bar then. It was nighttime, and I was behind the bar. A couple came in, and the woman looked sort of distraught. I asked them, "What's going on? You don't look too good."

She said, "Oh, I've been crying."

I said, "Crying, why?"

She said, "Padre Pio died today."

And I happened to know who Padre Pio was because my mother had made me read a pamphlet about him when I was 13 or 14 years old.

Padre Pio was the Catholic saint who had stigmata— bled from his hands and feet the last 50 years of his life. So I instantly knew who Padre Pio was and what it meant. Although I don't think 1 out of 10,000 people in Chicago ever heard of Padre Pio.

Anyways, the next day, I got up, I got my newspaper, and started looking through the entries. Out at Arlington Park, 7th race, there was a horse named Padre Pio, spelled the same way. I looked at it and said, "Oh my God!" I had about $100. I went over to a buddy and borrowed another $100. I went out to the track and bet the whole wad on Padre Pio; he won the race easily. I forget what I won, $1200 or $1400. After that one, I thought, "Oh, this is reality. If a person like me— and there aren't many with my makeup— if I can pay attention to symbols and horses, sometimes they match up."

Not too very long after, I was working at a different bar. I opened the bar at 10:00 a.m. and at about noon, the owner came in. He had a paper. I hadn't heard any news or anything from the day before. He put the paper on the end of the bar. I had no customers so I went and picked up the paper, and the headline was "Elvis Presley Dies." We talked about it for a while, and it was obviously quite a significant event. Anyways, after lunch I went and got the paper and opened it to the horses, and I think it was at Hawthorne racetrack. In the last race was a horse called Rock and Roll King. And I said, "Oh boy, here's another one."

So I was at work, and couldn't take off work to go to the track. I knew a bookie and called the bookie, and I said, "Terry, I want to give you a bet on a horse this afternoon."

He said, "Okay. What do you want?"

I said, "In the last race, I want Rock and Roll King."

He said, "Why are you betting that horse? Because Presley died?"

I said, "Exactly."

He said, "You're nuts. How much you want?"

I said, "200 to win."

He said, "200 to win?! You're a 20-dollar player. What do you want to bet 200 for?"

I said, "Terry, take my bet and bet it yourself." He said, "I wouldn't put a nickel on that nag."

He came in a few days later and gave me $2300 or $2400. Rock and Roll King won easily.

Again, in that same time period, there was an airplane crash out on the north side of Chicago, out past O'Hare, farther out northwest. I don't remember the details of the crash, but a lot of people were killed. In my life-time it was the only airplane crash near Chicago that I remember. Again, the very next day, I was at the bar that I worked at. I picked up the paper and was looking at the horses, and this was Arlington Park for sure. There was a horse called Plane Crash, and I knew it would win. So I called the bookie, and I bet something like $100 or $200. Again, the horse won, and I won money.

So those kinds of events have happened sporadically through my entire life; things that happened out in the world were cosmically associated to horse racing, and there was a way to link the event to the name of the horse. And in that time, I can barely remember one that lost. It was a way of showing me to pay more attention and have more awareness of what was happening out in the world. Later, I started seeing names of people that I may have just the day before had an encounter with, and then I started play-ing those horses. And most often 80% to 90% of the time, I would win on those. The last big one I had, I was looking at the horses running at Louisi-ana Downs one day. In that race were 4 women's names. Within the 24 hours prior to then, I had encountered 4 women with those names. Of them,

1 was an officer at a bank I went to, another was a woman, an old friend of mine who had called me the night before and out of the clear blue. The third was an old girlfriend of mine who had also called me the previous night. And the last one was a woman I had met on the phone that I had to do some legal dealings with. And I even asked her to spell her name. So there were 4 women's names that I had encountered in the prior 24 hours. So I made an exacta box and a trifecta box of the 4 names. And I bet it at a track. But this was a later race, so I went home. The next day I got the results, and the 4 women's names were the 4 longest shots in the race. And they ran 1st-4th. I had an exacta (betting that 2 specific horses will be first and second) that paid $700 or $800. The trifecta (betting that 3 specific horses will be first, second and third) paid $8,000 or $9,000. I went and cashed my tickets the next day.

But if I had made a superfecta box, I would have won $175,000. The superfecta paid $175,000. It would have only cost me $24 to make that bet, but I didn't even think about that at the time because they were all long shots. But I won over $9,000. So for me, it was a way of broadening my awareness, a way of understanding synchronicity and symbology, a way of making me link events to gambling became a very, very financially profitable thing for me. It was an offshoot of the premonitions that came through the Harold Sherman work.

This was sort of another gift to me. I always felt it was a gift given to me by the universe; it was a way for a guy who never had much money, who didn't know how to save much money, and these events often pulled me out of the fire. Again, it was the process at work.

Close Encounter with Disaster

This was the late '60s, and I was living on a commune in Arroyo Hondo, which is right near Taos, New Mexico. There were about 50 of us living in this big, adobe house. The guy who ran the place, Nick, came over to me, it was about 1 in the afternoon on a boiling hot sunny day and he said, "Look, some of the girls have been working real hard. And I'd like to have them take some time and go to the swimming pool." He said, "You've got a car big enough to take 5. Would you take them all over to the swimming pool?"

I was one of the only people who had a car. It was a big four door Chrysler. I had never been to the swimming pool. So I said, "Okay."

So these 5 beautiful young hippie girls, all of them really quite attractive, piled in my car with me, and we started down some side roads and some dirt roads; one of the girls knew where we were going. We drove about 5 miles up into a real rural area where the dirt road was the size of just one car. So it turned out that 20 or 30 years before that, somebody was going to build a big resort hotel out in this rural backward place. They were going to build this hotel, and they decided to build the pool first. So they actually built an Olympic-sized swimming pool, and it was fed by hot springs. So the pool had been refilled continuously for 20 to 30 years. Few people in the area knew about it.

So we get to this pool, and I park the car, and they all jump out, and they're all excited, and they all just take their clothes off and go in the pool nude. They wanted me to come in, but I was too shy. I just said, "Nah, I'll just hang out here." I was probably 25 or 26.

Anyways, they're all frolicking around, and they're happy, and everything is wonderful. Across the pool from the parking area where I was standing, was a big hill that maybe went 200 or 300 feet up to the top. And all of a sudden I saw a head pop up. And then there were 2 and there were 8 and then there were 20. And they were drunken Chicanos. At that time, Chicanos were defined as a mixture of a Mexican and Native American. From my understanding, they were historically not highly regarded by either Mexicans or Native Americans or by any white people; they were outcasts. These guys poured over that hill, stood out there at the top, and started coming down. So they had about 300 feet to cover. And I start yelling at the girls, "Get out! Get out now!"

I was absolutely screaming at them because I knew this was going to be bad. I could see half of them had bottles in their hands, wine bottles. I knew we were in a horrible situation. So the girls get out and start scrambling into their clothes, and when the guys see that, they all break into a full run. But before I can ever get them into the car, we're surrounded. Every one of them is absolutely drunk. They're all between 25 and 40 years old. They're all almost literally dripping saliva out of their mouths at what they just came upon.

So we're surrounded. The leader walks up to me; they're about 10 feet away from any of us in the circle. The leader comes up; he's maybe a foot shorter than I am. His eyes are absolutely bloodshot; he looks like he's been drinking for 2 days.

(Pardon my language—I have to tell it like it was, or it won't work).

He comes up in front of me and says, "You really fucked up, didn't you, white boy."

And I said, "Yea."

He said, "You know what we're going to do, don't ya?"

I said, "I think I know what you want to do."

He said, "Oh no, this ain't about what we want to do. This is what is going to go down. First, we're going to beat you to death and throw you to the bottom of that pool. And then we're raping all of them."

The girls are all huddled together, scared to death. And I said, "I would really appreciate it if it didn't go down that way."

He just laughed, and they all laughed. He said, "Dig this, gringo, he would appreciate it, if it didn't go down that way."

He turned to me and said, "How are you going to stop it?"

I said, "I'm not in any position to stop anything."

He said, "You're right! You're screwed."

I said, "It looks that way."

Now I can feel he's starting to be troubled by the fact that I'm not going to throw a punch, I'm not going to beg him, and I'm not going to run. He doesn't like that I'm just standing there, relaxed and calm.

He says, "What made you think you had the right to come in these mountains and pull this shit off?"

I said, "I've only been here a couple of months. I don't know any of the ground rules. I don't know any of the street rules."

He said, "You sure don't because you just did the biggest blunder of your life."

I said, "I'm very aware of that. I agree completely."

He said, "You agree?"

I said, "Yea, I got no right being here. This isn't my turf. This isn't my area. I've got no right being here at all."

Meanwhile the girls have not said a word; they're all just crunched together, holding each other.

And all the guys are starting to get a little antsy. They're sort of tired, and they start telling him about it. They're speaking Spanish to each other. I see they want action; they're tired of him playing around with me. So he says to me, "You know, as dumb as you are, at another time and place, I might like you."

And then there was a big groan from the rest of the crew.

He had a bottle of Thunderbird Wine half empty in his hand. I thought he was going to smack me with it, when he picked it up. He said, "How about having a drink with me?"

And I made my first mistake. I said, "Oh no. I don't drink, no thanks."

He says, "OH! You won't have a drink with me?! You're too good for me to touch my bottle, right??!"

And I reached out and snatched it out of his hand and guzzled it. I put it back out, and he took it. He pulled in close to me and he said, "You know, I don't know if it's going to work, but I'm going to try to hold these guys off. You go ahead, get those girls in the car, and get out of here."

I think some of them might have heard because the guys started groaning and grumbling.

And I told the girls—we were standing right next to the car— "GET IN THE CAR. GET IN THE CAR FAST."

They get in, and I grab my keys. One of the guys starts to reach out for me. And the leader, who is real small compared with most of them, he knocks the guy's arm away and he starts screaming at him. Then 2 or 3 others are coming at me, and he jumps in front of them and gets in their face. One of them says, "You're crazy. These women, we got them!"

He says, "I'm the leader…"

And they are screaming in Spanish. Meanwhile all the girls are in the car, and I'm in the driver's seat. I start the ignition, and he starts being pushed by 3 or 4 of them that he's holding back. They're pushing him back toward the car. So I realize that I've only got split seconds, and I have no chance to turn the car around. And I looked back in the mirror; there's only this skinny little dirt road. I bang it in reverse and start down that dirt road. And this guy literally gets overwhelmed. They swarm over him; a couple of them knock him to the ground; then he's on the ground, and then they're all coming at me.

They get to the front end of the car, and they start pounding, banging on the hood. I'm only going about 10 mph. I realize I gotta go a lot faster, or they're going to get me. So I just step on it. I'm leaning over the back seat where I'm looking right at the road and driving in reverse. And I'm balancing the steering wheel. And then I go faster and start pulling away from them. They as a mass and a horde are running at top speed, throwing their wine bottles; a few of them broke on the front of the car. I knew I couldn't even turn to look at them, or I'd lose control of the car. So I drove probably a mile before they gave up chasing. Then I could see they were all panting and stopping. I saw a little area where I whipped my rear into it, spun the car around and took off.

That was as close as I've ever come in my life to being in a nightmare that no person would ever want to find themselves in. And that little guy—he wouldn't fire on me because I wouldn't fight him. He wouldn't fire on me because I wouldn't cower. I have no idea what happened to him. I have no idea if he fixed it, made up, or if the next day he was still the leader, or if the next day he was still alive.

San Francisco, 1968

WHEN I WAS ON A SHORT TRIP TO SAN FRANCISCO, I had this particular experience, which at the time I really didn't think much of. I asked myself, "Why do I have these kind of experiences? What does this mean, and should I do something with it?" At that time, experiences like this were not uncommon to me, and they were not uncommon in the crowd that I ran in. They were not uncommon among people who were writing all manners of books about psychic phenomena and altered-state experiences. It happened at Golden Gate Park.

Golden Gate Park is this beautiful little park in San Francisco. I went there with 2 friends; they were just there picnicking. I remember the sun was shining brightly and there was a hill close by. I decided to go up on this hill and no one was on it. I started to meditate facing the sun. It was maybe 3 in the afternoon; the sun was beginning to set. So I sat down and put my hands on my knees, and crossed my legs which was my usual meditation posture.

I had been probably meditating for 10 or 15 minutes, getting very quiet. I could hear all the carryings-on in the park—people in the distance running, laughing, playing. I could hear kids. Then I became aware of hearing birds, and I became particularly aware of one bird chirping off to my left. I imagined that it was actually chirping at me. It seemed to be coming right directly at me, a continuous chirping sound. So I moved my head and opened my eyes. About 20 to 25 feet away from me was a low-hanging branch off of a tree. And there was one sparrow in the middle of the branch looking right at me and chirping. As soon as my eyes opened, he stopped chirping and hopped down the end of the branch, closer to me, until he was at the very tip, and then he started chirping again. I felt something unusual was happening and something more was going to happen. I felt a rise of anticipation me and of excitement in me. I closed my eyes again and went back to meditating, and the chirping stopped totally; it stopped so completely that I was surprised. I was sure the bird had turned away. After about a minute, I again turned my head and opened my eyes. The bird was right on the edge of the limb, and right when I opened my eyes, he started chirping almost wildly. I just laughed and thought, "Okay, you've got my attention. What are you going to show me? What are you going to tell me?"

I closed my eyes, the bird stopped chirping, and I went back to the meditation. No more than 1 minute passed. I had my hands on my knees with the palms open and facing down. I felt something. I was sitting on a grassy hill. I felt something touching my little finger. I thought I had just moved and I was touching a blade of grass. But something was moving. I didn't pay much attention at first. And then, I clearly felt something wrapping around my little finger. I was almost startled, except that I was in such a calm place that I looked down, opened my eyes, and watched a blade of grass finish wrapping itself 3 or 4 times around my finger and then gripping my finger like a little baby would hold a finger. I didn't move a muscle. I never had anything like that ever happen. I was fully aware, and again this excitement and anticipation was starting to well up in me. I kept my finger in the same position. I closed my eyes and went back into the meditation.

Maybe a minute or two later, still with the blade of grass wrapped around my finger, I heard a fly. I thought it was a bee at first because it sounded so loud. But then I decided it was probably just a fly. It was circling my head and buzzing. I became very aware that I was starting to almost rock in a circular motion as it continued to circle my head, buzzing.

I knew something was going on. I could feel my breathing starting to get rapid. All of a sudden the buzzing stopped, and the fly landed right in the middle of my upper lip and just sat there. Normally, in that situation in annoyance anybody would shoo it away. I didn't move a muscle. I felt the fly was waiting for me to do something. So I thought to it, I thought *at* it. "If you know what I'm feeling and thinking, walk down my lip, walk down the top of my moustache." The fly instantly traveled down my lip, all the way to the end of my mustache. And then I said in my head, "Okay, walk back and go to the other end." Instantly the fly—I could feel the little feet across my hairs—went to the other end. Then he came back to the middle, and I sat there in amazement with this fly that I had obviously just communicated with, with this blade of grass holding on. Then I wondered about the bird. I opened my eyes and looked up at the tree; the bird was right on the edge of the limb. It started chirping. I closed my eyes, and it stopped. And I just sat there and said, "Okay, if you're going to show me something, show me."

And then I just sunk back into my meditation. Probably 5 or 10 minutes went by. The fly didn't move an inch, the blade of grass held my finger, and all of a sudden I was just like shot out of a cannon out of my body. It's hard to explain if a person hasn't experienced something like this. It's hard to use words to draw a picture. But in the language that might be understandable, I felt my astral body, or spirit or essence, shot like a cannon out of the top of my head, and in a split second I was in a place of incredibly brilliant light. It wasn't white light; it was orange, reddish.

I knew I was in a place of incredible heat because I perceived instantly that the light was something like burning gas. In my mind, I asked, "Where am I?"

And a loud voice came from outside of my head, not inside my head. An exterior loud voice said, "You're in the vortex of the sun."

I seemed, at that time, to just be totally satisfied to be there. I looked around, and again it's hard to explain what I saw. Everything was molten; everything was moving; it didn't seem to have form. All of the lights, the dazzling, incredible bright lights, seemed to be the result of a gas burning like the fire off of a gas stove or something. And I was just in that place, completely aware. Not afraid in any way or even dazzled in any way. I was like in the center of the sun, just out of nowhere, experiencing in my astral body as I'll call it, experiencing what it would be like to be in the center of the sun. There were some brief other words that were said to me. I can't remember them at this moment. I have them written down someplace.

One of the words was illumined. I stayed in that place for what seemed like a long time. I had no discomfort; I had no concern; I had no fear, no worry. I was in a total state of complete amazement and awe. But my mind seemed to be calm and rational. I didn't need to ask questions. I didn't need to wonder anymore. I just stayed there for some time. Then I don't know why, but suddenly I was like shot out of a cannon again, into my body. And I realized that I had astral projected for some period of time and I was now back in my body. I couldn't feel the piece of grass on my finger anymore, and the fly was gone off of my lip. I opened my eyes and looked for the bird— no sign of him. And I closed my eyes again and sat there for some 10 minutes trying to understand what had just happened.

I went where my friends were. I asked if they had a pen and paper. The woman took a little pad of paper out of her purse, and I scribbled down the experience. That was a powerful experience that I told my friends about, and they just took it like ho-hum. Both of them having had altered-state, mystical-type experiences, both with drugs and without. At this time there were no drugs involved, no pot, no nothing. No booze. That was, another light experience that I had, which I would have more of later on. Another part of the process unfolding.

Meeting Remarkable Masters

To close out the events of the '60s, I want to talk about a couple of the many remarkable people I met in my lifetime. First, I'll talk about 2 friends of mine at the Spirit of '76, who took me to upstate New York, the Syracuse area, to meet a woman yogini whom they had talked to me about for some time. I wasn't too thrilled to do it, but they wanted me to go to New York with them and drive a vehicle back to Chicago for them. So they got me to make the trip, and then when they got to Syracuse, they said, "We're going to go meet Margaret Coble."

Margaret Coble was a very ordinary-looking middle-aged, suburban Syracuse housewife. Upon our first meeting, she immediately impressed me as being a very elegant woman, I could say of noble breeding. We were introduced, and she immediately invited my 2 friends and me down into the basement of her home, where she said, "I begin all meetings with young people with meditations." And we all sat down and meditated for an hour.

It turned out that this woman was no the ordinary housewife that I had perceived her to be. She was truly a highly enlightened being. She was profoundly well trained and taught in the different yoga philosophies. She was a master of meditation. She was a mantra master and had a never-ending number of Sanskrit mantras that she would sing in a most beautiful, angelic voice. Our meeting was brief, only a couple hours, but it impacted me tremendously. I knew I was in the presence of an enlightened human being for the first time in my life. Later, I was to meet her teacher and her guru, who was a little brown man from the Himalayas. He had long black hair and always wore orange robes; his name was Dr. Rammurti S. Mishra. I found out that Dr. Mishra was considered in India to be a national treasure. Also, unquestionably, undeniably, as I knew from our first meeting, fully enlightened. He was at this time a psychiatrist, a medical doctor; he had 2 or 3 degrees from universities in America, but I think he had 10 or 12 degrees from universities all over the world—South Africa, England, India, etc. He was a profoundly charismatic, powerful, vibrational, super-intelligent, super-aware human being. He had a history that was absolutely stunning. He had become a doctor, after being born into a Brahmin family, the highest caste in India. As a young man he had shown tremendous powers, extra sensory powers; he could control the weather. As a young boy, he could do magical, mystical things. He became a doctor in India and he was considered to be the reigning Sanskrit master in the world. The expert on Sanskrit language. He was considered to be one of the leading neurologists in the world. He was considered to be one of the top endocrinologists in the world. He spoke, I believe, 25 languages fluently. He could speak Swahili, I remember. He had only been taught 3 or 4 languages, and then when he mastered Sanskrit, he was able to speak other languages by just understanding the root words. He was a profoundly amazing, man. At one time he was the head of the Belleview Psychiatric Center at Belleview Hospital in Manhattan. At the same time, he was on the board of 4 or 5 other psychiatric hospitals. He was a most delightful creature to be around. He and Margaret were just an incomparable pair who could actually alter the consciousness of everybody in the room. I was to have many, many years of subsequent interactions with them. Going back and forth from Chicago to New York.

Finally, at one point, I became a yoga teacher at their ashram in Syracuse. These 2 people awakened my spiritual awareness. At any given time in their presence, I could go into altered states; I would see visions and feel elevated. I was profoundly affected by their presence.

Alongside of Dr. Mishra and Margaret Coble, in this same period of time, I also met a man called Baba Ram Dass. His name was Richard Alpert. I believe he was a psychology professor at Harvard University, a close friend of Timothy Leary. The 2 of them were thrown out of Harvard for turning their students on to LSD. I met Ram Dass in Chicago after he had returned from a long trip to India. He had left the States in search of a guru in India who could show him how to get into altered states without LSD. And he had found that man. I picked up a *TIME* magazine one day and read a little blurb that Dr. Richard Alpert had just returned from a long stay in India and was staying with his father in a small town in New Hampshire. On a whim, I called the information operator and got the father's home phone number. It was Franklin, New Hampshire. I called and got Richard on the phone. And I bumbled along. I didn't even know what to say. I just said, "I just wanted to meet you on the phone." He inquired who I was and where I was. I told him I lived in Chicago.

He said, "I'm leaving tomorrow to go to Taos, New Mexico. Could I possibly stay at your house for a few days on my way to Taos?"

I was thrilled. I told him, "Of course!"

Two days later, he arrived at my front door in his robes and his long beard. He spent about 4 or 5 days with me. I arranged a number of talks. I had a friend that was a psychology professor at the University of Chicago. I arranged for him to have Baba Ram Dass speak to his classes. It was quite an enlightening few days for me. He taught me much; he was an avid student of several religions. He was Jewish and knew much of the Kabbalah of Christianity and had knowledge about Hindu and Buddhist religions. We had quite a close connection in the time that he stayed with me.

Then when he left, he gave me an assignment. His guru had told him to come back to the United States and do two things: write a book about enlightenment and also to start a center for the dying. This was before there were any hospices. Baba Ram Dass asked me if I would get in touch with a certain professor at the University of Chicago who he knew was interested in death and dying to extract certain information from him and then relay it to Ram Dass, who would be in Taos, New Mexico. So I finally got this professor. He told me he no longer was involved with trying to set up a center for death and the dying because the powers that be were threatening him. He told me that he was turning over all of his work to Elizabeth Kubler Ross. So a week or so later, I got Ram Dass on the phone and reported everything to him. He thanked me for what I had done and for giving him the information that I had. We were to meet a number of other times. He set up the Lama foundation outside of Taos. That was a teaching and learning center. Later, I was to be down there a number of times. So at the very end of the 60s, I had a tremendous thrust into my spirituality by these meetings with amazing teachers—I don't know if Ram Dass was enlightened, but Margaret and Mishra were definitely enlightened. These 3 people had a tremendous impact on what was to happen in my life in the '70s.

Trouble in Taos

ON MY SECOND TRIP TO TAOS (the first was on the commune), a friend of mine in Chicago, told me he wanted to take me to Taos to get my ankle repaired. I had a very torn-up ankle; I wouldn't go to a doctor or hospital, and after 6 months it was still swollen and black and blue, and I was limping badly. I had dived down a whole flight of stairs from a landing down into an alley, and my right foot hit a patch of ice and my left foot hit solid concrete. My right ankle was badly torn up.

This friend of mine was called Trader John, but I called him Johnny. Johnny told me, "I want to take you to meet this rolfer to get your ankle fixed." What he didn't tell me was that several of his partners were in a war of words and disagreement about large amounts of money that didn't go where it was supposed to go in the past. And I knew nothing about any of that.

My friend John, actually used to think that I had spiritual and magical power, and he used to tell me that. So he decided to bring me to Taos as a shield for him to try to get large amount of money that these men supposedly owed him. So we get to Taos and we find the rolfer and he, with absolute miraculous abilities, fixes my entire ankle in one day, in one session. The next day I'm not limping, and a week later all the swelling and discoloration are gone.

That was like a miracle for me. I thought that was the whole purpose of the trip. This rolfer's name was Jan Sultan. Jan is probably the best rolfer and one of the best body workers currently on the planet (as well as a good friend).

After my ankle was fixed, we go into Taos, and we go this little house; he knocks on the door. I'm standing behind him, and the guy who opens the door is absolutely frightening to look at. He looks like the toughest, meanest person walking the earth. Not big, not muscular, maybe 50 years old, but a face that would stop a clock. He glares at my friend and says, "What in the hell are you doing here?"

Johnny says, "Oh, I'm with my friend here."

The guy looks at me, and what am I? I'm a skinny, long-haired hippy; I weigh 150 pounds.

He says, "Who are you?"

I say, "Oh, I'm Johnny's buddy."

Johnny says, "Can we come in and talk about the money you owe me?"

"Money I owe you? You haven't got the message yet, have you?"

He lets us inside and I meet his wife and his 2 little kids, and Gordon and Johnny go in the back room where they have about a half hour of heated talk. The wife and I sat there. I could see on her face she was scared to death. I couldn't make out what they were talking about, but after a half hour, Johnny came out and said, "Okay, let's go."

So we go back to the motel that we were renting. We went back there, and I said, "What is all this about?"

He said, "Oh nothing, just an old disagreement."

So we hang out in Taos for 2 weeks. In this time, Johnny goes back to this man, who is an old Virgo and one of the community leaders in the whole Taos area. He was the first white man ever born in Taos and had lived there all his life. Had all the respect in the world from every Mexican, every American Indian, every law enforcement person, and everybody. This man was one of the most highly respected people in the entire Taos community.

The next day, Johnny takes me to another place. This was the place where I met another very big, tough old guy. He was called—well, I won't mention his name—he was another staunch community leader and another tough, tough man. We went to see him in a garage, and he took Johnny into a room—again a long, heated argument. I heard some of that. This guy kept telling Johnny, "You don't have anything coming from us, and you're crazy for coming back here because we've already told you that if you come back here, you're a marked man."

When I heard that, I thought, "Oh my God..."

So that night I said to Johnny, "You want to tell me what's going on now?"

He said, "Oh, it's nothing."

I said, "Oh no, no, no, not nothing!"

It turned out that the week before we went there, he had called down and talked to these men and said, "I'm coming down here with my bodyguard, and you better not push me off. You better give me the money." Johnny felt he had put money in for some land there. Together they had all bought land, and Johnny wanted his part. But they felt he didn't have anything coming. Which turned out to be the truth

So before it all ended, the man Gordon, who was the leader of all these guys, he and I started talking maybe the 3rd or 4th day there, just the two of us.

When we first talked, he asked, "What do you do?"

I told him, "I'm sort of a quack healer."

And he was so interested. He just started picking my brain. He also had done some healing of his own. He started asking me all sorts of questions.

"Well, what do you do? How do you channel energy? What do you think when you put your hands on someone?"

He was immensely interested, so I gave him everything I had. I shared everything.

Gordon asked me, "How did you get involved with Johnny?"

I said, "Ah, we're just friends."

He said, "Johnny doesn't have any friends."

He told me, "When I opened my door and saw Johnny and you, it was like looking at a dirty whore and the pope. There was something about you that I could see, and I knew immediately I had to be careful with you. I knew I couldn't do what we normally would have done."

He said, "Johnny will leave this town in a week. He won't get anything that he came here to get, except personal property that he has strewn around. He's not going to get any money, but because he's with you, he's going to get to leave here with his skin intact."

This man Gordon turned out to be an incredible healer. He started healing people all by himself, no guidance. He started channeling energy; he turned out to be an incredible healer. He had me work on about a dozen people with him before I left. We remained friends until he passed away.

Woodstock- Mind Blowing

ONE OF THE HIGHLIGHTS OF THE '60s and, in fact, of my life happened in August 69. In early August, I was managing Moody's Pub on North Broadway in Chicago. I received a phone call from a dear old friend, named Bob Molnar, the man who gave me the *Tibetan Book of the Dead* that started my spiritual quest in a lot of ways. He called from New York; he was tending bar at a big nightclub in Manhattan. He got me on the phone and said, "If I pay for your ticket, will you come out to New York on the 15th of August? That's a Friday."

I said, "How about if I fly out there Thursday night?"

He said, "That would be perfect."

I said, "What do you want to do?"

He said, "You and Carol and I are going to take a drive upstate. We're going to go to my grandmother's."

Carol was a waitress at the Spirit of '76 who worked with Bob and me, and when he moved to New York, she moved with him. And they lived in Manhattan for a long time together.

He said, "My grandmother passed away, and she left a farm on the New York and Massachusetts border. You know about communes. You've done that stuff. I want your advice to see if my grandma's farm could be turned into a commune. I'm thinking of starting a commune."

I said, "Sure, you're paying for the tickets? I'd be glad to go."

So I made reservations. Thursday night the 14th, after I finished the shift at Moody's, I took the weekend off. I flew into LaGuardia and took a cab to my friend's bar. I just hung out with him and some of his friends until the bar closed. Then we all piled into his car and headed upstate.

When we got on the road, it was like 4:00 a.m. or 5:00 a.m. He said, "We're gonna make a little detour."

I said, "A detour?"

He said, "Yea, we're going to stop at a place called Woodstock. I've got tickets for the 3 of us. They're going to have a big music festival."

It didn't even interest me remotely until he said some of the names of the bands that were going to be there.

So probably at 7:30 a.m. or 8:00 a.m., we got near Bethel, NY, where the actual festival was going on. The roads were all clogged; there were already massive numbers of people there. So we parked the car on the side of the road and grabbed the cooler and our gear and probably walked a mile or 2 to the front gate.

The front gate which had been cyclone-fenced in was flat on the ground; the crowd had just run the gates over. There was no one collecting tickets. They weren't even pretending that you had to have a ticket to go.

So we were at Woodstock on Friday morning. We found a camping place, maybe about a ten-minute walk from the valley where everyone collected. At the bottom of this valley was this giant stage. And up the walls of the valley, already every square foot was filled. So we found a little place back behind the valley, across a road and back through a little forest. People were already setting up tents back there. We set up a tent.

This was so unexpected; none of us could believe the size of the crowd. Bob told me that there were supposed to be 30,000 people there. Well, we could easily see that there were hundreds of thousands already there on Friday morning.

So we wormed our way about a quarter of the way down into the valley. We were maybe 200 or 300 yards away from the stage. We cleared a place and put our stuff down. And we waited, and we waited and we waited. Every once in a while, they would give an announcement: "We're trying to put the electrical together," or "We're having trouble with [this], trouble with [that]."

Finally, sometime around noon, maybe a little after, they announced that the first person that would speak would be Swami Satchidananda, the famous New York swami. He was a love swami. He had a big white beard and just vibrated incredible love. So he got up in front of this crowd and gave a little speech about music. He said he was delighted to see the youth of America. All the youth of America. He thought every kid in America was there. Then he gave a speech about music and sound.

What happened next was incredible. He did a most amazing thing, which in the movie they never talk about; no record of what he actually did have I ever encountered. But he told everyone that he wanted us all to chant OM together. And slowly but surely, everybody in that vast audience—I'm guessing at that point there were probably 350,000 or more people in that valley—chanted OM. We all OMed. I looked around; every single person was OMing. It was like a thunderous roar going up. It was almost something beyond description. The OM sounds turned into almost just some thunder. Continuous thunder.

We OMed, I guess, for about 10 minutes. In the actual history of what happened to that festival, it has to be understood that the beginning—Satchidananda's insistence on everybody OMing for all that time—set the pattern for the 4 days. That set everything; that set the mind-set for the crowd, for the environment, for the elementals, for the musicians. The days were often called "3 days of peace love and music." I would say Satchidananda was more responsible for that vibe of Woodstock that any other individual person.

So when he finished, there was a long wait. They had a schedule of performers, but the majority of performers that were supposed to be playing on Friday morning and through the day weren't there yet. They couldn't get there because the roads were all blocked off, traffic was gridlocked.

So they were looking for someone to start the festival, and it took a couple hours I think. Finally, Richie Havens came out. I didn't know much about Richie Havens. I had heard he was a folk singer. He came out, and from his very first song on, he lit the place up. Everybody was so hungry for music at that point, and he just lit the place up. And he played for hours. In the movie they don't talk about that. Few people probably even remember it, but he played for hours. He played every song he had in his repertoire. His last song, he made up a song, an old Mississippi religious hymn song that he improvised— "Freedom." And then after him, there were a few other nondescript performers. I had taken off and gone back to our campsite to get something to eat. When I came back, it was late afternoon and Ravi Shankar was playing. And I knew who Ravi Shankar was. I had albums of his. I would meditate to his sitar music at home. He was phenomenal; he was just tremendous.

Then it was dinnertime. I went back searching for food. I went back out of the playing area not being able to see what was going on back through this little forest, but the music could be heard anywhere within miles. The rest of the day, I basically remember as scrounging for food. There were no concessions. They didn't have a stand to sell a bite of food. They didn't sell t-shirts; they could have sold a million t-shirts.

The only food that was available was in the tents scattered around the periphery of the valley, which the Hog Farmers of Taos, New Mexico, had set up. The women of the Hog Farm, for 3 days, continuously cooked brown rice. Sometimes there were beans. But they were the main supplier of food for this giant throng, other than what people brought in for themselves. So that very first day, the realization that food was going to become an issue really got brought to light.

At nighttime, probably one of the most outstanding of all the performers was Joan Baez. She followed a number of groups that I didn't pay attention to or get to see. But she went on at about 1 on Saturday morning, and she played a magnificent set. Many times she was singing a cappella; I found out later from a singer girlfriend of mine that singing a cappella to 300,000 or 400,000 people was almost impossible, and Joan Baez just had us totally immersed. Basically, I sort of wound down there; we found our sleeping place and got some sleep.

Saturday morning, the first performer that I remember was Santana. Santana rocked this crowd into a frenzy. In my experience, having seen a lot of rock groups play already in my life, I'd say at least 50% of the performers over those days played the performance of their lives at Woodstock, absolutely the best of their lives. Santana blew themselves into national recognition at Woodstock. They were just a little San Francisco group. Pretty much no one ever heard of them, but after Woodstock, they were on the map. Then the next group I remember really, really impressing me came on after the Grateful Dead. As for the Grateful Dead, the only way to describe their performance was, for me, a virtual flop. They were fighting on stage. They were afraid of being electrocuted. There had been a lot of rain, so the stage had water all over it. They'd play a song, and then 20 minutes later they'd play another. They were frustrating everybody. And they were flat. They just weren't together. I had seen them perform out at the Fillmore West in San Francisco, where they tore the house down. This was not a Grateful Dead performance. It was almost total disappointment.

After that it was almost nightfall. Creedence Clearwater came on. And they had, up to that point, the most powerful effect on the crowd. They were impeccable. They were so together. They were flawless. It was just like watching magic. They were so powerful. They had the crowd, just everybody, up on their feet. They did a set that was just unbelievable.

Later, they complained publicly that their set would have even been greater if the Grateful Dead hadn't stalled and wasted time. But as I remember it, they were magical. A little bit later—it was now past midnight on Sunday Morning—Janis Joplin came on. But when the original film came out—it was actually a documentary about Woodstock that won the 1970 Academy Award for documentaries—they didn't even put Janis Joplin in it. And I've read over the years many different reviewers and critics said that she was just nothing. That she had lost all of her skill. They were absolutely crazy.

Janis Joplin just had that place in a frenzy. It was like 2:00 a.m., and she came out on the stage with a full bottle of Southern Comfort in one hand and her mic in the other. And she talked dirty to us. Then just started going through her whole repertoire. She sang all her great songs. She didn't have her great band that she used to have, but she had a good band. To me she was just marvelous. And the crowd wouldn't let her stop. Every time she would try to stop, they'd force her back on for another song and another song, and finally she came out; it was probably 3 in the morning or so. She came out and held up her now near-empty bottle of SOCO, took a big slug, and said, "Okay, I'm finished. I'm drained. I'm gonna give you motherfuckers the last ounce of energy I have." And she sang, "Take a Little Piece of My Heart." And the crowd went crazy. Everybody loved her. I'll never understand where these critics got off saying she was flat. She was magnificent.

After her, Sly and the Family Stone came on. They also were so charged up, so together; they were flawless. So many of these groups fed off the crowd and just channeled the energy of hundreds of thousands of people in their instruments and their performance. At that time, I knew there was more performing but I was finished. I went and found our tent and slept. Sunday morning at about 530—I was still in bed— The Who came out and played til the sun came up. I got up Sunday morning and went down; there wasn't an empty space in the whole valley. Not a square inch. At this point there were many, many more people than on Friday morning. As I was getting ready for Sunday's performance, everybody was still buzzing about the performance of The Who So at about 8:00 a.m. on Sunday, Jefferson Airplane played. Gracie Slick, she owned the crowd anyways; she was the queen of rock and roll on the West Coast. She was magnificent; she was just flawless. That was another group that performed that was never even put into the movie or the documentary. I never understood that.

I went off and did other things in the crowd, and when I went back to the stage area, an unknown British rock star named Joe Cocker got on the stage. He was electric. He was on fire. It was like he was plugged into 220 volts. And again, the whole place was going berserk. He was just great. And then right after Cocker played, came the rain, the downpour, which I'll talk about more in a while. Sunday at 6:30 p.m., they finally repaired the stage from the biggest rainstorm I've ever seen in my lifetime. They got the stage put together, and Country Joe and the Fish played. It was tremendous. Groups actually played all night and into the morning. Blood Sweat and Tears played. Different performers played through the night, and I slept through some of it.

But on Monday morning at 9, Jimi Hendrix, who was supposed to close the festival on Sunday afternoon or evening, he finally got up on the stage. By the time Jimi got up on stage, I'm guessing there were about 20,000 of us left. After the rain on Sunday, the place was destroyed, and everybody was just trying to get out of there. But my friend Bob and Carroll, they didn't want to miss Hendrix. So we stayed up all night, and when Hendrix came on at 9:00 a.m., we were right down in front of the stage. He played for 2 hours; he played all his great songs. And then he closed the festival with a rendition of the "Star-Spangled Banner," which I think is classic in rock and roll history. And for the most part, that was the music part of the festival.

In retrospect, Crosby Stills, Nash, and Young were playing together for only the 2nd or 3rd time. When they were playing, they were all noticeably frightened and intimidated by the crowd, and they couldn't get in sync. They couldn't get in tune, and everyone in the crowd could hear the mistakes they were making. They looked petrified. I think the whole crowd felt so sorry for them and I could feel everybody in the crowd start pulling for them—get it together, get it together. And all of a sudden, and this is recorded in the movie in the documentary, in the middle of one of their songs, they hit a lick together; they merged into a group and finished that song on an incredible high note and played out the rest of their set superbly. What everyone there got to watch was the coming to life of what turned out to be one of the greatest rock bands of all time. They came to life on that stage. They had just played the day before in San Francisco and were barely able to communicate to each other with their music. When they went off the stage, they made history for themselves and made their future.

I always felt that Janis Joplin's performance was probably the greatest of her life. I felt that about Jimi Hendrix, even though he had nobody there to listen to him. Of course, shortly after Woodstock, both Hendrix and Joplin left the planet. When I heard about their deaths, in my heart I knew, they had given everything they had at Woodstock. They had reached their pinnacles, and because of who they were, they left the planet.

One whole story of Woodstock, the one shown in the documentary and movie, was the story of incredible performances, the incredible music. Another whole story was what I replayed of the event to my friends in Chicago. Everyone told me, "You've got to write this down. You've got to write this down." I did actually start writing. I got 2 or 3 pages written, and then I just let it go. I lost the pages later. But the real story of Woodstock was what happened between the people.

Between the musicians and the people there was an interaction and a powerful exchange of energy that I'm sure none of those musicians ever saw in their life before or after. But what happened between the people and the people was to me the great story of Woodstock. And I'll just narrate some of my observations.

There was no security there other than a handful of state troopers, who had been hired by the promoters. Just a handful. They all wore Woodstock t-shirts to identify them. They had no pretense of trying to control anything, trying to control the crowd or anything like that.

Some of the sideshows were phenomenal. That first day, a lot of the early attendees had gallon jugs of wine. I never saw a whiskey bottle. There was virtually no alcohol, and by the end of the first night, whatever alcohol that had come into the place was consumed. There was no violence. There was no fighting. There was an atmosphere of peace and love that pervaded the crowd from the very beginning. And it held up through the whole festival.

There was one point when I was hunting for food, for anything (I think it was on Saturday afternoon). I had wandered far out of the stage area to a road leading out of the front exit. A big truck came rumbling in and everybody started yelling, "FOOD! FOOD!" Everyone thought there was going to be food in it. By the time it pulled up and parked, there were 200 of us that circled it immediately. I envisioned they were going to open the door and start throwing out packages of Twinkies. So the back door opens, and there are 5 or 6 young hippies. They pull out some folding tables, put them up, and they start putting up a bunch of printed literature on the tables.

It turns out, these guys were SDS guys—Students for Democratic Society, who had bombed banks; they were revolutionaries. They started yelling about overthrowing society, and it was absolutely miraculous what I saw next. One young girl, she ran up to the front of the tables and said, "No! No! Peace! Love! PEACE! LOVE!"

Within seconds, there must have been a thousand of us chanting, "PEACE! LOVE!" Literally shouting it. It impacted these guys, it scared them. You could see fright on their face. They were probably afraid that the crowd was about to turn on them and rip them to pieces, which wasn't going to happen. But this one little girl started screaming, "PEACE! LOVE." And then there was more than a thousand people screaming, "PEACE. LOVE."

These guys took all their literature and threw it in the back of the truck, put their tables in the back of the truck, and started backing it right out on the road. They were driven right off of the property. They had come there to disrupt or to start trouble, or whatever their intentions were, and they were driven out by a single person starting to chant "PEACE LOVE" at them. That was an incredible thing to watch and be part of.

The next important event is not something easy to explain and might not make any sense to anyone. The Hog Farmers from Taos had built, in the weeks before Woodstock, a lot of almost playground-type things—out of big boulders and big logs. Actually you could climb on them and sit on them; they were very sturdy. But they had one thing that looked like a 3-poled teepee. All 3 poles came together and crossed at the top. The poles were big, big tree trunks, probably 12 to 15 feet high. At the top they were chained together. Hanging from the middle of that joining of the 3 poles at the top was the biggest piece of rope I've ever seen. It must have been 6 inches around and looked like it was from an old sailing ship. It hung down into the middle of this old teepee, maybe 8 or 10 feet from the ground. They had a flat rock, a round flat rock that had a big hole that had been drilled in the middle. The rope had been put down through the rock and then in a big knot. So there was a rope hanging from this teepee frame with a flat round rock. The rock was maybe 6 inches thick; it must have weighed a ton. And it was so heavy that 4 or 5 people could get on it without even tilting it.

So this is what I came upon. I was walking through the forest. I came out and saw this big teepee thing with the rock hanging. There were 3 guys up on top of the rock, and there was a young girl in between them, and they were OMing. I went over. I was curious about what was going on. There was a ladder propped up and attached to one of the poles so that you could climb up the ladder and climb on the rock. There was a guy at the bottom, and I said, "What's going on?"

He said, "These guys are from the Hog Farm, and they're taking kids who are freaking out on acid, and they're bringing them down."

I said, "What do you mean 'bringing them down'?"

He said, "They're OM-shocking them."

I said, "OM-shocking? What is that?"

He said, "Have you ever OMed?"

I had some many hours of OMing in my back pocket, so I said, "Yea."

He said, "One of these guys needs a break, stay right here."

I waited about 5 minutes; they finished OMing with this girl, and she came down the ladder. There was a young kid that 2 guys were sort of trying to calm down; he was freaking out on acid. They sent the kid up the ladder, and then they yelled to one of the guys, "Hey, we got a replacement!"

A guy came down the ladder, and I went up the ladder. They put the kid right in the middle, his arms and legs around the big rope and sitting down. The guys said to me, "We're doing OM-shocks."

I said, "I don't know what that is."

He said, "Just follow our lead. We're going to OM so strongly and so powerfully that it's going to change the kid and take him out of the paranoia."

The 2 guys that knew what they were doing—they each touched their frontal lobes, their foreheads, to this kid's forehead. I was behind him, and the guy said, "Do what we're doing." So I leaned over and touched my forehead to the back of this kid's head, and then the 3 of us circled our arms around each other, and around me. So we had this kid in the middle of us, all of us touching him with our foreheads and our arms circled around each other. They started OMing. They OMed like I had never heard before. They OMed, beginning with a low-pitched, deep, almost guttural OM. They would with each OM raise up the volume, the intensity, and the tone a little bit more. Every OM I was drawn up with them because these 2 guys were so strong; they must have been doing this for years. And they just sucked me right in. After about 5 to 10 minutes, the 3 of us were at such a high, intense pitch that it was as though we were screaming at the top of our lungs. The roar that came out of the 3 of us, all of that vibration, were going right into this kid's head. He never resisted or reacted. At first, he was jittery and shaky;

after a minute or 2 he calmed down; then he was still like a statue. At the end of about 10 minutes, it sounded to me like we were virtually screaming OM. Then the 2 stopped, they let go, and they yelled, "Get the next one up here!" And they helped this kid over to the ladder, and he climbed down.

Then came a young girl, maybe 18 years old. Very scared, tears running down her face, she was frightened to death. We got her in the middle, wrapped her arms and legs around the big center rope, circled her body, put our heads to her, and picked up right where we left off, starting slow and in a few minutes having a massive OM coming out. I lasted about 6 to 8 kids, maybe an hour or so. At the end, the very last one I did, I had a feeling and a sensation where right at the end of the OM, I took in another big breath and started blowing out the OM. And then something happened that had never happened before or after. I no longer was the OM; I no longer had to OM; it was as though someone had plugged a big cable into my chest. I didn't inhale or exhale anymore. What was actually happening was that I had plugged into the actual OM sound. It happened to the other 2 at the same time, and none of us were trying to OM. An OM was roaring out of me, and I no longer was breathing, trying to hold the intensity, trying to have more volume. The 3 of us experienced the same thing. When we finished with that kid, one of them looked at me and said, "You did great. You're through."

The other guy who had taken a break was ready to come back. He said, "You were great." And I said, "What just happened?"

He said, "Oh, every once in a while we hit the OM Car."

It was an expression I had heard before explaining that there is a level out there in the universe where OM vibrates every second of every day for eternity.

He said, "We plugged into the OM Car. It's happened with us many times," he said. "I'm glad you got to experience it."

I went down the ladder and literally wobbled away. I was in such an altered state. I was so high it was amazing. I just wobbled away, and as I got about 100 feet away, I heard them start up on the next person. And they did that for 3 days. Instead of taking people to the medical tent, when they were overdosing on acid or other drugs, people were now being taken to the OM station. It worked on every single kid. Everyone, when they climbed down the ladder, they were clear, they were no longer afraid, and they could talk. It was something that had happened, even though I described it as best I can, on a level that was indescribable. So that kind of thing happened all over the place.

The Sunday-afternoon rain was very slightly covered in the documentary film. I clearly felt and always believed that it was almost like the heavens were saying to the crowd, "You're going too far. It's too hedonistic." I would guess that at any given time in the 3 days, at least one out of every 2 people was on LSD. Many times, perhaps, a greater proportion. Possibly as many as 75% of the people there took LSD or mescaline or peyote on the 3 days.

On the Sunday afternoon when Cocker finished, these clouds came out of nowhere over the horizon. Just the biggest, blackest clouds I'd ever seen in my life. No one had time to respond; no one had time to do anything. Then there was a deluge I've often described as of biblical proportion. It was the hardest rain I've ever felt on my body in my life. It literally pelted a lot of people right to the ground, and it went on for hours. It was so powerful that it destroyed everybody's little encampments. Everyone had blankets spread out or tarps or their purses, their belongings, their shoes, their clothes. This rain was so powerful that by the time it ended, it had washed all of the belongings of most of the people in the entire valley down into a giant pool at the bottom, near the stage. Everybody seemed to have lost everything they had. We were fortunate because we had our campsite back by the woods and we had a tent; so my wallet and belongings were all soaked, but they weren't lost. After the rain, people started evacuating immediately. Just started pouring out. Some of the roads at the top of the valley and then into the woods became very treacherous. Everything was inch-deep or 2-inch deep mud. I remember there was one guy that broke his leg. Trying to crawl over a tree stump, he fell and his leg just shattered. Right away without anyone saying a word, 6 different guys grabbed him and picked him up and started carting him off toward the medical tent. There was a sense of survival. It was almost as if nature said, "This is too hedonistic. You're having too much fun. You've got to look at reality. You've got to take a bit of reality pie."

That rain just crushed everything. The stage was all broken up, and the speakers were torn up out of the places they were fixed to. When it finally stopped, it probably stopped about 4 or 4:30 in the afternoon. The people who weren't evacuating were like hardliners that wanted to hear the rest of the festival. Everyone started going up into the woods; there were hundreds of people going up into the woods and finding wood to burn. It had turned very cold. Maybe from 85 degrees to 45 degrees in 2 hours. There were hundreds of little bonfires all over the place. People huddled around, everybody sharing everything they had. A few people had a little food or they had pot. Everybody sharing everything with everybody else. Each one of us soaked to the skin. Muddy, soaked, dirty, hungry, cold, and hearty. Just committed to staying and watching the performers at night. It was biblical. It was a sense of something that the heavens had proclaimed. If you weren't there at the end, there's no way of even comprehending what I'm talking about. I lay there in the mud. Lay in cold wet mud and slept on and off during the night, waiting for Hendrix. Everyone wanted to wait for Hendrix; unfortunately, the conditions got so bad. I can't even remember the performers; a lot of the speakers weren't working. But the festival went on after this torrential, biblical downfall that drove probably 7 out of 10 people into the cars and out of the area.

There were so many things that happened among the people. There was so much camaraderie. There was such a sense of this being like a disaster area, or like an earthquake area or a hurricane area. What it showed me was that everybody in this type of crisis would pull together. I saw no type of greed or anybody being out for themselves. Everybody tried to help everybody in any way they could. The people who stayed through that night—it just sort of linked us together in a common misery. Misery loves company.

In this powerful commitment. Through the whole festival, people talked all the time about Jimi Hendrix closing the festival. Everybody knew he would finish with the Star-Spangled Banner. That's what we wanted.

One of the most incredible events that I never heard mentioned in the film or in reading was on the afternoon on Saturday. All of a sudden there were 3 or 4 army helicopters, green camouflaged army helicopters surveying the whole area and filming the whole thing. This was the only time that I saw the crowd on edge. There were some people yelling, "Get out of here!" or various things. Not a lot of people, but you could hear them in the crowd. The crowd was being agitated by these helicopters suddenly in the area, flying over. We could see they had cameras pointing down; they were filming. It was the only point where I felt something bad could happen. Somebody could do something wrong.

Then the helicopters were gone. And then they were back again about maybe 2 hours later; this was late afternoon. And these helicopters came again. Again, the crowd started getting edgy; some people shook their fists up in the air. All of a sudden, all of the helicopters started dumping something on us. They were dumping was flowers. These 4 helicopters had gone back to their base. They had arranged to wipeout every single florist probably within 20 or 30 miles around. They took every flower from every florist in the whole area, piled them into the helicopters, and then flew over the crowd and dumped flowers on us. The crowd went insane. Screaming at them, "LOVE" and "PEACE." It was an eruption of love between the helicopters throwing flowers and hundreds of thousands of people. There must have been tens of thousands of flowers dumped on us. It was just a magical moment that, for some reason, no one ever even wrote of in any Woodstock book or eyewitness report. No one ever talked about this. I don't doubt that everybody in that crowd at that time was impacted tremendously by that event. At that time—this was Vietnam time—the military was not very beloved in the eyes of the hippies of this country. But anyone who was there for that experience had to have their heart touched in a profound way.

The people of the Hog Farm from Taos have never really been truly honored. When I was living in Taos, the Hog Farm was not far away. It was the big commune. It was the granddaddy of communes. It was incredible what they did for 2 weeks before the festival and what those people did during the festival. They must have brought thousands upon thousands of pounds of brown rice. 24 hours a day they just kept cooking and feeding and cooking and feeding. Other than them, there was virtually no food available to anyone. I got in line one day. I got my paper dish of brown rice, and they had tamari sauce. And it was like a godsend for me. But these Hog Farmers, they didn't get paid a penny. I found out that the producers didn't pay them. They had volunteered to work on the property, build the stage, and clear the area.

And then when Jimi Hendrix quit. I turned to Bob and Carroll and I said, "Well, we did it."

And Bob said, "Nah, we're not through yet."

I said, "What do you mean?"

He said, "Look at this horrible mess." Somebody had shown up with giant boxes of big, thick, heavy garbage bags. He said, "Let's clean up some of this mess."

So from 11:00 a.m. until about 1:00 p.m., we filled big bags with the debris and garbage that was left. Maybe 300 of us stayed for hours, just filling up garbage bags.

As we were driving out of Woodstock on Monday afternoon, one of the troopers that my friends and I had met and talked to, gabbed with quite a bit, he was directing traffic. He recognized us and pulled us over to the side and we talked about what had happened.

We asked him, "Do you have any idea how many people were here?"

He said, "We've been officially ordered to essentially say there were between 350,000-500,000… But our state trooper estimate is that in the three days there was an absolute minimum of 750,000 people were here."

He said, "This is something that no person who was here will ever forget for the rest of their lives." And Woodstock turned out to be that way.

My friend Bob, I don't know how he did it, but he drove like a madman. He drove straight from Woodstock to LaGuardia. I got my plane back to Chicago by about 15 minutes. I was riding home on the plane still covered with mud; everything I had was muddy—my pack, everything. The stewardesses on the plane were very patient with me because I was a mess.

They said, "You must have been at Woodstock, huh?"

I said, "Yes!" And they crowded around and wanted to hear stories.

When I got back to Chicago, for weeks when I got together with groups of people, I told them everything I had seen, everything I had experienced. It was, on one hand, the fusing and joining of the entire youth of America with that festival. The movie didn't come out for maybe 9 months; there were no reporters there, and no newspapers sent film crews. Nobody recorded it. Nobody thought anything was actually happening while it was happening. But the intensity of the energy of the crowd in a positive and powerful way was an awesome thing to be a part of. There were times in the first and second day when rumors would start going through the crowd that just had everybody higher than a kite. The first rumor was that the Beatles, who were all in London, had heard about the festival and were flying a private jet over to be able to perform. Then that Bob Dylan was going to show up. It was just absolute magic. It affected me for months afterward. I had a whole different perspective on the entire youth of America. I had a whole different feeling about the SDS. I used to feel they were crazies and crackpots, and I just had compassion and empathy for the misguided and negative path they were on. For the anti-war movement, it was probably an immense injection of peace and love instead of anger and bitterness. So that was Woodstock for me.

We never got to grandma's farm. We never got up to find out about turning a farm into a commune. My friend never took over the property; he let other relatives have it.

Our original plan was to stay Friday and then leave Friday night; it was impossible to leave. There were no paths out. Our car was buried in the middle of thousands of cars.

I'm guessing there were maybe 100 porta potties. I don't know where everyone did their business. I saw people in the forest areas, but I don't know where the mess from all the bodies went. I really don't remember more than 100 porta potties near the main entrance. And you'd stand in a line for the porta potties for about an hour. And there was a guy, who was even in the documentary, who had like a giant gasoline truck and a hose, and he was going from one to the next to the next, all day long, sucking all the waste into his big tanker. He was happy; he was the happiest guy there; he was laughing; he knew he was doing a much-appreciated service.

There wasn't much water to drink. I don't remember drinking water at all for the last 2 days. I must have been massively dehydrated.

No one was ready for it—the promoters weren't ready, performers weren't ready. I read later in an underground magazine that maybe a third or a quarter of the performers drank electric Kool-Aid acid before they went on stage. They had a big five-gallon orange cooler that they kept full of some sort of juice and LSD. Many, many performers were rocking on LSD as they were blowing the crowd away. Sometimes you could tell; you could see some of the performers were just tripping their brains out. This was an awesome, life-changing event.

LSD Rescue Service

AFTER WOODSTOCK and returning to my very sedate life as manager of Moody's pub, there was one more event in the latter part of 1969 that comes to mind. There was a man in Chicago named George Peters. He was the son of a wealthy banking family in New York City. He had become a very good psychiatrist to say the least. I met George through a mutual friend of mine. He was one of George's inner circle. George had lived on the north shore of Chicago on Sheridan Rd. To the best of my memory, at one point he had seen how the police in Chicago dealt with kids, hippies, who were on bummer acid trips, freaking out on acid. At that time there was no real humane way of dealing with a young kid freaking out on acid. They would commonly be arrested and taken to a jail. Which would only deepen their trauma and their paranoia. So as I understand, George went personally to Mayor Richard Daley.

He got a one-on-one meeting with him and proposed to Mayor Daley, "You know there are a lot of kids being arrested for drugs who are in precarious mental states. They're overwhelmed by the power of the drug; they're often in deep paranoia, and they often have somewhat shattered psyches. And the last thing in the world they need is harsh treatment or brutalization by police. Yet that is the common way of dealing with any kid found on the street having a bad trip on acid." George said, "Let me take the problem off of your hands. Let me intervene instead of giving arrest records and criminal records to young kids who might not even understand how they got into the situation of being on LSD." He said, "Why don't you have the police, instead of taking kids to a hospital, or to a jail, why don't you have them bring them to my place on Sheridan Rd?"

He had a very large apartment. And he had a group of people who were pretty conscious; they were all young people, some of them degreed, some not, but all of whom understood the vulnerable state of someone being overwhelmed with LSD. So he proposed to Daley that instead of running these kids through criminal arrest records and making their situation worse, have the police just take them to his place on Sheridan Road, leave them with him, and he'd be responsible for them. He was a psychiatrist; he had the ability to talk them down and guide them out of their paranoia or fears and back to their homes or parents. So Daley went for it. Much to his credit, he went for it. He saw, this was a possible solution to a growing problem that, in truth, his policemen were not trained in any way to deal with; they were not trained to handle this kind of a mind-set. So he went for it and let George set up the LSD Rescue Service.

I had met George through a mutual friend who told George I'd be interested in being a volunteer. I already had some small skill in dealing with people who were having hard psychedelic trips. So my friend Joe Martins and I became a tandem, became a team. Sometimes we would get phone calls on a Friday or a Saturday night (these situations most commonly happened at night) from the LSD Rescue Service that there were some kids in trouble at this and this address. We would drive there and would often walk into very bizarre situations. Most commonly it was kids that were afraid. Most of the fear was because they were hallucinating and seeing pictures of tigers in the wall now jumping out at them, or imaginary boogeymen coming out of shadows. So Joe and I would go in; we didn't have any tools. At the time, hospitals would use Thorazine, and they would inject the kids with a powerful tranquilizer. We didn't have that to work with, our tools were a bottle of vodka and a big jar of honey. The inclusion of alcohol into the bloodstream of someone on LSD would start negating the symptoms and the side effects. Or a tablespoon or 2 of honey would change the blood sugar rapidly, and that would often start bringing down a kid who was freaking out. So for 6 months or a year, Joe and I on call would go out and knock on doors, find scared kids, and talk them down. If you talked carefully to a kid freaking out, you could make them understand. That they were just real high.

What I used to say to get their attention was, "You took a drug to have an experience, and now you're having the experience. Don't be afraid of it."

So Joe and I did that for some period of time. It was very rewarding because we were always successful. Sometimes it would take an hour or two, or sometimes we would spend a whole night with someone who was in real bad shape, but by the time we would leave, they would be calmed down, usually ready to fall asleep; often we'd wait till they fell asleep. We felt good about it because every time we did it, we knew we were saving some kid from a nightmare with their family or the police and courts and judges. George Peters was quite a wonderful man, quite a humanitarian. He never received a dollar for any of this work he did. I don't know how widespread it was. I don't know how many people he had going out on these missions. Sometimes if the police found these kids, they would take them to George, and sometimes if it was just reported on the phone, then one of the many volunteers, like Joe and I, would go out. And that was a very fulfilling piece of volunteer work that we did for that short period of time. We did that through the end of '69 onto the beginning of '70.

Comments on the '60s

ESSENTIALLY, I AS A 17-YEAR-OLD, entered the '60s with a certain mind-set. I was, for the most part was living in a shell and extremely shy. Even my mother once in a while used to refer to me as a young punk street tough. I had no comfort zone in talking to human beings. I avoided conversation, especially with strangers, at all times. I was very introverted. I was very uptight. I was very scared, like the animal part in me was always on edge. I knew little to nothing about any of the positive mental experiences that people had. I was mostly sullen, angry, and introverted. I was a committed workaholic, perfectly trained worker ant. All I really cared about in my life at that time was going to work and working harder than anybody else. I had extremely poor communication skills. I had a very deep-seated negative attitude about life. In those days I would find myself telling my friends or thinking to myself that I would never live to be 25 years old. I was surrounded by violence, but I truly hated violence. By the time I was 17, I had already had enough for anybody's lifetime, but there was a lot more ahead of me to come. I didn't embrace violence. I never started trouble or fights, but I was a worthy opponent for anybody who pushed me into a corner.

So in the beginning of the '60s, I was a very deeply troubled, very negative, very unhappy human being. As the '60s rolled on, all of my hard edge essentially got harder. My toughness got tougher, and my anger was greater. But by my early 20s, when I had switched to working on Rush St., I was on the brink of change. I was in a position as a bartender in the most popular nightclub in the city. I was in a position where I had to start a different way of interacting with people. I was literally forced into being—I won't say pleasant, because in those days I wasn't pleasant in any shape or form—communicative. Then just past the mid-'60s was when my 2 dear friends singled me out and decided that a sugar cube would be a good thing for me to experience. That day profoundly changed my life.

That day was the closing of the chapter of this hard-nosed angry young man and the beginning of the ongoing chapter that is still in progress. As the '60s wore on, I had experiences for the first time in my life of joy, bliss, happiness, awareness, and spiritual experiences of many types and forms. I had expansion of my consciousness at such a rapid rate that I can hardly even believe that I was able to maintain function from day to day with how rapidly the universe was opening up to me. I met many wonderful people— lifelong friends. I became deeply engaged in spiritual learning, understanding, and pursuits. I read voraciously for the first time in my life about important issues such as consciousness, awareness, higher realms. I essentially entered the '60s as a beaten-down, negative, self-destructive, hurt kid. And when the '60s unfolded, I was a completely different human being. I had, for the first time in my life, experienced compassion, empathy, love. I had relationships—friendships and love affairs—that took me very deep inside of myself to places that I didn't know existed. I don't know if in a 10-year-period many people could possibly experience the immense change that I experienced in my life. When the '60s came to an end, I was filled to the brim with hope. I knew hope for the first time in my life. I had dreams. I had my consciousness just blasting wide open. I had the whole world seeming to unfold. The whole universe seemed to be trying to wedge itself into my mind, into my awareness. And as powerful a change as can happen, I believe I experienced it in those 10 years. A maximum level of change. And as I shot out of the '60s into the '70s, I was catapulted at a high rate of speed. I was empowered with a belief, trust, and hope that I didn't know existed when that decade started.

Basically, the '60s in my life story were the turnaround from darkness into light. From ignorance to the beginning of wisdom and knowledge. From fear and anger to love and compassion.

'70s

Dr. Liss

As **MY LIFE MOVED OUT OF THE '60s AND INTO THE '70s,** one of the people who I met that had an immense impact on me that I hadn't understood until just recently was Dr. Joseph Liss.

Dr. Liss was a naturopathic doctor, but when I met him, he was behind the counter of a little storefront of a health-food store on Devon, right near Ravenswood. I had been told to shop there by a friend, and for some reason Dr. Liss made an incredible connection with me. He came out from behind his counter when we were introduced and either read me or scanned me; he knew me. And he welcomed me with his heart wide open, and it somewhat floored me. Joseph Liss was, maybe 5 foot 3, 110 pounds. When I met him, he was in his early-to-mid-70s. In that encounter, where it seemed no one else came in the store for a long time, he told me his story. He just opened up and told me what he wanted me to know about him. As he talked to me, I was incredibly aware that his eyes were magical. He had a perpetual smile on his face unless he was speaking seriously. But when he was listening to someone or not talking, he had a smile that was like branded on his face. It was so powerful and deep; it was captivating. And his eyes, every time I went to the store for the next 10 or 12 years, his eyes absolutely captivated me. His eyes seemed like they were black. They were dark. I don't even know if I could say brown or blue, they looked almost all black. In the middle, it was like a burning coal. His eyes looked like they were on fire, and the fire of his soul showed right through his eyes. So that first day we were introduced, he said, "I opened the first health food store in Chicago, right here in 1926."

That was already 45 years that he had been in that store in Chicago. He said, "I haven't had a bite of cooked or dead food in 50 years." He said, "I eat nothing but live food. I take no poisons in my body."

He began guru-ing me. I used to tell people that Dr. Liss was my nutritional guru. He was more than that. He was a spiritual powerhouse and a very enlightened man. He stayed in his place of joy and happiness all the time. Everybody who walked through the door into his place received an equal share of his joy, his wisdom, his knowledge, his healing ability.

He wrote book; I think it was called *Heart Attack or Gas Attacks*. He told me at one point that in Chicago in the '50s, he challenged the cancer doctors of Chicago to bring him a terminal case that he couldn't heal. There was a newspaper at that time called the *Herald American*. One of the editors wrote about his challenge, and over the next 2 years, I don't remember how many, but multiple AMA doctors actually brought him terminal cancer patients who were very close to dying. In the back of his store, he had just a curtain separating his little storeroom and the area he lived in. He had some cots back there like army cots. He would take these terminal patients, and for the 30 days, if they agreed, they would stay on a cot in the back of his store. All the cases that were brought after 30 days were considered cured. The AMA debunked that, even though *The Chicago Herald American* admitted that he was healing terminal cases.

I asked him once, "Doctor, what did you do with them?"

He said, "If you can take control of what goes in a person's mouth, no matter how bad their cancer is, they can be healed."

So he essentially, as a naturopathy doctor, put them all on raw food juices and water every day, along with other treatments.

He had such a strong connection with me. He liked to write postcards. I'd be in New Mexico in a commune and I'd get a postcard with a poem he'd written for me. Or in upstate New York at the yoga ashram, I'd receive a postcard from Dr. Liss, telling me how much he missed me. This was an amazing man, who I now fully realize, was actually in a perpetual state of joy and bliss. He affected the lives of every person who entered his world.

I think by the time he died, he must have been in that store for 55 years. He healed and taught and shared love and light. He was an amazing mentor and an amazing teacher. I think it was maybe his 83rd or 84th birthday. I remember asking him, "Dr. Liss, how long do you think you'll live?"

He said, "I've decided on my 100th birthday to decide whether to live until I'm 120." Phenomenal health and phenomenal strength.

Unfortunately, he left the planet prematurely, when he fell off a curb on an ice patch in front of his store one day. He landed down in the gutter. Somebody who was right there at the drugstore ran in and called 911. Two blocks down was a firehouse, and a paramedic was on the scene within a few minutes. He had gotten up and was on his feet. These 2 young paramedics told him to stay still; they'd get him on a stretcher and get him to the hospital.

He said, "No, no, no, you can't take me to the hospital. I'm okay."

They said, "No, your hip is broken."

I wasn't there, but this account is from the woman running the store who told me exactly what she saw. The paramedics were forcibly holding him down, and he was trying to get up, out of the street. Then a police car pulled up, and the paramedics yelled for the policemen to hold him down while they got a tranquilizer. They said, "He's got a broken hip, and he's freaked out!"

He yelled, "No! You can't put drugs in me. My body has never had drugs! Don't do it."

The police held him down while the paramedics got a syringe full of tranquilizer, and they shot it in him. Then, with 4 men controlling him, they put him on the stretcher, strapped him in, and took him to a hospital.

The woman who ran his store went to the hospital, as soon as she closed at 6:00 p.m. He was in a room, and they had given him many more drugs. They told him that he was right that there were no broken bones and there was no severe injury other than the shock of falling.

The store lady said, "My husband and I will come tomorrow to get you out of here."

He said, "No, it's too late. I feel my kidneys and my liver shutting down. I feel all my organs shutting down. I won't live through the night."

She told him, "Oh, Doctor, you're going to be fine."

She left and came back in the morning, but he had passed in the middle of the night.

This man was somewhat hidden from the world. He was an enlightened man, living in joy and full spiritual light every day and sharing it with every person who came in his store and never wanting anything, asking anything; his life was serving human beings. That was his fulfillment and joy. He was a powerful, powerful influence in opening up my consciousness to the need to understand and take control of my body. He taught me how to fast. He taught me how to do different forms of healing using poultices. He was just an unending source of love and joy, and he lived this life—almost as though he was a spiritual powerhouse in disguise—as a little Jewish man running a health-food store.

Cab Driving

IN THAT SAME PERIOD OF TIME, the very end of '69 and the beginning of '70, I had cut myself loose from Rush St., from the nightclub scene, from being a bartender, a bar manager, a bar player. I had realized that I had to go somewhere else with my life. In the interim, I decided to leave the bars.

As a way to support myself, I became a cab driver. In late '69 and in '70 for some months, I made my living driving a cab, which was a very interesting period for me because I felt the strength in me to not be afraid. I felt the strength to do things I shouldn't do, to trust my feelings. These realities were beginning to emerge in me, so when I became a cab driver, the general rule for all white cab drivers in Chicago was to never drive south of Madison Avenue, the dividing line between north and south in Chicago.

I would regularly drive out into the south side. When I was trained, I was trained not to pick up black people. To never pick up young black men. To never go on the south side of Chicago. To refuse any fare that would take me out to the south side. Well, I just thought all that was ridiculous. From all my experiences in the '60s, I was beginning to feel and understand the concept of brotherhood. I had already had many experiences where I embraced all races, all types of people that prior to the '60s I would have no contact with, no communication with. I truly understood the oneness of all my brothers and sisters on the planet. It was in a fledgling state; it was in an early state. It was in the beginning of the end of any racism that I had in me, which, from my father, I had a tremendous amount. The judgments on other people and other races and other religions. All of that was dissolving in my consciousness. So in my cab, I would defy the rules and would go out on the south side. I probably had at least 3 close calls with death.

The first one that happened was on a Sunday night. I picked up 4 young black men. I was out around 47th and Halsted. These guys thought it was hilarious that I picked them up, and they started talking about what a dumb white boy I was. To come out on their turf and think that I could be safe. They ordered me to stop at a nearby drugstore. One of them went in and came out with bottles of terpin hydrate with codeine. They were all cough medicine codeine junkies. I realized quickly that I had gotten myself into a serious trick bag. But I didn't panic. At one point one of them leaned over the seat and had a pistol in his hand; he said, "After you take us to our drugstores, we're going to take you out to 63rd and Cottage Grove under the L tracks. We're going to take your money and your cab, and we're going to put a bullet in ya."

There already had been that kind of murder of cab drivers out there. Where they had found them under the L tracks and their cabs and money gone. So I knew I had a very interesting night ahead of me.

I probably was with them for 2.5 or 3 hours. Probably took them to 15 different drugstores. They seemed to have a load of money. Everybody had wads of money. Each drugstore a different one would go in and come out with 2 or 3 bottles. Then they'd just slug them down. Meanwhile they all were continuously telling me or goading me that I was going to end up dead under the L tracks. I remember clearly not panicking inside at all. I remember at one point thinking, "How can I convince these guys that we're all brothers?"

I wrestled with that in my mind. Meanwhile there were times where I would see police cars. There was temptation to just jerk the cab over in front of the police cars, do something like that. And then I thought, "No, don't do that. That's not the way to handle this."

So they finally went to their last drugstore where they knew they could get this stuff. Now they were all extremely high, and a couple of them were very frustrated that all this time I never pleaded, never begged, never tried to make some deal. I had stayed centered all the time, just calm, quiet, did everything they said, didn't question anything. We got to the point where one of them said, "Okay, let's get this guy, get his money…"

Then out of nowhere the guy who was sitting behind me—whom I never saw in the mirror or made any eye contact with, while I saw the other ones—said something like, "Why don't we let him go."

One of them, he really didn't like me, he said, "Oh, that's BS. Give me the gun. I want to be the one to shoot him."

The one with the gun sort of liked me because I did everything he said, and he pulled the gun away and said, "No, maybe he's right. Let's let him go."

They started arguing. In the meantime, I pulled the cab over on State St.—maybe 70th and State. I pulled the cab over, and they didn't seem to be concerned about pulling over. They continued to argue; finally, the guy with the gun said, "Look, we don't have to kill this guy. He hasn't given us any trouble. He hasn't done anything wrong. We're just gonna let this guy go."

And I just sat there, so relieved, and the guy who had wanted me dead opened the backdoor and got out the passenger side. And then 2 other guys crawled out after him. Finally, for the first time, I saw the guy that first stood up for me, who had been seated behind me. And I really did something dumb, but it just came out of me. I reached out as he was getting out and tapped him on the shoulder.

I said, "Wait a minute, there's one more thing."

He sat back on the seat and said, "What?"

I said, "The meter, you gotta pay for this."

And he laughed and laughed. He said, "You are so crazy! You gotta be nuts!"

He went in his pocket. I think the meter was $27 or something. He took a 10 and a 20 out of his pocket, threw it on the seat next to me, and said, "You're the craziest white boy I ever saw."

And the 4 of them went staggering down the street.

About a week after that on a Sunday night again, I picked up a lone, older, maybe 50- or 55-year-old, very big-bodied black man. He waved me over. I scooted over to the curb; he sat in the back seat and just said, "Drive." And I said, "To where?"

He said, "Just do as I said. Drive."

I realized I was in another trick bag right away.

I looked at him in the mirror, and he looked incredibly troubled. He looked like he was in anguish. And I said to him, "Is there anything I can do to help ya?"

He said, "You want to help me?"

He said, "I'm going to kill you, and you want to help me?"

I looked in the mirror; he had gone in his coat and had pulled out a big butcher knife. I drove for maybe 10 minutes.

And this time, in contrast to the previous incident, I felt like I had to continuously talk to him. I had to try to befriend him or help him with whatever was making him look crazed. He said at one point, "I need to kill someone, and you're the perfect one."

He said, "I'm going to slit your throat. I'm going to kill ya."

I said to him, "You really don't have my permission to do that."

I had said this at a few other times when I was in trouble. I had told people they didn't have permission.

He said, "What are you talking about? You're going to die. There's no permission involved."

I said, "Look, we're brothers."

That set him off. He came out of the seat, leaned over the seat, and had the butcher knife down by my rib cage. He screamed at me, "What do you mean we're brothers! We're not brothers!!!"

I said, "No, we are brothers. I feel you're my brother."

We started a banter back and forth. Me holding tight to my argument that we were brothers, he sometimes furiously screaming that I should stop saying that and that I had no right to say that. That we weren't brothers.

At one point, he lapsed back in the seat with the knife in his lap and said to me, "Do you really believe what you're saying to me?"

I said, "About being brothers? Yes, I do."

He said, "No white man has ever even spoken to me decently in my lifetime, much less say that he was my brother."

I said, "We are all brothers whether we know it or not. I just happen to know that you and I are brothers."

He was quiet for a long time. I think I was at 79th and Stony Island. He told me to pull over at the corner, and I pulled over. It was a big, busy intersection. He put his knife back into his coat and said to me, "You should never come out here. Every time you come out here, you'll be in danger."

He started to get out, and he saw the meter. He threw 5 or 6 dollars, whatever it was, over the seat. Then 3 tough-looking young kids came rushing up, trying to push into the cab; he knocked one of them right down onto the sidewalk and pushed the others away. And he said, "You're not getting in here."

He said to me, "You get going and don't you dare stop until you get to the north side."

Then out of the L station came a black man and a woman with 2 little kids, and they rushed over while he was still warning these 3 street guys. And he told them to get in the cab. He said, "You take them where they're going and get out of the south side."

I took off. This couple had to go to Cabrini Green, which was on the north side, and I took them there.

That was another cab-driving experience where I put myself in jeopardy, empowered my belief system that was growing in me that there was basically good in all people.

In these 2 instances, I tested myself to the max but drove away from both situations. I drove a cab for some time. I had more dangerous situations, not as clearly deadly potential situations as those 2. But driving a cab for me at that time was very therapeutic; it was very freeing to me, not being trapped behind a bar for 10 or 12 hours, having the liberty to get in and out of my cab when I wanted, drive where I wanted.

In those few months, I really transitioned my habit patterns nightlife and bar stuff into the next phase of my life, which was essentially a powerful call to do healing work.

The Healing Path

IN THIS SAME PERIOD OF TIME, in the late '60s, I met a man, whom I'll call JA. He was part of the LSD Rescue Service. He was one of the leaders or teachers. And one day, in front of a number of other people, he offered to do a physical therapy treatment on me while I lay on the floor; in the treatment he was going to put me into a profound state of relaxation. He said this therapy technique had been put together by a group of Harvard doctors. I volunteered and lay on the ground. He essentially had me focus continuously for probably an hour. He had me focus on deep breathing, keep my eyes closed, and do nothing voluntarily. Use no muscles for anything. Then he started with my arms, lifting them up, shaking them, and rubbing them. He moved through my whole body, down my trunk. He would massage; he would do deep manipulation in joint areas. He kept saying, "Pay attention to your breathing. Focus on your breathing."

At one point I began feeling buzzing in my head. Then I began feeling tingling throughout my body. Eventually my inner vision, which is always just like blackness when my eyes are closed, my inner vision began to light up. In a short period of time, I began to realize that his voice was trailing off, and this light inside was getting brighter and brighter and brighter. The buzzing was getting louder; the tingling was more intense, like waves through my whole body. I began to lose contact with what he was doing with my body. He was working on my head and neck, massaging them, moving them around.

I felt as though he had trailed off into the distance. At one point, I couldn't hear him talking to the other people in the room anymore. Then I just realized that I was in a white light place. I had all these sensations going on of waves of energy and light and sound. I was not conscious anymore of him having his hands on my body. He actually put me into, for lack of a better phrase, some level of Satori or Nirvana. It wasn't as though it was a state of realization as much as him pushing me through a doorway that I didn't conceive even existed or had any idea that that could happen. I thought I was going to get a massage on the floor and was going to be relaxed. Well, it was much more than that. At one point, he lifted one of my arms up high and then let go of it, and my arm crashed down to the floor. That sort of brought me back to that arm. He went to the other side and did the same thing. Lifted my arm up and let go, and it crashed back down onto the floor. And then I started coming back into my body. Well, I don't know if I ever actually left my body, but I came back into awareness of my body. And then he said, "Okay, I'm through."

I just laid there in this place of diminishing light, but still there was an immense experience of peace and bliss. Quietude. Whatever is 10 degrees beyond relaxation, or 10 levels beyond relaxation, is what I had experienced. When I came out of that, I could hardly even talk about it. Everyone was asking me, "Well, are you relaxed?"

I don't think I even tried to tell anyone what I had experienced. But from that point on, I started to have a strong, strong desire to heal people—something that had actually never occurred to me as any kind of desire or choice or path. I had never thought of or considered healing. Well, I started doing this same technique on friends.

Some of them also had, though not similar to mine, very profound levels of relaxation and some visualization. Some sort of revelation. At one point, one of my friends who watched me do this on a man said, "Do you know what you're doing?"

And I said, "No."

He said, "Don't you think with all those movements and all that stuff you're doing to people's bodies, don't you think you should know what you're doing?"

It actually sort of stopped me in my tracks. And I thought, "Maybe he's right."

One of the most famous massage schools in the United States was downtown on State St., the Kellburg Institute. And the old woman who ran it, an old Swedish doctor, Esther Swanson, she had run the school for I think 40 years downtown. Anyways, I went in there and signed up and started taking classes. I decided he was right. I should at least know if I was pushing or pulling on joints. If I was going to be twisting necks or ankles, I should have a little bit of knowledge about what part of peoples' bodies I was moving. So I did my stint at the Kellburg Institute. During the time I was there, a couple of my friends also decided that they too wanted to be healers, and they joined.

We were all young; probably everyone in the class was under 30 years old, except one man who was in his mid-to-late 40s. His name was Maurice Paulsen, and he ended up telling me that he had to have a massage license in order to go to Rolfing school and become a trained rolfer. I didn't know anything about that. And later, Maurice, after he finished at Kellburg, and having finished the Rolfing, he settled in Downers Grove. He became Chicago's first rolfer. (Even though I had met Jan Sultan years earlier in Taos, Maurice took me through the whole 10-hour "recipe" of complete body rolfing.)

Idaho Springs and Yosemite Sam

I GRADUATED FROM MASSAGE SCHOOL ON SEPTEMBER 15, 1970. I immediately took the invitation of a friend of mine who wanted to drive out to California to see some mutual friends that we had outside of San Francisco. He said, "You're out of school. Why don't you come with me and help me drive?"

So we took off for California. We had a very interesting ride; we were almost lynched in Texas for being hippies. We went to LA, saw friends, and went up to San Francisco to see the people we had set out to see. And on the way back, we were driving on, Highway 70 through the mountains of Colorado, heading back for Chicago; it was a very hot, muggy day. He didn't have an air conditioner. We had been driving, probably, for 16 or 18 hours. We were both sweaty. It was late afternoon, and we came up on a town about 40 miles west of Denver, called Idaho Springs. They had a big billboard about a mile before the exit to the town, and the billboard talked about the radium hot springs.

My friend Paul was driving and I said, "Paul! Why don't we stop at this town and go in these hot springs and clean ourselves up and get something to eat and then drive the rest of the way to Chicago tonight?"

He thought it was a good idea, so we went into the hot springs place, which were some caves that the Nez Perce Indians had dug out in the late 1800s. It was their spring healing ground where they would go—the tribal people that had injuries or were sick. Everybody would get healed before they started their trek to their place where they spent the summer.

These caves were very magical. The caves and the mineral water that came up into these pools were quite different than regular hot springs. They were dug deep under the ground. In 1900, they built a hotel over the caves. We had quite an amazing time in these hot pools. There were 3 different pools with different temperatures. They had a cot room on the side where you could get out of the hot water and go wrap yourself in a sheet and lie on a cot. So after a couple of hours of soaking, I did that. I was lying there in this dark room, and I had a very clear, unintentional astral projection. I was up on the ceiling of this room, looking down at myself and 8 or 10 other men lying in cots. I had no fear. I had had astral projection before, so I recognized it right away. At that same time, my friend came in the room and yelled at me, "Come on, let's shower and get on the road."

So I went back in my body right away, but I got up and thought that this experience was too powerful to just walk away from. So we got dressed in the locker room after showering. On the way out, I went to the front desk. The owner was there, though I didn't know that at the time.

I said to him, "Does this place ever need masseurs?"

He said, "Are you a masseur?"

"Yes."

"Are you trained?"

I said, "Yea, I just graduated from the Kellburg Institute in Chicago."

"You live in Chicago?"

"Yea."

"You want a massage job? You want to come back here? I need a masseur right now."

I got his phone number. I told him, "I'll call ya when I get to Chicago." I did just that. He confirmed that he wanted to hire me.

A week later, I got my car packed and drove out to Idaho Springs and did my first 1,000-plus massages. I began to understand and allow energy to come through me. In getting the massage diploma, I had sort of given myself cover and a reason to put my hands on people. But what actually was happening with me was that my intuition was starting to come into play, and I was being guided to do things with peoples' bodies. Therapies, different movements, different techniques that were coming through me intuitively. I was becoming an intuitive, somewhat empathic healer in the disguise of a professional masseur. So this experience was out in Idaho Springs. I stayed there for about 6 months. I saw incredible things happen at the hotel in my time there. I could actually write a whole book just about the experiences down in that massage room and in those caves.

One man, who was a geologist for the state of Colorado, came in one day and I happened to strike up a conversation with him. He told me he was a geologist and I said, "Do you know anything about these waters?"

He said, "I know everything about them. I've studied mineral hot springs in the state of Colorado for the last 20 years, and I know everything about Idaho Springs."

I asked him if he could tell me any reason why the healing potential of the water of these springs seemed to be so high. I had met dozens and dozens of people who had been coming there for years, when the first time they went into the waters, they were crippled, they had terrible distortions in their physical body, and the water seemed to have removed all their afflictions. Especially people who would go in the waters often. There was one room in the basement of the hotel at that time that was filled with crutches and wheelchairs and all sorts of braces and devices that people had to live with who came to the hotel. They would spend a couple weeks or a month or a couple months there and then be able to walk out normal and healthy, and leave their devices behind.

He told me, "This is a radium hot spring. There are only three radium hot springs in the world. One is in China, one is in Poland, and this is the third." He said, "What makes this water different is that under the mountain there is a gigantic lake that this water bubbles up from." He said, "It's a tremendous body of water. The contents of that water come up through the tubs. Each of the tubs is fed by holes in the floor of the tub, where the water comes right up from under the ground." He said, "That water was rain water between 600-800 years ago and it filters down into that lake. The lake sits on a radium deposit. So the radioactivity speeds up the molecular structure of the minerals of the water and the water itself. So the water is actually empowered by some magnitude, we can't really guess what it is. But the healing potential of the minerals in the water become highly activated and then they can do things that normal hot springs are not capable of doing." He said, "This is potentially the most powerful healing water of any area of the United States. This place is very rare and very special."

I'm going to backtrack for a moment, to the beginning of the road trip where I found Idaho Springs. When we left Chicago, before we headed to

California, my friend actually wanted to drive to Virginia Beach to the Edgar Cayce Foundation. He said, "Why don't we go and spend some time there in their library?"

I agreed. I had read Edgar Cayce's life story. I was excited about it. We spent about 4 days at the Cayce Foundation. Each day early in the morning, we went into the library and read various readings. It was just like an old-time library with little pull-out card catalogs. I decided, when I got there, I would read anything I could about healing. I would look up "massage" and there would be 20 or 30 readings listed. I would then go to the library and get those numbers and read Cayce's explanation of how to do massage or how to do adjustments. So in the time at the Cayce Library, I had a notebook, and I took notes. And one of the things I read about was tinctures, ointments, and concoctions that Cayce would put together to use for massage. There was vast information about how to use different oils. One of the things that I wrote down was an ointment that could be used for very painful, serious arthritis and rheumatism.

Now back to the Radium Hot Springs Hotel, where I had been working for just a couple weeks. A man came in, and as soon as I looked at him, I thought of Yosemite Sam. He was a little prospector, and he was bowlegged. And his knees, as well as bending outward, were bending forward, and they were locked. He walked in the strangest manner; he was only about 5 feet tall. He came in and went into the baths right away. Somebody came down and said, "Oh, the old miner is here, isn't he?"

I said, "I think that's the guy that I saw."

They said, "We know because his burro is out front in the parking lot."

He came from the other side of the mountain than the hotel was at the base of. He would come over the mountain every couple weeks, once a month for sure. And he would soak those legs for a long time, usually for a whole day.

So maybe 6 hours later he came out of the tunnel where the caves were. He had never seen me. I could see he knew I was a new guy. He said, "You know how to work on arthritis?"

I said, "Yea."

He said, "You look pretty young. I don't think you know too much about it."

I said, "I probably know more than most people."

He said, "You got any tricks? Or do you do the stuff that everybody else does?"

I said, "What's going on with your legs?"

He said, "My knees are frozen. They've been unable to bend for 20 years now. I live up in the mountains, and the winter is hard on me."

We were heading into winter then.

He said, "Most of the masseurs who have been here over the years don't know how to get into arthritis."

I said, "Are you going to be here again soon?"

He said, "I don't have time for a massage now, but I'll be back in a week."

I said, "Okay, I've got an idea of some liniment that I could put together that might help you."

So in that week I drove to Boulder and bought all the things in Cayce's recipe—cayenne pepper, alcohol, and a couple different oils such as peanut oil, almond oil, and wintergreen oil. Cayce's instructions were that it would take 5 days to make up this liniment. So I made up a batch of liniment for this old guy. I didn't know if he would come back.

The next Saturday he showed up; he came early in the morning. He went in the baths and came out maybe at 5 or 6 in the evening. He said, "I want you to massage my knees. I don't want you to touch any other part of my body, just my knees."

So when he lay on the table and tried to straighten his legs, his knees were like 10 or 12 inches up in the air. That was the position they were locked in. So I got a bunch of pillows and put them underneath his knees and had him hang his feet off the end of the table. And I went and got the liniment.

I started rubbing it into him. It was hot; it was actually hot. His pores were wide open. I said, "This might burn a little bit."

He said, "I don't care."

I started rubbing it in gently, and right away he said, "If you're going to be like all the other masseurs and be afraid to get in there, you ain't gonna help me."

I said, "Can you handle it? I'll go deep if you can handle it."

He said, "I can handle anything you can do, but don't waste my time with rubbing over the surface."

So I had both knees saturated with this liniment, and I started digging into that arthritis. The deeper I dug in with my fingers or my knuckles, the more he encouraged me. I finally was almost brutalizing him. I was digging my knuckles as hard as I could into those joints, into the back of the knees, into the side, into above and below the knees. I was sweating furiously.

At one point I was moaning and groaning. He didn't have to encourage me to go deep anymore because I was tearing into those legs. On one hand it was actually pretty foolish to go after injured joints that way, but he pushed me to do it. And once I started doing it, I felt totally confident that this was the right thing to do.

I worked on each of his knees for a half hour, and continuously, every couple minutes, put more liniment on. I dug into him so hard that when we finished, the skin on my fingers and knuckles was almost raw and burning from the liniment. We did some strange dance where he convinced me to not be afraid and to do what nobody could or should do to anybody. When we finished, I wiped his legs off. I was exhausted. It was the end of a long day anyways.

He got off the table and stood up and said, "Oh, God."

I thought I had hurt him. Right away, I thought, "Oh my God, I've hurt him now."

But he was bouncing himself up and down. Only moving a couple of inches, but both of his knees had come loose, and he could flex them just a little bit.

He said, "I didn't think I'd ever be able to do that again in my life. I'll be back tomorrow."

He came back the next day, and we did the same dance.

He came back the next weekend, Friday, Saturday, Sunday. We did the same dance. I dug into those knees with all the strength I had in my body. I would make him lie him on his face and put my knuckles down into the cavity of his knee joint and put my whole weight down into that area behind his knees. I did things that not only weren't taught to me, but that I don't know anybody has ever done.

By the time we finished that second week, this man's knees were free. He was actually able to stand up straight. He was still somewhat bowlegged, but the frozen inability to even bend the knee joints was completely gone. His knees were half the size they were the first day that I had worked on him.

What I had done without plan or understanding, but by his continuous prodding of me, was I had actually dug into the calcified material and broken it up, and somehow the liniment went in and helped burn it up. Then I broke up the crystallizations with my knuckles and fingers.

I think what the 2 of us experienced in that time was his body being able to handle the severe pressure and heat of my hands and that liniment and then my willingness to follow his lead and actually go after the arthritis. The last time I saw him, he could do almost a deep-knee bend. He could bend his knees so well and then stand up straight. It was maybe a month and a half from the time I got there to the last time I saw him. And I never saw him again, don't know what happened to him, but he was like Yosemite Sam. He was hard and old and gruff.

He and I did an amazing dance that taught me that things that seemed not possible could actually happen. That was maybe the first time that I fully understood the limitations of the people who run massage schools, or the people who write books about massage, or people who teach massage. What they held as limitations I had violated in totality. I had dug into this man in an almost brutal manner, and then end result was that he could move his knees for the first time in 20 years. He was a profound, deep, important person for me to meet because his intuition was telling him from the beginning, "This guy can do something that no one else has ever done for my knees."

He pushed it; he put the pedal to the metal. And I responded. I put the pedal to the metal. And afterward, I knew arthritis is something that can actually be assaulted. It can actually be confronted. If the person that had the problem was willing to let go of their suffering. It was one of my first experiences of watching a person let go of their suffering, which he had carried with him for 20 years.

Hannah Kroger- Healer

THE TIME THAT I SPENT AT IDAHO SPRINGS was rather impactful on the rest of my life. I settled into a routine. I lived in a little 1-room cabin across the parking lot from the hotel. I settled into a routine of taking care of the expanding massage business that the hotel was experiencing. When I began working there, I would do a couple massages a day. Within a month, I was doing 10 full-body massages every Friday, Saturday, and Sunday. I had Mondays off, and then Tuesday, Wednesday, and Thursday I would do 6 to 8 massages.

So I settled into a very easy routine of finding out what I could do with my hands. I was in what I felt was a spiritual healing power place. The hotel, built over the hot springs, was just a mecca of healing potential. Pretty much everyone who came to the hotel was looking for some sort of healing, either from the waters or from people who worked there. The routine went on for some months. Very easy. On my day off I would usually drive to Boulder and go to Hannah Kroger's Health-Food store on Pearl St. I would have lunch there and do my shopping. I knew a little bit about Hannah. She was the kind, beautiful, blue-eyed grandma who ran the store, who already had quite a history in Boulder and the whole area of being an amazing healer. I don't think she had credentials. But she was an amazing woman.

So one day I was shopping, and she came out of her office. I happened to turn and see her standing by her door, surveying the whole store. At one point, she made eye contact with me and just started waving to me to come over. I looked around and I was the only one she could be waving to.

So I went over. She grabbed me by the arm and pulled me into her office and said, "I need your help."

I said, "Okay."

So she had a young woman lying on the floor of her office on a blanket. She said, "You have to give this young girl a grapevine. She's pregnant and needs one desperately."

I said, "I don't know what that is."

And she said, "I'll show you."

I said, "Wait a minute, what do you want me to do?"

She said, "Just don't talk. Listen to what I say and just do what I say."

It was rather intimidating.

So she had this girl sit up with her legs stretched out and feet together. She told me to take my shoes off and sit behind her. So I sat behind this girl.

She said, "No, get up close to her!"

So I scooted close to her; she had her back to me.

Hannah said, "No, no, no."

And she reached down and pushed me right up, flush with this girl, pelvis to pelvis, chest to back. She said, "This girl has a twisted sacrum, and if we don't get it straight, she won't have a good birthing. She could have a miscarriage."

At this point, my head was spinning. I was sitting on the floor, my pelvis pushed up against this woman whom I didn't even know the name of.

Hannah said, "Okay, now put your legs around her."

So I put my one leg on this woman's lap and then the other. And I reached out and made a lotus out of them. So I literally had her pelvis locked between my crossed ankles.

She said, "That's good."

She had the girl put her arms out and grab her elbows straight out in front of her. I had to reach around and with my right hand, grab the girl's left elbow, and with my left hand grab the girl's right elbow. So that's where the grapevine name came in. I was entangled with her. I had her by the elbows; I had her pelvis pinned to the ground with my legs. She said, "Now I want you to rock back and forth."

She said to me, "You control the rocking, just rock with her back and forth. Pull her arms down to her body, hold her close, and rock back and forth."

So I started doing this and started getting in a motion, nice gentle rocking. She said, "Now I want you to close your eyes and wait until it feels right. And then rock all the way as far as you can. And then when you know it's the right time, lay down very fast, very hard, keep her pelvis pinned with your legs, pull up on her elbows, and forcefully drag her back down on top of you."

Well, at that point I thought, "What in God's name am I doing here? What is going to happen here?"

I was confused and I was befuddled. But she was orchestrating and ordering both of us in this situation with such confidence and such strength and clarity that I just decided at that moment to surrender. So I closed my eyes and started rocking more forcefully, as far forward as I could and then backward, and then forward. I did that for I don't know how long…in my head I said, "I don't know what I'm doing. I need help." No more than a couple seconds later, I just felt a shiver of energy go through my brain down into my body. At that second I pushed forward, pushing this girl down, and then I really powerfully lay back as fast and hard as I could, pulling up on her elbows. I heard her vertebrae, almost the entire length of her spine, I heard the vertebrae moving, and then right at the end, the last pull I gave, I could hear her lumbar vertebrae adjusting.

Then Hannah said, "Okay, get out! Get out from under her, scoot out!"

I scooted out. She made the girl lie down and said, "Everything's good! Everything's good."

Then she said, "Come here and look at this."

She took the girl's ankles and touched them together; her ankle bones were perfect; they lined up touching. She said, "When you came in here, those bones were an inch and a half apart." Then she had the girl roll over, and she pulled her trousers down and exposed the area of the sacrum. And she put her fingertips on the tips of the sacrum (the sacrum is an upside-down triangle that the spinal cord connects to at the base of the spine) and said, "See, they're perfect! They're perfectly even." She said, "When you came in here the left one was an inch higher than the right one."

She said, "Okay, you've done it. That was a good job. This girl won't have any more trouble with her pregnancy." And she ushered me out of the room. I went back in the store with my head spinning, not fully comprehending what had just happened. I had lunch in the store and later saw her standing near her office. And I went over and introduced myself. I told her I was a masseur at the hot springs. I said, "Hannah, you've got to tell me what I just did there."

She said, "You gave a perfect perpendicular pull up the entire spinal column that caused the spine to go straight. And then when you laid down flat, you arched her lower back and put a powerful pull onto the sacrum, which pulled it straight. You accomplished exactly what the grapevine is supposed to do."

She said, "This girl won't have any trouble with her pregnancy now."

I said, "This was a very strange maneuver. How did you learn it?"

She said, "It was taught to me when I was 18 years old in Germany by an old doctor who could no longer do it himself. He taught me how to do it, and I would do it to women with these sacral problems. I had to get your help because I can no longer do it. I don't have enough flexibility or strength."

She said, "You've got a perfect body for it."

I said, "Are there many people who know this?"

She said, "I know of one doctor whom I taught it to 30 years ago in Southern California. Other than that, you and I are the only other people I know who can do this adjustment."

So that was my initial meeting with Hannah Kroger. Very famous, very dedicated healer, light bearer, and servant of the people of the planet.

I had another encounter with her, with similar circumstances, maybe a month later. I was in the store shopping again, and a woman came through the front door with a 3- or 4-year-old little boy in her arms, who was screaming at the top of his lungs. It immediately disrupted the whole store, everybody stopped. Hannah came out of her office, grabbed the woman, and took her in the office; everybody could hear this kid just screaming. He wasn't crying, just screaming. A long loud scream and then a little break and then another scream. He was intermittently just screaming. After a couple of minutes, Hannah's door opened again, and I was over at the tea area picking up some herbal tea.

Again, she saw me. I didn't have any eye contact with her, but she yelled my name. I turned, and she frantically waved again. So I scurried over into the office; the little boy was lying down on the blanket on the floor. I could see his body was all distorted. She had the mother sitting in a chair, and the little boy was just sort of thrashing around and doing this screaming thing. I looked down at him, and she said, "You have to help me with this one."

I said, "Okay. What's wrong with him?"

She said, "He's possessed. He's been possessed since birth."

She turned to the mother and said, "You tell him."

The mother was in tears. She said, "My little boy has never talked, he only screams. He eats, and then he screams. He screams all day long. My husband can't take it anymore and wants to institutionalize him."

She said, "I found out about Hannah and thought maybe Hannah could help, so that's why I'm here."

So Hannah said to me, "He's possessed by a spirit that I can easily push out, but I'm not strong enough to do the whole thing. You have to help me."

I said, "Hannah, I don't know anything about this."

She said, "You don't have to know anything. You just do as I tell you."

So she had me kneel down behind the boy with my knees on either side of his head. She said, "First I want to show you his problem."

She rolled him over on his stomach and pulled his shirt up and his pants down. And I was absolutely horrified to see his spine. His spine was so twisted. His spine came out of his head down through his neck area straight. But an inch or 2 below the cervical vertebrae down into the thoracics, it all of a sudden bent directly left, and his spine twisted all the way over to his left rib cage. Then it twisted back, and at where his sacrum was, it turned straight. So his spine was like a giant letter *C*. I couldn't even imagine how he could live like that, how he could even be alive.

She held him so I could see it, and she said, "The entity possessing him is living in his spine and has set up residence in his spine."

Then she flipped him back over on his back. Meanwhile he was not resisting too much; his arms were just sort of fluttering around, and there were his intermittent screams, which I had started to get used to.

She said, "What I am going to do is that I'm going to hold his pelvis by both hips, and you have to pin his shoulders down on the ground."

She said, "Lean up on him, put your hands on each shoulder and pin him on the ground."

So I did that. But I didn't want to hurt him, so I didn't put any pressure.

She said, "No, you have to listen to me. I need him pinned to the ground so he can't move. If you hold his shoulders so he can't move, then I can force this spirit out. If you don't hold his shoulders, this won't work."

"Okay, okay," I said.

I got up closer to him, and I literally pinned him down as though I were holding down a 200-pounder. I used all of my weight and all of my force. I was afraid of hurting him, but she said, "Don't think about that. Just pin him."

So I pinned his shoulders down to the ground; his screaming turned up in intensity and volume. I thought I was hurting him. At that moment, Hannah grabbed both sides of his pelvis, his hips. And she pulled real hard downward. I had to push harder so his body wouldn't slide. And then she started turning, like cranking in a circle, like a corkscrew circle. She started moving his hips up off the ground into circles. First real small, and then bigger and bigger. He was trapped between us contorting and twisting his little body. She became like a whirlwind almost, pulling harder and harder, twisting harder and harder. Meanwhile the mother was just becoming hysterical.

The little boy's screams became just one long scream. Then Hannah started talking. I don't know if it was in German or what, but I couldn't understand it. She started ordering the spirit to leave his body. And she raised her voice to a high pitch, screaming at the little boy, twisting him into these rapidly moving circles. The boy was now absolutely screaming at the top of his lungs. And Hannah was screaming whatever invocation or whatever words she was saying to the spirit. All of a sudden the little boy's whole body quivered like there was an earthquake under us. And it shook violently and almost knocked her away. She sat back down on her haunches, and let go his pelvis; it just dropped to the ground, and the little boy went unconscious—no sound, no movement, nothing.

The mother was down on the floor, hysterical. Hannah pushed her back and said, "No, don't touch him yet."

She told me to let go of him and move away. We all just sat there and looked at him. Just staring at this little unconscious 3-year-old.

Then Hannah rolled him over, after a minute or two. She pulled his shirt up and pants down, and his spine was perfectly straight. It came out of his neck, it went right down the middle of his back, right down to the sacrum. She just beamed and turned and said to the mother, "It's done. It's finished. The spirit is gone."

She rolled the boy over on his back, and his eyes started fluttering. The mother pushed past Hannah and reached down and grabbed him and pulled him up to her chest, and there was not a peep coming out of him. Now his eyes were open, and the mother was crying— with so much relief. A minute or two later, the little boy said, "Mama."

And the mother almost lost it. She was just crying profusely. She said, "That's the first time he ever said 'Mama.' That's the first word ever out of his mouth."

Hannah got up and grabbed me by the arm. And she said, "Okay, okay, you've done it. You can go now."

She hustled me out. And I was back out in the store again, again my head spinning, having just been a part of and witnessed a powerful exorcism. Hannah was obviously working totally intuitively but with a masterful ability to control the entire room, the entire situation. Somehow, she intuitively knew exactly what to do with this little boy's twisted spine and possessed spirit. I just stood out there, and I was so grateful. I just felt profound, profound gratitude at being allowed to be used as a tool in that situation. A few minutes later, the mother came out, the little boy with his arms around her neck, eyes wide open, and they headed for the front door. I never knew anything about either one of them again. Hannah came over again and said, "Thank you for helping me."

I said, "Hannah, I'm truly honored."

She said, "You'll be a good healer. You already know some things, but when you learn to let God come through you, you'll be a good healer."

In subsequent visits to her store, I encountered her and talked briefly with her about various things. She wasn't much for talking; she was a workaholic. She had the most popular health-food store in all of Colorado. She took on any kind of healing challenge that walked through the front door. Everybody in Boulder or Denver area knew that Hannah could do things that were impossible. I can certainly attest to that.

Harvey Bevier- Healer

SHORTLY AFTER THAT, RIGHT AROUND CHRISTMAS TIME, I had another encounter with another healer. It was sort of a lonely Christmas for me. I was in the hotel. There was very little business on Christmas Eve, and I remember feeling sort of sorry for myself. A day or two after, it was a

Saturday. I actually had 12 massages scheduled that day, which meant I couldn't have lunch or dinner. I just worked 12 straight, full-body massages.

I remember in the middle of the day, somebody came down from the lobby—one of the employees of the hotel—and came over and said, "You should see this guy up in the lobby. There's a healer up there. And he' got people lined up, and he's working on one after another after another." It sort of piqued my interest in the moment, but then my next client came walking through the door and I went back to work. Later in the afternoon, at 3 or 4, again another different employee came down and said, "This guy in the lobby, he's already worked on 50 people or more. He's an incredible healer."

Again I thought, "Geez, I wish I could go up and watch him." But I had more work to do. Finally, at about 7:00 p.m., I finished my last massage, and I put together a big laundry bag of all my old sheets and towels. And I had to take them upstairs to the lobby and then down about 100 feet to another stairway to another part of the basement, where the washers and driers were. I felt like Santa Claus with this giant bag on my back. I got up to the top of the stairs, headed across the lobby, and saw the owner of the hotel with this little man who was working on someone's head and neck with his hands. I realized, "Oh that was the healer; he is still there."

We made eye contact for a split second; he seemed to recognize me, and he nodded his head at me. I went down and put all the laundry in the machines. When I got back up, he was finishing that last person. I stood about 20 feet away, and the owner of the hotel was telling him, "Okay, that's all! You've worked on 65 people. Now I want you to come to the dining room and sit down and have dinner with me."

While the owner was talking, the healer turned and saw me standing there and waved his hand for me to come over. The owner turned and looked and said, "Oh no, he doesn't need any help. That's just the masseur. We don't have to talk to him. Come in the dining room."

This man said, "The masseur is why I am here. The masseur is why I'm at the hotel today."

I heard that, and it shocked me. He pushed past the owner and reached out his hand and said, "I'm Harvey Bevier."

I said, "I'm Corky Matson."

He said, "You're the one that I have to talk to. Have you closed the baths yet?"

I said, "No, they'll be closed in just a little while."

He said, "Come on, let's have a little bit to eat. Eat lightly."

We walked into the dining room area. The owner was beside himself. He didn't want me near this man. He didn't want me to be interrupting what he wanted to do, which was to essentially set up a situation where this man could work on the owner's wife (she had MS and was living in a wheelchair). So Harvey quickly told him, "Yes, yes, I'll come back tomorrow, and I'll work on your wife." And then he directed the conversation back at me.

He was a slightly built man. I'd guess 60 or 65, something like that. He had beautiful, beautiful shiny eyes. He had a deep smile. He was very gentle and yet charismatic to the nth degree. He just exuded power, spirituality, kindness, and love. He was a very charismatic, powerful man. So we had a little salad, and he said to the owner, "I'll talk to you later. I need to go down into the baths with this man."

So we went down there; it was closing time. I got all the men out. When they all left, he said, "Lock the door."

Then he quickly disrobed and threw his clothes on a bench. He said, "Let's go back in that water."

So we got into one of the tubs, and he said to me, "I'm a real estate broker. I live in Aurora." He said, "I also know how to do healing. The main kind of healing that I do is adjustments."

He gave me a cervical adjustment. He stood in front of me, took my head in his hands, moved my head around, and then gave me a powerful thrust to the right and then instantly turned the other way with a powerful thrust to the left. Every vertebra in my cervical area moved and sounded like piano keys. When he finished and took his hands off, one of my ears was roaring —the only way I could describe it was like I was standing next to Niagara Falls. That was my right ear. My left ear sounded like I was in a Com Ed power plant. As if I was in among turbines and electrical generators at maximum output. The pitch of the vibration was so high and so loud in that ear that I looked at him; he was talking to me, and I couldn't hear one word. In both ears just these 2 separate sounds were screaming. Then after a minute it wore off.

He told me, "I've come here because you need to have help right now, because if you don't learn what I'm here to teach you, you will not last as a healer." He said, "Have you ever noticed in the morning or when you get up, any physical problems?"

And I said, "Oh yea, I wake up some mornings, and my knees hurt or my back, the next day sometimes my shoulder, or a headache! This has been going on, and it's very concerning to me that every morning I wake up, I feel all these bodily issues."

He said, "You haven't put 2 and 2 together yet, have you?"

I said, "What do you mean?"

He said, "Think of the most recent trouble you woke up with."

It had been that morning; my left shoulder ached. But by the time I was dressed and headed for the hotel, it was gone.

He said, "Did you work on anybody yesterday who had a problem with their left shoulder?"

I immediately flashed back on this truck driver whose shoulder was so locked up, I worked on it for almost the entire massage. I worked on it intensely. I did things intuitively—pulling, pushing, and yanked on his arm down at his side. By the time I was through, he could move his shoulder around, and he thanked me. He was grateful.

So I told that to Harvey, and he said, "Okay, so do you see what happened?"

I didn't see what he was getting at. He said, "What do you do when people unload on you?"

I went back to my bar days, thinking about people who would come in who had trouble with their boss or their wife and would just start talking it out. I was real good at letting people just do that. I would just listen. So I said, "If someone unloads on me, I try to just listen and understand."

He said, "No, what do you do if someone *unloads* on you?"

I was just baffled. I said, "I don't know."

He said, "Well, you better know if you want to continue on your path. I'm here to tell you what to do when someone unloads on you."

So I just sank back in the hot water, opened my ears, and cleared my head. And the way he expressed it to me was this: "There's a universal law that protects healers." He said, "The law is stated this way; that all unseated negativity must follow running water." He said, "If a person desires to heal another, even if they desire that that person isn't afflicted or in pain, the mere thought of wishing that someone who is in trouble could be relieved sets up a situation where the empathic person can take on the illness, disease, pain, suffering. Healers who use their hands, they are very vulnerable to pushing physical ailments out of people and then having that vibration go right back into their own bodies."

He said, "The intent of a healer to help makes them vulnerable to taking on whatever it is that they're trying to free a person from." The light bulbs started going on in my head; I started flashing back instantly on many guys whose knees I had helped or ankles I had fixed and I would wake up with a bad knee or ankle. I started seeing the picture.

He said, "If you take on someone else's suffering, what you have to do to get it out of you immediately on finishing your treatment. You have to go and find running water. Go in the bathroom and turn the faucets on. You can put your wrists together under the water, let the water run over your wrist, close your eyes, and just for a few moments, center yourself, get quiet inside, and just ask the angels of the water, the spirits of the water, to pull out of your nervous system and your body all unseated negativity. You spend 10 or 15 seconds doing that. The law is that all unseated negativity must follow running water. In 15 or 20 seconds, but 30 seconds for sure, everything you may have picked up from your last client—physical, mental, emotional—will be pulled out of your body and washed down the drain."

He said, "You have to do this after every single person you work on for the rest of your days. Then at the end of the night, someone like you who is in touch with continuous misery, pain, suffering, aches, dilemmas, trouble- you must get under a shower. Let the water run under your whole head. Let your arms fall out to your side and again ask the spirits of the water to remove all unseated negativity."

"Unseated means that when you pick up something from someone else, it starts traveling through your nervous system, looking for a place to settle in. It will travel around and will try to settle there and become part of you. If you can do this work with the water within 24 hours, nothing will seat itself. But if you were to work on someone and pick up their negativity or suffering and you don't do the water, it will find a place in your body. It will seat itself, and at that point," he laughed, "And you become the proud owner of that ailment."

We were probably a total of a half hour down in that pool. In that time, this man changed my whole future. I never asked him, "How did you know about me?" Or, "How could you have come to the hotel to see me and then worked on 60 or 70 people?" I never questioned what actually made him come to the hotel. But it was apparent to me that he was a messenger. He was a messenger to help me be able to survive because my sensitivity was very high, especially in those years. My compassion was growing by the day. My empathic qualities were coming into reality in a strong way for the first time in my life. Somehow, he knew that if I didn't have the information about what I would be absorbing into my own body, it would be impossible for me to continue on my chosen path—to help people with my hands.

Harvey and I had several more encounters. I won't go into any more detail about them, but the last time I saw him was outside the Denver airport. I had taken some of his friends to the Denver airport. He told me, "I want to tell you something that I want you to remember." He said, "You have some buried fears in you about atomic destruction." He had hit the nail on the head because I was very young when Hiroshima and Nagasaki were bombed. By the time I was 5 or 6, I had heard so much talk of eventual atomic war with Russia, and it was a very scary thing to hear that so much when I was a little boy.

Anyways, he said, "I want to tell you this: every government, every army, every police force on this whole planet is already infiltrated with spiritual beings." He said, "There will never be an atomic war allowed on this planet. It will be controlled and stopped before this happens. So for the rest of your days, any further talk you hear, any news you hear, any governments threatening each other, understand an atomic war will not be allowed on this planet, so it will never happen."

Then he told me, "I know you're going to go traveling. At one point I'd like you to come back and look me up in Aurora. I'm a realtor, and I'm in the phone book. I have so much more to pass on to you. But it would have to be at a time when you have no commitments and are very free and can hear all that I have to offer." I never saw him again.

I did talk to him once well down the road, when I was married. Probably in the early '90s. I found him in the phone book and called him up and had a brief discussion with him. He remembered me, but I had a feeling that the offer that he had extended to me was long past expiration. So I talked to him and he was about to do a treatment on someone. He said, "You call back in a couple weeks and we'll see if we can get together."

So I called back a few weeks later; his wife as always answered the phone. I asked her if I could talk to Harvey. She said, "No, it's too late, Harvey passed away." I was sort of crestfallen and immediately aware that I should have gotten back to him many years earlier. So I'll never know what it was that he wanted to show me or teach me or share with me. So this was another very powerful healer that I encountered at Idaho Springs.

How to Be Your Own Doctor

IN THE SPRING OF '71, early on, maybe March or February even, I got a letter from the Syracuse Ashram friends of mine. My friends who had originally taken me to meet Margaret Coble had moved to Syracuse and lived in an old Victorian house. Probably a 17-room house. They sent me a letter saying that Margaret Coble wanted me to come to Syracuse, move into the ashram, and teach a class. She was designing a class called *How to be Your Own Doctor*. She wanted me and another "ashramite," as she called us— to be co-teachers. She had a young man living there, who was in his last year of medical school at Syracuse University; I had never met him before—and she wanted us to co-teach an 8-week class on how to be your own doctor.

So I read this letter; it was an open invitation to move to Syracuse, New York, and become a yoga teacher. Only, I didn't fancy myself teaching people how to stand on their heads, although at that time, I could bend myself into pretzel positions and do many yoga postures. Anyways, in the ensuing months when I had to make a decision, I decided that my experience at Idaho Springs was finished. I had been able for 6 months or so at that time, every day, bathe in these healing waters. I now had an understanding of why I had been there. I had been drawn out to that place for many areas of growth in my consciousness, in my healing ability, in my understanding of human bodies and human beings. I had been brought to expand my connection with nature, to empower my constant desire to understand spirituality in my life, in nature, and in other people

I realized when I got the letter from New York that it was time to move on. I was literally being invited by the most incredible, enlightened woman I had ever met to come back to Syracuse, move into the ashram and start teaching a class that was, to me, not anything that I had ever thought of doing, and yet, it was part of my path. I had some years before that, decided that I would take on the responsibility for my body and for its upkeep and care and healing; I would do that myself. I had read a book in my early 20s that a friend gave me. It was appropriately named *How to Be Your Own Doctor* by a man named Beiler. And he was the doctor for all the Hollywood movie stars all the way back into the '40s and '30s. He was an AMA physician. And the essence of the book was his message to take on responsibility for your own body, not leave it to others, and not require others to keep you healthy. So I had read that book and decided, "I'll do that myself." And then my meeting with Joseph Liss had greatly sent me along the path of being able to take care of my own body. Now, this enlightened woman was inviting me to come to Syracuse and teach a class on "how to be your own doctor."

So I decided at that point to give my notice, go back to Chicago, settle some business, and drive on to Syracuse in time to get there for the start of the class. They had already put the class in the yoga studio schedule. The class had already filled up before I got there. I said goodbye to Idaho Springs and reluctantly moved on, realizing that probably everything I was supposed to learn or experience in the mountains of Colorado had been accomplished. So I got in my vehicle and headed east to return to Margaret Coble and Dr. Mishra's turf, move into one of their ashrams and become a teacher.

Ashram Class

WHEN I ARRIVED IN SYRACUSE, I believe it was mid-April, the class was supposed to start within a week of my arrival. I sat down with Margaret Coble and tried to figure out why I had been chosen from afar to do this. Margaret was incredibly perceptive and truly enlightened. She was in a spiritual place of illumination every minute of every day. Rarely could anything pull her out of her center for even moments. And she told me (she would make references to spirit guiding) "Spirit will guide you. Spirit guides people."

She made some reference to being guided to have me come back and do this class. She said, "Just do it. You know all the stuff. There is no plan for the class yet."

I said, "What are we gonna teach?"

"I don't know. You and Robert will know."

So I settled into the ashram, had a room of my own. We had our routines. There were maybe 10 people living at the ashram. Several of them were friends of mine from Chicago. The other people I had met, it was all very friendly, and everybody got along pretty well. I settled in a routine. We got up early in the morning, we meditated.

Margaret would assign people different teaching jobs. We would teach some classes at the ashram. But most of the Hatha Yoga teachers would go out to schools or businesses or YMCAs where they would teach regular yoga. Sometimes I was called upon to go to a YMCA or go to some group. I got very good at doing Mantras and chanting. Everyone had their expertise and we all functioned together under the direction of Margaret.

So upon moving into the ashram, I met with Robert. He was very likeable. A very sharp, clear, pleasant, red-haired young man. We sat down, and I said, "Do you have ideas of what you want to teach?"

He said, "Not really. What do you want to teach?"

I thought, "This is the goofiest thing. We're a week away from 20 people coming in to be taught what neither one of us know what."

I said, "Let's start throwing stuff out that you know about or that I know about."

"Okay," he said, "Well, I'm real good about sprouting."

I said, "Okay, one class will be totally about sprouting. Just teaching people everything about sprouting. You can do that class and I'll assist." He had been at a Wigmore center, so he knew about the whole sprouting deal.

I said, "Good, that's one out of our 8 weeks."

He said, "Okay. How about you throw one out now."

I thought a little bit and said, "Okay, I know a breathing technique from Guru Rajneesh that can put people into altered states with 30 minutes of intense breathing." And he said, "Okay, we'll call this one Rajneesh breathing."

I said, "No, let's keep Rajneesh out of it. Let's call it deep breathing to connect a person inside."

So we figured out a name for that class.

He said, "I also know reflexology. I know how to do reflexology real well."

I said, "Great! I don't know anything about reflexology."

We had another class, foot reflexology. We paired people off and taught them how to do reflexology.

So we put together 8 weeks that way. We put together our whole curriculum and our whole game plan in that first meeting. And then a week later we started. The classes were every Wednesday from 7:00 p.m. to 9:00

p.m. The very first class, we had 20 students I think the youngest girl was 16, a young boy at 18, and then middle-aged people, and then a 78-year-old man.

Anyways, the classes started out very successfully. I'm not even clear what they were. One of them was a massage class that both Robert and I taught. I think the 3rd class was one where I had decided, from the Woodstock experience, to do a class on OMing. I had been taught the OM-shock at Woodstock, and in subsequent different times, I had done OM-shocks out in Idaho Springs. So I decided to make that a class.

The class was essentially 20 straight-laced people. Most of them were housewives or people with regular jobs. The OM Shock class really set our group into a motion, a powerful motion. What I had designed was that we would, through the 2 hours, do a group OM-shock on every person. And the way I planned that was to have 1 person straight up on the floor. And 4 people kneel around that person, everyone touching their foreheads to the head of the person in the middle, as I had been shown at Woodstock. So the first person that we put in the middle was a 50-year-old woman.

We told her, "You just be passive. You just go into your center and be still and we will do the OMing."

So I had a very good, strong voice, for doing OMing. Robert too had a very strong voice, so I put him opposite of me and then took 2 of the other students, and the 4 of us put our heads down on this woman. I gave directions as we went along.

I told everybody, "Let's just start out with several OMs where we try to breathe together, fall in a pattern of breathing, and chant OM together." After a few minutes, I said, "Okay, let's raise it up now." And we OMed a little bit more intensely and a little bit louder. With Robert and I anchoring the group, after 8 minutes or so, we were really in unison, and we were very, very focused. We spent about 10 minutes on this woman, and then when the pitch had gotten high enough where I didn't think the 2 students could go any higher, I said, "Okay, one more good strong OM," and we finished up that woman. I had everybody sit back. This woman sitting in the middle, it was a full 5 minutes before she moved a muscle. I told her, "When you can, come into the room, open your eyes, and if you can, relay what you experienced."

So this woman had had the first high of her life. When she could finally talk, she said, "I've heard people talk about being high my entire life and never had any idea what they were talking about." She said, "I elevated to a place inside that I have never been. The noise coming in through my head from everybody touching me and their voices, it just took me into another place that I couldn't even describe."

So then quickly I had another person sit down and methodically we went on. Robert and I realized that we had to anchor every one of these groups for it to be as successful as the first woman. So we continued this on, 2 different people coming into each session. We had the students rotating around until every one of them had had a time in the middle. No one seemed to have been aware whatsoever of the time. And when we finished, everyone, every single one of the people in the class had had an experience. They ranged from very minor experiences of clarity and relaxation to some people saying they saw angels, and they felt their hearts open. Everyone had a remarkable experience of one form or another. And then when we finished the last person, Robert announced, "Oh, we've run over time." It was past 10:00 p.m. The class was supposed to end at 9:00 p.m. Somehow that day, we bonded as an entire class.

One of the subsequent meetings was a shock to everybody. I taught a class called Enemas 101. Each week when the 20 would get there, Robert and I would explain what was to happen that day. So I spent 2 hours one night with Robert's help, explaining colon therapy. Explaining how to be aware of the GI tract. How to take care of the GI tract. Robert added in a tremendous amount of holistic and medical information about digestion, assimilation, and elimination, and I gave graphic explanations of how a person can purge themselves using teas, laxatives, implants, enemas or high colonics. Again at the end of the class, everyone was delighted. Like they had really learned something that none of them had conceived of learning that day.

So this class was very powerful. Everybody attended every single session. Not one person took one day off. No one missed a class. These people each had to pay 20 dollars for this class. And Robert and I got to split the money for the whole venture. Actually, we got a quarter each and the ashram got a quarter. So I think I got $100 for my 8 weeks, and the ashram got $200. And these people for a 20-dollar-bill had probably 5 or 6 of the most exciting classes they had ever had in their entire life.

The last class was worth talking about because there were some real dynamic experiences. The last class was the one in which I was going to teach a breathing technique. I had everybody do deep rapid breathing called "bhastrika breathing" or "bellows breathing" for 10 minutes, sitting down. And then an alarm would go off, and then they had to continue the breathing where they stood up or rolled around or jumped. What they had to do was let their body express, let their body move in any way they wanted. I very carefully monitored this class. This one I felt was potentially the most powerful experience they would have. So in 2 large rooms, I had 20 people breathing through their nose very rapidly. Each person was breathing as fast and hard as I could get them to breathe. Essentially, Robert explained to the class, one did have to be afraid of hyperventilating. According to the yogis of India, there was no such danger as hyperventilation, and if you oxygenated your bloodstream and brain at a very high degree, then the brain would go into higher realms of functioning. He explained it medically and physiologically, and I explained that the intention was to use the rapid breathing as a methodology of becoming free.

So the second 10 minutes, there were people bouncing around, walking around, and waving their arms. I told everybody, "Don't do what other people are doing. Let your body express. Let the energy come out the way it wants." So pretty much everybody did that. So after 20 minutes when the alarm went off, I explained that the last 10 minutes were continued deep breathing with the bodily movement and, at the same time, internally screaming inside their own minds, screaming, "WHO AM I?"

The whole intent at the end of the 30-minute-method was to program powerfully into the brain the question, "Who am I?" So I had shown them all these 3 sections before we started, and at the end, they were breathing, moving their bodies around, and internally, as I had instructed them, saying, "WHO AM I? WHO AM I? WHO AM I?"

The yogi who put this together said that this kind of powerful demanding internally of one's computer or one's spirit, demanding to know "Who am I?" would be shown to them after the 30 minutes ended. When the bell went off to end the 30 minutes, I had instructed everyone to immediately lie down right where they were at. To lie down flat on the ground, be totally still, no one talk, no one move from their place. And then I explained, "Whatever happens is the answer from your spirit to the question that you ask, 'WHO AM I.'" So I told people, "Any kind of thing might come into your consciousness. There's no telling. There will be 20 different experiences. As you come out of it and you feel like getting up, slowly get up, totally quiet, without touching anyone or communicating, and walk through into the kitchen, where there is hot tea and different little treats for people." So right when the 30 minutes ended, I directed the people, "Lie down right where you are and experience who you are."

Maybe 5 minutes later the youngest girl got up and went into the kitchen. I had a couple other ashramites in there to talk to them to make sure they were feeling okay. Then every couple minutes another person would get up and creep into the kitchen. I was more concerned about the old man than anybody. I walked around those bodies and carefully knelt down at each one to make sure that they were breathing rhythmically. Everyone was in a very, very quiet pattern of breathing. Their chest hardly moving. Like every 45 seconds I could see their chest move up and down. They were all very, very deep into their experiences. About maybe 45 minutes after the class ended, there were still 4 or 5 people on the floor. The old man had got up, and I helped him to his feet. He looked bewildered, but he was fine. He walked straight, and he went in the kitchen. And then I realized in the very middle in one of the rooms was the last person who had entered the class. Actually, I don't think he had made the first class. He was moving from NYC up to Syracuse. I think he missed the first class, but he was at every class after.

He was a very amazing-looking young man. He was about 30 and had jet-black hair. He was always in a business suit, the only one to ever wear a suit; he was impeccably dressed and impeccably groomed, and his nails were manicured. He was incredibly soft and gentle and respectful. The only thing I had been able to get out of him in earlier classes was that he had been a Catholic priest who had left the priesthood—3 or 4 months before. He had left the priesthood because he could not have a spiritual experience.

I remember him telling me, "I can't explain it to you, but I joined the priesthood in hopes of getting closer to God. But nothing in the seminary or nothing after I took my vows ever gave me a spiritual experience." He said, "I don't know if it's possible to have a spiritual experience. I heard of Margaret Coble, and I went to her and asked her how to have a spiritual experience. She said, 'Go to the class. Join this class.'"

So he ended up being the last one. Everyone else, all 19 people, had gotten in the kitchen in the adjoining room; they were all drinking tea. It was about an hour after we finished doing the breathing. I sat down on the floor next to this man, and I just watched him, watched him breathe.

He opened his eyes and said to me, "I've just had a miraculous event happen."

I said, "Can you explain it to me?"

He said, "When I lay down after the breathing, I felt like I had a 3-inch-wide steel band around my forehead. I've had this feeling for a long time. For 10 or 15 years I've had this feeling of a band around my forehead. A stainless steel, screwed-on band." He said, "When I lay down and stopped the breathing, I heard you tell everyone to lie down and be quiet and not disturb anybody and go and find out who you are." He said, "I heard you say that, and then I relaxed. All of a sudden, I felt that my body was slipping down, and the band fell off my head. Then all I can tell you is that I went up through the roof of this building, and I was shooting up into the heavens."

He said, "I'm going to give you a little bit of it, but not try to explain all of it. I went very high and very fast. I was traveling, I don't know how fast, but stars were whizzing by. Then I heard OMing. I slowed, down and I was in an area of the universe where there were millions of angels, all of them OMing. There were angels below me, alongside me, above me. He said there were angels everywhere, and everyone was OMing."

He said, "I'm not supposed to tell you any of the rest of it." And he sat up.

I said, "Come in and have some tea, and we'll talk more."

He said, "Oh no, I have to get home and continue this." He had his coat on a hook by the door, his suit coat, and he walked right to the door.

I said, "Are you sure you don't want to stay a little?"

"Oh no, I have to get home because they are going to show me more."

And then at the door he stopped and turned around and reached out to shake my hand; he said, "We'll never see each other again, but all I can say is to tell Margaret my profound thanks for sending me here. I've had my spiritual experience now, and I don't know if it will ever end."

That class, that night, the majority of the people stayed till after midnight. Everybody talking about their incredible experiences. That night Robert and I hugged each other and acknowledged to each other that what was almost an impossible task, we had successfully pulled it off. From not having any idea what to do for any 1 of the 8 weeks, we had actually had an extremely successful 8 weeks. Margaret told us the next week that 18 out of the 20 people had already inquired to her when they could sign up for our next class.

We never did another class, but it was very fulfilling to be able to help all these people in the things that we introduced them to.

A Communal Healing

VERY SHORTLY AFTER WE RETURNED TO THE ASHRAM from a two-week convocation and the yoga retreat, again I was in this quandary about what to do. Should I leave? Should I leave right away? I actually couldn't leave because I had back weeks of rent, or back months. So I went out and found a job. There was a Jack Lalanne's health club, and I went in there and asked if they needed a masseur. The regular masseur had quit the week before, and they hired me on the spot.

They didn't have much of a club, I mean much of a clientele in the club. But I started working every day from noon to 4 in the afternoon, and then they started having anyone who wanted a massage come in at that time.

At the same time, Margaret left a message for me one day at the ashram when I got back from work that a woman was going to come that night. This woman needed help, and Margaret had decided that I could help her. And the only other part of the message was that she might want to do a fast. So an hour or so later, this older woman showed up. I don't know how old she was, probably 65 or 68. She was very crippled up, walked with 2 canes, and had a hard time getting up the stairs to the ashram. She came in, and I sat down with her. I had a couple other people there, and I said, "How can I help you? Margaret just said you needed help and that I could help you."

She said, "I went to Margaret with a particular issue and problem that is facing me."

She said, "As you can see, my knees don't work. They're arthritic, and I haven't been able to bend my knees correctly starting 40 years ago, and now I can't bend them at all (shades of Yosemite Sam)."

She stood up, and I asked her if she could stand up and pull her dress up so that I could see her knees. She also was stooped down, and her knees were frozen up with arthritis and swollen to double the normal size. She had to keep herself steady with the cane and pull her skirt up so I could see. And they were slightly bent; they weren't locked as when you're standing up straight. Her knees were just slightly bent like you were beginning to do a deep knee bend. They were sort of locked in that position. So I looked at her legs and said, "What is your whole situation?"

She said, "I'm married for 40 years. I've had this arthritis coming on since I became a school teacher. I've been teaching in the same school. My classroom for all these years is on the 2nd floor. All these years I could go up and down the stairs okay. All the kids in the school learned to be careful if I was on the staircase, and no one ever bumped me. Then I had to start using a cane and then 2 canes. The school board has just informed me at the end of the last semester that they're going to retire me. They're going to require me to retire."

She said, "I went to Margaret for help because I know if they force me to retire, I'll die. My whole life is the kids, and my whole life is teaching. I've pleaded and begged with the school board, and they said I've become too great of a risk with the stairs. In our school, on the ground floor, there's only auditoriums and administration places. There are no ground-floor classrooms. So," she said, "basically I went to Margaret and asked for her help.

Immediately Margaret said, 'Oh, there's a fellow in our ashram that can help you.' And I was told to come here and seek you out."

"And what is the issue about fasting?" I said.

She said, "I've heard a lot about fasting and about how bodies can be healed when they are fasting. So what Margaret thought was that maybe you could guide me on a fast, conduct a fast for me, and help me. I've got through the summer to make my condition better, or I'm finished with teaching."

So I started formulating a plan immediately. Robert had come into the room; I had called him over to confer with me about what I was planning.

I said, "If I agree to guide you on this fast, will you agree to move in here to the ashram?"

She said, "Oh, I thought I could do it at home." And I said, "No, no, I won't be involved with you if you do it at home."

She had told me she had never fasted a day. I knew a lot about fasting from my days with Dr. Liss. I said, "It would be too hard for you to fast the way that I'm conceiving, a straight water fast."

She said, "Oh, I thought I would do juices and stuff like that."

I said, "No, if we want to put your body in a healing environment, through fasting, we have to do a straight water fast. You have to agree to do nothing but water for a whole 30 days. And you have to live in the ashram here. I have to be able to see you all of the time."

She said, "I've spoken to my doctor about these possibilities and he has forbade it."

I said, "If you agree to this plan, you move in here in 2 or 3 days, and we'll start the fast immediately. You'll have your own room. I'll put together an entire program. I'll get the other kids here at the ashram to pitch in and do different things with you. And we'll monitor you day and night. And every Friday you have to agree to go to your doctor and have him check you up." (This was the suggestion of Robert, the doctor. He said it would be good for her to be monitored once a week by her own doctor).

She said, "I'll talk it over with my husband." Sunday afternoon, I hadn't heard from her, but her husband pulled up, put 2 small bags up on the porch of the ashram, and took off. She hobbled up the stairs and into the place. We were all there waiting.

She said, "I'm ready to start."

I said, "Do you agree about the doctor?"

She said, "My doctor has an appointment for me every Friday afternoon for the next 4 weeks."

I said, "Okay."

I had set up a game plan with the people at the ashram. I put together more of the liniment that I had used on the old miner at Idaho Springs. I had Robert agree, every night after classes, to sit with her for an hour, do reflexology on her feet, and essentially go over her vitals and make sure she was okay. I had another woman at the ashram, who would help her go to bed every night. She would help her if she needed to be showered or bathed or whatever woman stuff she needed. I had a girl who agreed to be with her for the next 30 nights.

I had another ashramite, who was going to sit and read with her every afternoon from various yoga writings. I had another woman who was very, very good at doing neck and head massages. And she was going to work every morning when the woman woke up and give her head and neck massages.

I planned twice during the day if possible, but once for sure, to go after those knees, the way I had with the old miner. I didn't expect that she could handle the intensity that I had worked at with him. But I thought at some level, getting that liniment in and working as deep as she would allow may start freeing those joints up a little.

So this is what we planned, and this is what we agreed to. And this is what we did. We took her up to the second floor; we put her in a bedroom, and the girls helped her unpack her stuff. It was a nice bedroom. I talked to her before she went to sleep. I told her not to be afraid, something wonderful was going to happen. I felt absolutely confident with our team and with

Robert overseeing me and with her doctor overseeing both of us, I felt tremendous confidence. I had estimated she was 30 to 40 pounds overweight, so I knew her body could handle the weight loss that would come. We had charts up on the wall that kept track of her weight every day. I had a journal at that time where I kept track of what we did.

The first week went very smoothly. The first 2 days on water only, she talked about starving, about being ravenously hungry. And sure enough, on the 3rd day she told me, "I don't have any more hunger"

I had the girls, the one who worked with her at night and the one who worked with her first thing in the morning, make sure that her bowels were moving. And there were even a few times where we had to do enemas to clear out impaction. The girls handled that with no problem. The first week went by, and the first Friday came.

We helped her downstairs. She went outside, and we called her a cab. She went to see her doctor and came back about 2 hours later. She was just totally depressed; she was crestfallen. I asked her what happened.

She said, "The doctor examined me and said I had lost 4 pounds and that if I didn't stop what I was doing I would probably die. He ordered me to end this fast and end this nonsense immediately."

I didn't want to hear any of that, but I let her tell all the things he said. He filled her with fear and negativity. I said to her—to be honest, at this moment I don't even remember her name— "I don't think he's right. You're okay. You've gone through the first week, almost the first whole week. I see no sign of any debilitation. I see no signs of any sickness, and your energy is still good. I'll make a change in the program if you'll agree to stay." She said, "What change?"

I said, "I won't keep you on water only for 24 hours a day."

She said, "Oh, you're going to have me eat?"

I said, "Oh no, no, no, I'll let you have a cup of chamomile tea before bed every night."

She said, "That's all?"

I said, "That's all! But if you want to keep going, I think you should stay. What do you feel? What do you think?"

She said, "I don't want to stop. I know if I stop, I'm through, my teaching is through."

I said, "Okay, let's stay with it then." So she agreed, and we got her back up into her bed. The next day, all the same program. On weekends, when I had the time, I would do 2 sessions on her knees. One in the late morning and one in the late afternoon.

I had explained to her from the first one that this liniment was going to seep down deep in the joints, it may be hot, and it may be uncomfortable. She at first didn't like it because it was hot but got used to it after a day or two. And then after about the second and third day, I was pretty gentle with the massage. Then I asked her, "Can I dig deeper into your knees? I would really like to talk mean to your arthritis."

She laughed and said, "You're going to talk mean to my arthritis?"

I said, "Yea, I want to be a brute with it. Can I dig deeper?"

She said, "You do whatever you want. I need help, I came here for help. You do what you want."

Very surprisingly to me, she could handle some real, real intense work. I started going that day very deep into her, and for the rest of the period, I never let up. I would spend one hour each time and really went deeper and deeper. And she never expressed any discomfort or pain. Everything sailed along in the second week beautifully. I got one of the girls to help her get out to a back porch down the hallway from her room. We set up a rocking chair with padding in it. We would take her out there every morning and afternoon. There were trees everywhere and birds.

The 2nd week went beautifully. Robert said that as far as he was concerned, she showed no signs of any physical ailment or trouble. Her spirits were up, and she was getting her cup of chamomile, which she relished. She thought it was the greatest treat. She was sleeping well. Everything was working great. Everybody's report of their interaction with her was great. The second Friday came, and again we got her dressed and took her downstairs; the cab came, and she left.

I sat there with literal trepidation as to what was going to happen when she got back. She got back, and we helped her up into the ashram and sat her down. Again, she was just defeated. She was just literally hanging her head.

She said, "The doctor told me that I'm crazy. I've now lost almost 9 pounds. In his opinion I was starving to death, and it would be any time that I would collapse, and he didn't want to be responsible. He again ordered me and told me he was going to call my husband and order him to put an end to this insanity."

So we were all in that place again. Again I let her talk it out. And then I told her, "Look, I am looking at a woman who is starting to shine. I'm looking at a woman who is shedding weight that she doesn't need. I am looking at a woman who is almost halfway to fulfilling her goal of at least having a 30-day fast and trying to have her body heal itself. You've got a whole bunch of people here who love you, who support you, who do everything they can to get you through this."

She said, "You know, you're right. I don't care what that doctor said. Let's go on. Let's move on."

So when I reported this to my team, it was like everybody dug in. It was like I could see on everybody's face a new determination. We had to help this woman continue to be able to teach. Everybody more or less intensified their level of commitment, caring, and loving her. One girl started coming in and brushing her hair, and she would brush out this woman's hair every night. Our efforts seemed to double.

The third week went by so easily, so perfectly. Everybody reported every session with her, whether they were reading with her or sitting on the porch, or bathing her, everybody felt that we were making incredible headway even though there was no real strong change in her knees; but they were both starting to move very slightly by the end of the second week.

At the end of the third week, the dreaded Friday came again. We sent her along in her cab, and 2 hours later she came back, with the potential of being deflated and defeated, but her eyes were sparkling. She said, "He just screamed at me. He said I'm down almost 15 pounds. He yelled at me and screamed at me that I'm on a path to the end of my life and that I would at any time collapse. But I sat and listened to his ranting, and this time he didn't scare me. This time I realized I've only got one more week and I'm going to stay. So I told him I'll come back next Friday."

And he said, "Don't bother, if you're not going to listen to me, I won't be responsible."

So she said, "From his office, I called my husband. My husband is scared to death. The doctor has him frightened. But I told him, 'We're going to do this for one more week. We're going to stay until a week from Sunday.'" (which meant 9 days). "I told my husband that I'm staying that long, and then I'll come home on the following Monday." So she said, "Let's just keep going. I feel better than I've felt for years."

She said, "I feel stronger. I feel healthier. I don't have much energy, but I know my body is healing."

Then she turned to me and said, "I think you've really got to go to work and talk mean to my arthritis."

So we went into the 4th week. This time, everybody knew that something good would happen. We went through the whole week, and she was moving around better the whole week. She was using 1 cane instead of 2. I did intensify my work. I saw to it that I did at least 2 sessions every day on those knees. And the entire week just whistled by. She began singing in the morning. She would wake up before any of us, and then she would go out by herself on her chair and sing with the birds. We all knew something good was happening. And then when Friday came, there were about a half a dozen of us, she decided she was going to go back to the doctor even though she didn't have an appointment.

She said, "I feel like I've got to back and at least show him there is improvement." At that time, she was about 20 pounds lighter, down near her more normal weight. She looked radiant, she had great color, she had a twinkle in her eyes, and she was smiling all the time. She said, "I've got a gift for all of you. I want you to come out on the porch."

We went out on the porch with her, and she took her 2 canes and handed them to one of the girls and said, "Watch this!" She was right near the staircase, and she reached over with her left hand and took the railing, and walked down the stairs. One at a time. Each leg going to the next stair. Something she said she hadn't done in almost 40 years. When she got to the bottom, she turned around and walked back up, showing no pain.

She said, "For the last few days I haven't let any of you see how well my knees are." And then she reached out toward me and said, "Hold my hand."

I held her hand. She started bending down, stooping down, about halfway down, which showed me that her knees were almost completely free.

Then she stood up and said, "I don't feel right now that I'll ever have to use my canes." She said, "I may use one for a while, but my knees, I feel, are healed. If I can go to the school and show them that just by grabbing a rail, I can get up the stairs without help—no one in my school has seen me walk like I have just shown you kids—I know I'm going to be okay. I know they won't force me to retire now."

When she went to the doctor, and she didn't come back. The doctor apparently called the husband right away when he saw her in the waiting room. She went in with the husband to the doctor's office, and the doctor started yelling at her.

The husband said, "Wait a minute, are you better? You look wonderful. Are you okay?"

And she got up and put the canes down and held onto the doctor's desk and bent her knees up and down like she was going to do a deep knee bend. She showed the husband and the doctor that her knees were functional.

And then she told the doctor, "You've been my doctor for a long time. I've always appreciated you, but these young people at this yoga place, they've given me my life back. If you don't want to be my doctor anymore, I'll find another one." And she and her husband left.

He took her home right away, and she called the ashram and said, "My husband will come back tomorrow for my bags. I'm going to skip the last 2 days." She said, "I have what I need." She talked to me on the phone about the doctor. And she told me that her husband was gloriously happy. And she said, "What you kids have done for me, there's no way I can ever repay you other than the thanks from my heart." And I thanked her for being so brave. I had one of the kids pack the bags, and the husband came the next day and took them. And then it was maybe a month later. I was getting ready to leave Syracuse, and Margaret called me over to the ashram. And she said, "I just wanted to let you know that the school teacher has been told that she can continue to work for as long as she wants. They watched her go up and down the stairs. She navigated them better than she has in 30 years. She's got her job back, and she asked me to call and thank all the ashramites."

That was an experience that showed the cohesiveness of our group. Our intent and our commitment were so well grounded and was so deeply agreed upon. Our intent, our job, our work was to get this woman where she could continue to teach. All of us were gloriously happy. And Margaret was happy. Margaret said, "I didn't know all of those things you were doing with her. I didn't know you were going to make her live in the ashram. If I had, I might have not sent her to you!"

Margaret lived in her own house in Syracuse, separate from the ashram, with her husband and her kids. Margaret would never usually go to the ashram. For any meditations or meetings, we would always go to Margaret's house.

This experience for everyone in the ashram was so powerful to have and almost had an emergency-like state. It brought us all together, put us all on this program of getting this woman on her feet, and then her shocking all of us the last day with her putting her canes down and going up and down the stairs. We were all blown away. Then finally finding out that she was going to be able to retain her job. This was rewarding beyond words. There was never a dollar that passed hands. She never paid the ashram or Margaret a penny. None was paid, none was asked. It was a labor of love for the whole crew at the ashram, and this woman showed incredible trust and belief. Then finally she had 28 days of fasting, lost 20 pounds, and came back to life. We were all humbled and honored to have served this good woman in this way.

Wandering into the Light

In my 5 or 6 months living at the Syracuse ashram, I saw Margaret Coble on a regular basis and sat with her in meditation. In my experience, she had such a powerful meditation that she would just sort of drag people into deep consciousness. You could sit with Margaret Coble and, within 5 minutes of meditating get down into a depth that sitting by yourself in a quiet place, you'd rarely reach in an hour of chanting, breathing, and doing everything to get deep in a meditation. I was fortunate to have had this period of being around Margaret, who—I used to tell people—was probably the most enlightened woman on the planet. I still feel that way to this day. What Margaret never did was that she never gossiped. She never once talked about the world or world events or politics; she talked only yoga. Whether I was alone with her or with 40 to 50 people, she was totally centered on being a teacher of atman. She was a teacher of Satchyadanana; she was a teacher of Brahmin; she was a teacher of highly altered states of consciousness. And that's where she lived; that's where she vibrated from; and that's where she stayed. If you were around her, you were gonna get a piece of that, whether you wanted it or not. I had month after month after month of that delightful experience with her. And I also got to take classes with Dr. Mishra at the convocation and at his visits to our ashram. He had a big yoga center, an ashram in Monroe, NY. It was just up over NYC. So he was never more than a couple hours away. And I got to see him at the Syracuse ashram, at Margaret Coble's house, as well as at the convocation retreats. And I, several times, was down at his yoga center in Monroe, where he lived in a mansion. As this period of time wound down for me, it was becoming clearer and clearer that I wanted to move on. I'll talk specifically about the last month, and maybe the last couple weeks at the ashram.

It became more and more obvious to me that Margaret Coble wanted me to stay and take over running the ashram. At that time, 2 friends of mine were in charge of running the ashram. They had suggested that they wanted me to take over the ashram. In those days in my life, I could be rarely grabbed by anybody. People used to tell me that I was a slippery fish. I had more than a few women who wanted to grab me; no one had really ever done it. One, in my mid-20s, had grabbed my heart. But Margaret wanted to grab me. I think she saw light in me and potential in me that I didn't see in me, nor had any care to see or develop or expand. I had the road on my mind. So in the last month, I was working part-time, every weekday at the Jack Lalanne health club as a masseur. One day driving home at about 4:30 in the afternoon, I was heading to the ashram, and I was aware of an unusual desire to meditate. I meditated every day. Sometimes multiple times, but usually once or twice in the morning or the evening. But I rarely on my own felt this desire for meditation. At that time, I was living in the attic of this 3-floor Victorian house. I had my own space up there that was very private, very secluded. I wanted to get up there and sit down and meditate. I heard in my head what Margaret had often said. I heard her say this many times. She used to say that until you become a lover of meditation, meditation has not given you its benefits. She would say disciplined meditation is better than no meditation, but if you become a lover of meditation, then meditation feeds you. I never understood what she meant by "lover of meditation." But as I bounded up the stairs after parking my car, I was feeling that kind of sense. So I got up to my space, kicked my shoes off, sat right down on the hardwood floor, and crossed my legs. I looked up at my clock on the edge of my dresser. I was contemplating what would be a gathering for a meal usually at 6:00 p.m. I was aware of the time when I closed my eyes and started meditating.

When I started meditating, I honed in on what is called in Sanskrit, the "nadam" sound. Dr. Mishra, in both of his yoga books, clearly and distinctly explained what nadam is. As far back as 2500 years ago or so, Patanjali wrote widely of what the nadam sound meant. I had heard it months before, and I had asked Dr. Mishra about it. I had been meditating with him in a group, and all of a sudden, I was aware of buzzing in my ears. After that meditation I went to Dr. Mishra and asked him if I could ask a question.

He said, "Yes, yes, yes, yes."

I said, "Doctor, during my meditation I was just was hearing buzzing in my head."

He said, "Explain more."

I said, "Well, it was high-pitched vibration. I don't remember hearing it before today, but I may have heard it other times. But today it got loud."

He told me, "You are blessed beyond your understanding. The sound you heard is the OM sound."

He said, "Another way of understanding it is the sound you heard in your head is your spirit moving through your nervous system, and your auditory nerves were relaying that to you. In ancient times, men would sit 30 to 50 years trying to hear the buzzing in their head." He said, "You're blessed beyond your understanding. Having visualization ability is wonderful, but hearing nadam, the OM sound, hearing your own spirit, is much more powerful. When you hear it, attend to it, listen to it. That vibration is subtler than anything in the physical world, and it will lead you into subtler realms."

So after that, I heard the buzzing in my head every time I meditated. If I paid attention and turned my attention inward into my ears and into my head, I could hear it while I was listening to a lecture or reading a book or driving in my car. It became part of my ongoing life experience even to this day and to this minute, where now, focusing just a little bit of my attention, I can hear 2 different buzzing sounds, one in my right ear, one in the back and middle of my head.

So I was sitting in my attic, going into this meditation, and my OM sound appeared like I had gotten used to. But this time, I remembered what Dr. Mishra had said, "Attend to it, and follow it."

So I took all my attention and put it directly into my head into this high-pitched vibration. And I had never done that before. I had never put my attention and concentration into the interior of my head to listen to that buzzing sound. As soon as I did it, it started getting louder. I was immediately amazed that giving it my attention would make it louder. It got louder, and it got louder. I listened more, and it got louder, and I concentrated more, and it got louder. And at one point it was roaring. It was as though you had a radio on, off the channel, and just put the volume up all the way. Only it wasn't static; it was a clear, comfortable sound. My head was filling with this increasing level of vibration and sensation of being overwhelmed by it. Then suddenly from one moment to the next, I was in a place, I won't call it a room because there were no borders on it, I was in a place of absolutely brilliant white light. It was white light that if I would have seen it with my eyes, it would have blinded me in a second. I think I would have turned away or collapsed, but internally I was entranced by this brilliant white light. It wasn't a source of light like a light bulb—everything was white. I was in a field of pure, powerful, luminescent white light. Then I became aware that somehow, I had elevated my consciousness tremendously. Then again—this is hard to explain—in the ensuing moments or minutes, I so became part of this light that all thought vanished, all ability to think vanished, all comprehension vanished. I felt like I was a pinpoint of light within a giant field of light. I was sort of the classic observer, where I could see in my vision that I was part of this vast field of light, and it was part of me. And I felt no separation from it. I'm using words to describe what was wordless.

I'm using English words to try to describe a feeling that was indescribable. I sat in that place; the OM sound in that place was still at high intensity. The white light was at high intensity. My awareness was at a pinpoint. There was no thinking, no experiencing; there was no nothing. There was me in the light as part of the light and no thought. No patterns of recognizable conscious thought or intention. So I just sat there.

Then I was not there. Then I was sitting on the floor in my room. The OM sound in my head, or the nadam sound, was rapidly decreasing as my awareness of sitting on the floor in this room was increasing. As I was coming back to body awareness—I was sitting in a full lotus position; I always sat in a full lotus as I meditated—I saw no more of the white light. The interior vibration was decreasing, and I was aware that I was sitting on a hard floor, and I might have laughed out loud. I was aware that both of my legs were dead. I had no feeling, only tingling in both legs. I opened my eyes and looked at the clock, and I had what was almost a bigger shock than ending up in that white light place. Because the clock had clearly shown me that I had been meditating to the minute for 3 hours. Before I opened my eyes, I thought, "How could my legs feel this way in 15 minutes?" I didn't think I had been gone for more than 15 minutes. I stared at the clock; the room was now dark because the sun had gone down. I sat there and stared at the clock and realized that I hadn't moved a muscle in 3 hours. I unwrapped my legs, and they were useless; they were like 2 pieces of putty. It probably took me 10 or 15 minutes of massaging and stretching my legs to get the blood flow back to where I could stand up and almost feebly go downstairs.

So I had that experience. I didn't tell anyone. When I got downstairs everyone said, "Oh, we didn't even know you were home. We had dinner. There's some left for you." I went in the kitchen and ate by myself, and then I went back up and went to bed and slept. I got up the next day and didn't think much about the meditation. I went to my massage job, got off at 4:00 p.m., and started driving home. Only this time I was clearly aware that I wanted to get back up into that attic room as fast as I could. I was literally feeling hunger. I had never one time in my life felt hunger to meditate. At that time driving 5 to10 minutes to the ashram, it was almost like a craving, like an obsession that I had to get back up into that room. Not so much to see if I could go back up into that space because in truth, I didn't think I'd ever experience anything like that ever again. I again bounded up the stairs, threw my shoes off, and sat down—same position, same place. I looked at the clock; it was approximately the same time as the day before. The sun was still pouring through the window into my room, closed my eyes, heard the OM sound, focused my attention on it; and it immediately started getting louder. And then louder, louder, and louder. Then I sort of felt like, "Oh my God! It might happen again." Within a very short period of time, again I was overwhelmed with the sound in my head, roaring, just roaring. And then, in a flash I was in the white light place again.

This time, I only remember wanting to be there. I only remember the vaguest thought of great relief that I was back there. Then my total memory of any of these series of meditations was just the white light. In my adult life I've thought about those days a hundred times, or a thousand times. I've even nicknamed that place as my "Holy of Holies." When I think about it, I think about that time in Syracuse when I went to my "Holy of Holies." When that ended, exactly the same as the night before, I was first aware that I was sitting on something hard. Then I was aware of my feet and legs tingling. I immediately opened my eyes and looked at the clock, and literally to a minute I had sat for 3 hours, for a period that in my conscious mind said was no more than 15 minutes. Except for that, my legs were again dead. I unwrapped my legs and went through the same process of getting them feeling again. I don't remember what I did after that night, but—and this is the strange part for me, because normally I'm always journaling—I wasn't journaling at that time for some reason. So I don't have and never had a record of how long this went on. But I went to work the next day, and all day at work I was anticipating getting off work. This hunger to go back into that place was prominent but not distracting. I got in the car, and I felt the hunger, the powerful thrust to get back into that attic room. Again, I ran up the stairs and repeated the exact same thing, same time frame, and same 15 minutes in my conscious mind. Same 3 hours on the clock. This time, on the 3rd day, I didn't put my legs in a full lotus. I kept them flayed out on the floor, so this time when I came out of it, they were a little cramped, but they weren't dead limbs.

I remember clearly those first 3 times, but then for some reason, in all the years since then, I have never been able to pinpoint exactly how many times it happened. My intuitive sense is that it was maybe 5 times or as many as 10. Those following days I think was in a semi-trance state. I don't remember any desire to interact with the other ashram people. I think I had a couple days off that I was doing this. I can't really pinpoint how many total times I sat down and went into that 15-minute journey that was 3 hours of being a pinpoint in a field of brilliant white light.

I left the ashram shortly after. I don't remember when it stopped, this progression of daily going back up to the attic. But I remember that all of a sudden, my job was finished and there were several days of chaos before I was able to pack my car and head for Chicago. But that was the "goodbye" that I got from Syracuse and from that building that we called the ashram. I entered into these immensely deep, powerful meditations, and when they ended, they ended.

I left Syracuse and went to Chicago, and as many times as I attempted after that to be able to meditate myself back into that place, it's never happened once. I've tried. I can only say that I haven't been able to; since leaving the ashram, I haven't been able to get into the mind-set of wanting that experience enough to actually still myself, listen to the sound, the vibration in my head—I can hear it now as I speak. It's with me every night I go to sleep; before I sleep, I listen to it; every time I sit down to meditate all these years I hear it, but I have never been able to attend to it and concentrate to the point that I go back there. Many times, it starts getting louder again, and I get excited. I think, "Oh, I'm going back there," and then it's finished as soon as I think that kind of thought.

So out of frustration, sometime in my 40s, I sort of gave up and haven't really tried to bring that kind of experience back into my reality again. I've never told many people about that, about those days and that white light that I was in. I've read 100 books trying to pinpoint where I went. I've read books on Satori, on Samadhi, on Nirvana, on all manner of altered states of consciousness. And there are pieces and bits of my experience that I had. So I have no real name for it. I have the profound reality that I owned, that I experienced, for those days, exactly what I experienced. I've never lost any memory of it or the feeling that I felt in that place.

Through my life, it was always just a memory of a time—maybe the only time in my life—that I became a true lover of meditation—where I hungered for it; where I craved it; where I lost my consciousness in it; where I experienced illumination and high vibration. I've had that with me my whole life. I look back at it as though it was like a gift to me. Maybe like a parting gift from Syracuse. But it was the highest state of consciousness that I have ever attained in my lifetime. Much higher than any kind of consciousness that I've experienced on any kind of psychedelic, plants, sugar cubes, etc.

When I left Chicago originally and went to Syracuse to meet Margaret Coble, it was because I had come to the realization that psychedelics were very real, very powerful, very profound, and an amazing part of my life. But after some years of doing them, I realized there had to be some way to attain high states of vibration, high altered states without using substances. That's what headed me to Syracuse originally. That's what I wanted when

I met Margaret Coble. That drove me for many, many years—experiencing altered states in meditations, in chanting, through many different yogic practices, through breathing techniques. I read volumes and volumes to try to pinpoint where I was at in those days. All of it served me well into this day. But my departure from Syracuse was truly the highlight of my entire lifetime in regard to spiritual exploration, experimentation, and investigation, which drove me from my mid-20s and hasn't really ever abated or ended. That was my goodbye from Syracuse from the heavens.

The Worst Massage Ever Given

AFTER THE "HOW TO BE YOUR OWN DOCTOR" CLASS ENDED, I really wasn't sure what to do with myself. I had moved there with the agreement to do this class. It was the end of June, and I really didn't know what I wanted to do. Margaret wanted me to stay and be a teacher. I didn't have any money, and interestingly enough, we had to pay rent. I had to pay rent to be at the ashram. So I was sort of betwixt and between. Should I move on? Should I go back to Chicago? But there were more experiences to be had.

One of them was there was a 2-week yoga convocation that Margaret did every summer. She rented a spiritual retreat outside of Syracuse called Watson Homestead. It was a place with barracks and a big kitchen and meeting rooms and mediation halls. It had a lake; it was a beautiful piece of land. I had attended one of these convocations a year or two before that. But since I was there, I hung out and told Margaret that I would be available for the 2 weeks. I told her I would be part of the staff and would do whatever was necessary.

So she said, "At the last convocation you were here, you worked on a lot of people doing some sort of healing or something. You just worked on everybody for nothing. This year if you do that, I want you to charge."

I said, "Margaret, I'm not really comfortable with that."

She said, "No, I'm comfortable with it."

She said, "You don't have to give away your energy. You'll charge $2 if you do any treatment on a person. If you charge $2, you keep $1 and give $1 to the ashram."

Well, there were over 200 people at the convocation and we had beautiful weather for two weeks. So between classes when we weren't being taught by Dr. Mishra or Margaret, in all the breaks, I would just sort of plop myself someplace, and people would come, and I would do some kind of treatment for their necks or their back, or if there was anything bothering them. I would just do my routine, whatever came to me. Interestingly in the 2 weeks, at the end of the convocation, I had $300. So I had apparently worked on 150 people. And I gave half to Margaret and kept half.

Anyways, toward the end of the convocation, there was one day, where in a side building, they were having an "enlightenment intensive." It's probably too much for me to explain what an enlightenment intensive is, but there was a group from NYC putting on these 72-hour enlightenment intensives. So one of those was going on, and I found myself with a little gap of space. I was leaving the lunchroom, and I was going to try to find a place and write in my journal. Margaret was all a sudden in front of me, and she said, "I want you to give one more massage."

I said, "Okay. Who?"

"Dr. Mishra."

I was floored. I was immediately afraid. I wanted to back out; I wanted to turn and run.

I said, "Are you sure? He wants a massage?"

She said, "No, he doesn't want one. I had to bend his arm. He's never had a massage nor really let anyone touch him."

I said, "Margaret, what are you doing?"

She said, "You're supposed to give him a massage. Spirit has made it clear that you should do that, and he's in his room, waiting."

Well, oh my God…

I went and got towels and my oil and went and knocked on his room, and he told me to come in. And he looked at me like, "I don't know what this is about."

I looked at him like, "Can I turn and run?"

So we were both in the same position. He had a cot there with a sheet on it.

He said, "What do I do?"

I didn't know what to say. I said, "Gosh, Dr. Mishra…"

I realized I had to tell him to take his robe off. So I said, "Well, if it's okay with you, take your robe off."

He looked at me like I was asking something crazy. We just stood there, and then all of a sudden it was like Margaret was there telling us, "Come on. Get on with it. Cut it out. Stop this nonsense."

He peeled off his orange robes; he had boxer shorts on. I told him to lie down. He lay down on his back. I knelt down next to the couch (this wasn't a massage table) it wasn't a very good setup. But I put some oil on my hands and started on one of his arms, rubbing the oil on. This man was as stiff as a board. He was like petrified. I could hardly move anything. I could hardly raise his arm or move his head. We struggled mightily with me trying to figure out how to get him to relax and him in a position that he had apparently never been in his entire life, with some stranger touching parts of his body that had never been touched before. He was of the highest caste of a Brahmin family from India, and I don't think strangers were normally allowed to touch a Brahmin. So I did the front of him and toweled him off. It was, to say the least, the hardest half-massage I had ever given.

I got him to roll over, face down, and I did the back the same way. Only I hurried through the back because I knew there was no such thing as relaxing this man. He was literally stiff like a board. He never said a word through the whole thing. I never said a word. I finished toweling off his back and his legs.

And he said, "We done?"

I said, "Yes Doctor, we're done."

He leaped up, grabbed his robes, and put his robes on real quickly, and then he smiled at me and said, "Thank you."

And I said, "Doctor, thank YOU."

I headed for the door, and he said, "Wait a minute. Wait a minute."

He fished down in his robes. I didn't know his robes had a pocket. He pulled out a wallet. I couldn't even imagine him carrying a wallet. He pulled out this wallet and opened it up, and I saw all those bills.

He said, "I have to pay you."

I said, "No, Doctor. No, no, no."

If for no other reason, I could never have received 50 cents for that massage I gave because it was worthless. And I said, "No, no, no, no, you don't have to pay me."

I grabbed the door handle behind me, opened the door, and started out, and he was on me. He grabbed my arm. He had his wallet in one hand and grabbed my arm in the other, and he said, "Wait a minute. You don't want to be paid?"

I said, "No, no, no, no, no."

He said, "You don't want anything?"

I said, "No, no, no, nothing. You can't give me anything."

He said, "Oh, I can't give you ANYTHING?"

I said, "No, Doctor."

I was so nervous, I was probably shaking. And he laughed and laughed. He had hold of my arm, and he laughed. He said, "Oh, you want nothing?! And I can't give you anything?!"

And he laughed and laughed. He let go of my arm, and he said, "Thank you, thank you very much."

I walked out the door. I leaned over on the wall, and I was literally quivering. I was like, "What was this disaster that just happened?" I had a chance to massage this enlightened man, and I botched it. I blew it. He wanted to pay me…. I was twisted in circles.

I walked down the hallway into this beautiful green field and I put my gear down on a bench near the doorway. I thought I'll pick it up later. I was just going to go for a walk. I walked about 10 or 15 feet, and my hands started burning. Both of my hands just felt like they were flaming within a minute. They were on fire. I stood there and looked at them, I held them up to the sky, and I looked at them, and all I could feel was the fire. I kept walking out into this field, looking at my hands, feeling them burning, not knowing what that meant, thinking, "Did I do something wrong? Did I take his energy? I'm in a quandary of what just happened. What's going on?" I walked without intention over to this building where the enlightenment intensive was going on. There were 30 people doing the intensive; 10 of them were ash-ramites and friends. And I was just sort of in a daze. I walked over to the building; I opened the door, and everyone was celebrating; everyone was hugging. The intensive had just ended, and everybody was happy and joy-ous. I stood there by the door in the entranceway, not knowing what I was doing, why I walked in there, my hands burning, my head confused. One of the guys who was in the intensive was Bob Molnar. He's the guy who I tended bar with on Rush St. years earlier, who gave me the *Tibetan Book of the Dead* that started my spiritual reading. He was there and he saw me and he yelled, "Corky, Corky, come here and celebrate with us." And then he yelled out, "Let's do an OM-shock on Corky." And everyone joined in, screaming, "Yea let's do it!"

So I sort of crumbled to the ground. I had these people all over me, I had people touching me, had people with their heads on my rib cage, on my pelvis. I had people holding my feet; other people lay down and had their heads on my head, and everybody started OMing. It wasn't just the people touching me—all the people in the whole group formed circles around me, and I had this whole group pouring in OM onto me, and suddenly I started crying. And it was ambrosia. It was honey pouring out of my eyes. I've experienced it 3 or 4 times in my life. But this time, the energy of that group and the intentionality and the power of their OMing broke loose something in me, and I started crying. I cried and I cried. I laid there in the midst of all this love and all this joy and all this caring and energy. As I lay there, I heard Dr. Mishra laughing, saying, "Oh you don't want anything, and I can't give you anything?" I heard him uproariously laughing. And I realized that this was the first time I had cried since my father's deathbed.

The moment that my father had died, I made a vow to myself to never cry again for the rest of my life, and in all those years from 17 until whatever I was at that moment, 28 or something, in all those years I never shed a tear. In all those years, there were times when I needed to cry and couldn't cry, where I tried to cry and couldn't cry. Then that turned into in my 20s where I actually started praying that I could cry. And I must have prayed to Christ 1,000 times, just let me cry, let me feel crying again. And I had never gotten near crying. And I lay there with the tears falling out of me and the love being poured into me, and again I heard Dr. Mishra. I heard him laughing again and saying, "Oh you don't want anything, and I can't give you anything?" And then uproariously laughing.

That was a powerful, powerful experience. Neither Mishra nor I wanted anything to do with that massage; somehow Margaret Coble convinced both of us to do it; we were both totally uncomfortable through every minute of me touching his body, and then it culminated in me crying. Breaking a dam that I had put in my consciousness at 17 years old and being free to express myself in that way.

This was an incredible payment for the worst massage I've ever given in my entire life.

What a gift. God is good. Life is good!

Discovery and Investigations

IN MY LIFE UP TO THIS POINT, I had read some of the great books and autobiographies of the Hindu yogis and saints. I had become a voracious reader of all things spiritual since I was given the *Tibetan Book of the Dead* at 22. I had also read a wide variety of stories of the American Indian leaders, chiefs, and medicine men. I had read some stories of various tribes down in Central and South America as well. Anything I could learn, anything about spirituality. Various historical, cultural, and religious information from many cultures, religions, and spiritual pathways from all over the world. But in the 70's, I was directed to investigate the Huna System, the secret and spiritual way of the ancient Hawaiians.

There was one major book at the time that was published in the '40s; it was called *The Secret Science at Work* by Max Freedom Long. He was a white man, who apparently was possibly the first white man that any Hawaiian shaman had shared any of their spiritual culture with. The men in Hawaii who were the keepers of the culture were called Kahunas. "Huna" means secret, so they were the "keepers of the secret." They were also the medicine men, shamans, healers, the wise ones, going back thousands of years. Not just in Hawaiian culture, but the Huna system has been traced back all the way through Polynesia back to India, and the closest origin that can be found is actually in Egypt, 3,000 or 4,000 years ago.

So when I read this book, it opened up to me an understanding that I had, to that point, not even come close to grasping. Essentially, the Huna system is based upon a belief that each person on the planet has a high self, a middle self, and a low self. This system corresponds to Western psychiatry or psychology where they would say a person has a superconscious mind, a conscious mind, and a subconscious mind.

The Hunas would call the subconscious as the low self. And they looked at it not so much as a part of the conscious mind, but almost as a separate entity. As a separate source of information and potentiality. The Kahunas would say that the middle self was the rational thinking, planning, reasoning part of the human mind. And of course, this would be agreed by most psychologists. And then the high self, to the Kahunas, was the divine parent or guardian who looked over a person from birth to death and guided them or tried to help them grow spiritually or fulfill their life's purpose.

In Western psychology there is reference to the "superconscious," but there's little to no real understanding or investigation or scientific foundation of what this superconscious is or what it's capable of. So, in essence, as I read this book, I saw that the Hawaiians personalized the high self and the low self to the middle self. Their basic belief was that the middle self, as a rational, thinking, reasoning part of human consciousness had a responsibility to the low self to bring it from the subconscious up into communication or interaction with the middle self. And then down the road, if a person through their reasoning mind, could connect with their subconscious mind, then the 2 of them could work together to manifest, create, and build anything that the conscious mind could design or desire. At the point that the middle self would have communication and connection with the low self, then the 2 of them could combine their intentionality and then actually connect with the high self to bring about miracles.

This system so intrigued me that to this day, I use it on a daily basis. There have been times in the last 30-odd years where I essentially have gone to sleep with what the Kahunas felt was the responsibility of the middle self, to the raising of the low self; to help the low self rid itself of all repressed anger or animalistic desires or instincts, all stored or buried traumas, all kinds of negativity (what neuroscience would now call the "reptilian brain"). What Freud encountered through his early psychoanalysis, was the uncovering of a person's low self. When he would get that person talking about it and releasing what was in that person's subconscious, he often freaked out. He felt that he had opened a Pandora's Box full of nightmares and ugliness. So he never completely understood it, but he unlocked for the first time in recorded Western history the unconscious through psychoanalysis. He didn't know how to help the person to help themselves, to rid themselves of complexes, neuroses, abysmal fears, unrationalized traumas, and negativity; all of these things that all human beings bury in their subconscious minds. The Kahunas of the Huna system, they had a way of very methodically and very carefully teaching a middle self how to work with their own subconscious, with their own low self to bring about healing, release, and freedom from past traumas and buried nightmares.

So this became the most intriguing and most challenging mental work that I had ever encountered, or taken on, or applied to my life. My yoga teacher, Dr. Mishra, was a great proponent of Patanjali's sutras, which were essentially about self-analysis. Dr. Mishra named his international yoga organization The International Center for Self-Analysis. I had, for many years, already been taught by Margaret Coble and Dr. Mishra the importance of self-analysis. When the Huna information entered my consciousness, for the first time I understood what "self" was being talked about when someone would talk about self-analysis, self-realization, self-awareness, or self-knowledge.

I understood that in the Huna system, they were talking about the middle self, a conscious rational mind, working with a low self to bring forward the abundant gifts and energies and abilities that the low self has down in its world. They also knew how to release and expel the buried traumas from the womb on through childhood and even adulthood. This can be done by an informed and committed middle self.

So I won't speak any more about this right now, but this became a tool, a navigating tool, a power tool for the rest of my life in helping me to understand myself and helping me to understand others at a higher degree than I had attained up to that point.

Psychic Surgery in the Philippines

UPON RETURNING TO CHICAGO from my stay at the ashram in Syracuse, NY, and a subsequent period in Taos, NM, living in an ashram, I got a job working in a friend's bar. I sort of just muddled along for a while. For a period of time, I became the bar manager for The Brewery on North Broadway. I was sort of wrapped up in that world for a few years. Then I started having symptomology, strange symptomology, happening to my body. Which led me to the second divine intervention I've had in my life. The first was the fall from the porch when I was 17 and was moved away from sheer disaster by a hand under my rear end.

Now I was heading into another one. So from this point to explain all the events in a way that I can draw the best picture of how I arrived at this next divine intervention, I'm going to start from the very beginning of when I became aware that I had a serious physical problem.

I was about 9 years old and sitting by an empty baseball field, just after dinnertime. All the men in the neighborhood came and played softball at night. I was too young to play, but I watched every night. So I was at this field, and I was the only person there, no one around me. I was sitting on the curb, waiting for the players to arrive. All of a sudden out of nowhere, in my right ear, from outside, a voice screamed with such intensity that it actually knocked me over on my left side. The voice screamed in my ear so loud that it just froze me. It screamed, "YOU HAVE BRAIN TUMORS!"

I jumped to my feet and looked all around me. I thought someone had snuck up on me and screamed that. There was no one, no one in sight even, not even a person down the block. There was no one near me. I stood there just shocked at what was just said to me. I knew what my brain was; I had no idea in the world what a tumor was. I essentially did what I was to do repetitiously over the years: I completely buried within minutes the entire experience. I buried it so deep that I had no recall of it even later that day and not for many years afterward. I can look back at that moment and realize the power of the human mind to go into denial and to bury a trauma. That was my first warning or insight or revelation that I had brain tumors.

The next thing that happened—I was 17 years old, this was before my father passed—I was working in the same factory. I was doing an inventory, counting things on the shelf in the warehouse, and a box that was hanging over the edge of a higher shelf came down on me, landed on top of my head, and knocked me down. A couple of the other workers and the foremen were there and saw what happened. I told the foreman I was fine. I got up and shook it off. He insisted that I go to a medical clinic nearby that the factory employed. He had one of the drivers take me to the clinic. They gave me a cursory examination, looked in my eyes, and told the driver to take me to Alexian Brothers Hospital. That it's possible that I might have had a concussion or even a skull fracture.

I didn't like any of this, but I went along. The medical center called the hospital. So as soon as I got there, they admitted me. They took X-rays, and later that evening I had a couple doctors come in and tell me that the X-rays showed a growing mass on the right lobe of my brain, and they wanted to schedule me for a neurological exploratory. They felt that was absolutely necessary as soon as possible. Well, I just automatically, without thinking about it I rebuffed them. I told them I wanted out of the hospital. I told them I would go to my own doctor, I made up some story. I just wanted to get myself out of there.

The next morning, they again were trying to get me to agree to a time with a neurologist and a neurosurgeon. I just completely brushed them aside, and when I walked out of there, I clearly remember going just automatically, not thinking about it, not planning, just going into denial. Just as though nothing had happened. By the time I got to work and was back at the job, I had buried the entire thing. At work they asked me, "Well, what did they say?"

I said, "Oh I'm fine. There's no problem."

I just dismissed all inquiries as to what I might have been told. I never told my mother, never told my mother about the earlier experience with the voice, just automatically buried it, and from the day that I got out of the hospital on, I never thought about, not for one split second, for years.

Then I was 19 years old. I had an emergency where I had a bad appendix. Basically, I didn't want to bother my mother about it. I was staying with her at the time, working in the GM factory. But I had this sharp, deep cramping pain in my lower right abdomen. Finally, she came home from work on a day I stayed home, and I was moaning in the fetal position on the bed. She called our doctor who had been our family doctor since I was little, explained to him what she saw, and he said, "You call the police immediately and have them come and pick him up and take him to Cook County Hospital. His appendix is either burst or about to burst."

My mother called the police; a paddy wagon came, 2 big burly cops half-carried me, helped me down the stairs, and put me in the back of the paddy wagon. Then I was in Cook County Hospital. My appendix had in fact burst; they did an emergency operation and saved my bacon.

In the process, the next day of follow-up paperwork, the nurse who was filling out these forms, was asking me routine questions. I was drugged and not paying much attention. I was in a lot of discomfort from the surgery.

She asked me if I had ever had seizures. In the year prior to that I had had 2 epileptic seizures. Both of them I had after coming home drunk from hard drinking sprees. Both happened as I was going to bed at 4 or 5 in the morning. My mother was there and got me through each one. I didn't remember either one. I would wake up later in the morning, and she would tell me what happened. So, when the nurse asked that, not thinking, I said, "Yes, I've had 2 seizures in the last year."

Later they came in and said they wanted to do an X-ray of my head. I didn't think anything about it; they took the X-rays. Then the next day, they were going to release me, but instead they came again, more surgeons, with a clipboard and a release form. They actually just put it down on my lap in the bed and said, "We would like you to sign this paper." I read the top of the paper; it was a release form for the hospital to do a neurological exploratory on me. I said, "What is this about?"

They said, "The X-rays should a large growing mass on the right lobe of your brain, and we want to schedule you tomorrow for a neurological exploratory."

I was somewhat panicky because I thought in my condition, they might be able to somewhat force me to do this. So I concocted out of nowhere a story. The story was as follows: "I'll let you do that, but you have to let me go home first because my mother's got a bad heart (which was true). I don't want her to hear any of this from you. I want to tell her myself. And if you let me go home today, I'll tell her, and then I'll come back tomorrow."

They were very skeptical, but I was more convincing. I told them this is the only way this can go down.

So they released me with the promise that I would be back in the hospital at 6 in the morning. So I got up at 5:30 the next morning; my mother was doing her routine before she went to work. I sat by the phone. And she said, "Why are you up? You should be resting."

I said, "Oh, I just thought we'd gab a little bit." I knew instinctively that the hospital would call when I wasn't there at 6.

About 5 minutes after 6, the phone rang, I snatched it immediately; they started saying, "This is Cook County Hospital," and I said, "Oh, you have the wrong number, thank you." And I hung up.

My mother said, "Oh, what was that about?"

I said, "Just a wrong number."

I never heard from Cook County Hospital again after that. From that day on I again went into deep denial; from that day forward, I never thought, not for one minute, about having brain tumors. Or having a large growing mass on the right lobe of my brain. So that was at 19.

I merrily went along through my life, and when I was 27, I was on Clark St., sitting in my car, and I was rear-ended by a drunk. I was sitting at a light, and he smashed me pretty good. I had some sort of a whiplash-type injury. When I got where I was staying, I told the friend I was staying with that I was starting to get a headache. I told her about the accident and how I just left. I didn't even try to get police or charge the guy. I just told him to go home.

So my friend tells me, "You could have an injury. You should go see my doctor. My doctor is a block away."

She called, he was still in the office, and he said, "Yes, yes, send him over."

So I walked down a block to this doctor I had never met, and all he did was look in my eyes and tell me, "I think you have a serious injury. You've got to get to the hospital."

I started to protest, and he said, "You have to do this. I don't like what I see in your eyes. You have to go to Augustana Hospital." He said, "You go there, and I'll call and tell them you're coming."

So again, early evening, I'm taken into a room, after being X-rayed, where some doctor checked me out and said, "We have to admit you." They put me on a bed, and at about 8 at night 3 guys with white coats come in and a guy with a suit. One guy says, "I'm a neurosurgeon." The other says,

"I'm the head of the department." The guy in the suit says, "I'm the administrator of the hospital." So these guys get around my bed, and they tell me, "The X-rays show that you have a large growing mass on the right side of your brain, and we've got to do a neurological exploratory."

Well, now I'm a little bit older and a little bit tougher, and I just told these guys point-blank, "I don't want any surgeries. I want to be released out of here tomorrow morning." They became quite insistent, bordering on angry. They each had an attitude; they were throwing all sorts of fear at me. I got huffy myself and told them, "You're not touching me. You're not doing anything. I'm not signing any forms. I want out of here."

The neurosurgeon stepped forward and said, "Listen kid, if you don't let us do this exploratory, your life is not worth a plugged nickel." Those were his exact words.

I looked at him and said, "Well, I'm a gambler, and I'll just take that gamble."

They left the room. I had a feeling that they were going to try to do something to force this on me. I had a phone there, and I called my friend Joe Martins. I said, "Joe, you gotta get down to Augustana and spring me out of here."

About 9:30 p.m., he walks up in my room with a nurse telling him, "You can't be here. It's after visitors' hours." As soon as he came in the room, I jumped out of the bed. There was a closet there. I found my clothes, and we got me dressed. The nurse was yelling for the doctors, and we walked right out of there.

Again, as in all the previous times, my friend said to me when we got outside, "What was going on?"

I said, "Joe, I just didn't like the feel of the place. I wanted to get out. Thanks for comin'. And I'll see ya back at the house."

We both got in our cars and drove away. I didn't tell him or his wife, or the friend who I was staying with, a word about what actually happened.

From the next day onward, not one minute of any of the days that passed, day after day, year after year, I never thought one minute of my predicament, of my plight, which by now was a reality. There couldn't be 3 hospitals in a row that came up with the same story. But again, I went into denial and just went on with my life.

By 1973, I started having the aforementioned symptomology. I was managing a restaurant, and I started having (I won't give all the symptoms), blindness in my left eye that would last for about an hour, and then my vision would go back. That would occur to me while I was working. I wouldn't even stop working when that happened. I was also having what are called petit mal seizures where I would lose consciousness for 15 or maybe 30 seconds. I was having them on a regular basis. And then it got to be the summer of '73, and I started having a tremendous intolerance to noise. Even just the slightest noise would bother me. I had to take leave from the restaurant because I couldn't handle the noise. I stayed with my girlfriend at the apartment we were at. For weeks I just stayed home. I didn't want the television on, I wanted the windows closed, and I didn't want to hear cars honking, kids yelling, or birds chirping. This sensitivity to noise became more and more pronounced—where by the end of the summer it was real bad. I didn't know what was going on. I wasn't going to any doctors. I wasn't asking anybody for help. Even my girlfriend whom I had lived with for some years, I didn't tell her anything about my tumors or anything about my symptomology, except what she was aware of just by observing me.

Finally, I was on the phone with Joe Martins; he had moved to upstate New York. I talked to his wife and told her what was going on with me. She pleaded with me to come out to New York. She said, "Get out here. You'll be in the country. There's no noise, and we'll take care of you."

So I had a good friend of mine, in his car, drive me to upstate New York. When I got there, I decided to start a fast. I had been fasting for many years. I thought maybe a 10-day fast will get me through this. After 2 or 3 days, I went out. It was late morning, and the sun was brilliant; it was a beautiful day. A beautiful fall day. I went out and roamed through the fields and found a really large boulder. Maybe a 6- to 8-feet-high, big, round boulder. I climbed up on the top of it, sat on top of it facing the sun, and just decided to meditate.

Now the story will rapidly turn into events that all started happening very quickly. This was late October. I sat there with the sun bathing me. I remember having my head turned right directly toward it; my skin was hot, and it felt wonderful. And all of a sudden, as though on the inside of my eyelids, a movie went on. The best way I could say is that it was like a Hollywood production or documentary of my life. Normally when I meditate, I just have blank inside, darkness. With the sun, there was some illumination through my eyelids, but when this movie went on, it was like I was sitting in a darkened movie theatre. The movie was narrated by a voice. The first thing I saw, I actually saw, was myself as a little boy, maybe 6 or 7 years old. I had a dirty face; I just had been apparently out playing, sweaty dirty. And I was looking up at a person, and I had a big smile on my face. Out of nowhere into the picture came a hand that whacked me on my right ear so hard, it was like a slap, but it was so hard that it knocked my body up in the air horizontal, 3 to 4 feet off the ground. Then I crashed down on the floor, and without making a sound, I leaped up, ran through the house, and crawled into the back of a closet, not making a sound. I was in absolute total trauma.

Prior to this being shown to me in this vision, I had no recall of this event ever happening. When I saw it in the vision, I remembered it. The voice at this time said, "This is where the brain tumors started." Then I saw what I later understood was a picture of the inside of my cranium, the inside of my skull. It was like a white surface, a real thin white surface, almost like the inside of a coconut. There was a crack, like an inch or two long. The voice said, "Bacteria grew in that crack and then later became so big, it touched your brain and invaded your brain and grew over the years into tumor." And then that part of the vision stopped. I was so mesmerized, and I was so shocked as to what was going on. At that moment I remember opening my eyes, and I was sitting in the field; then the vision ended. And I sat there and looked around and thought, "What's going on? What's happening to me? Maybe I'm going crazy or something."

Then I closed my eyes again, and the vision picked up right where it left off when I had opened my eyes. Then I was shown each of the times that I had been warned about the tumors. I was shown the point where the voice yelled at me about having brain tumors and I was a little boy that I had remembered. And I was shown each of the 3 hospital visits and about how I almost methodically avoided and then went into denial of dealing with the reality that I had a growing problem. I was then taken forward in time. I was shown all of the symptomology, actual things that happened as early as 21 where I had symptomology where I just denied it, never told anyone about it, and just forgot it. I was shown each and every time that I had something related to those tumors happen to me, interfere with me, or be shown to me. When that period ended, it was almost like right at that time I had been shown the problems in Chicago, the growing problem with noise. Then it was like I was in the vision, in the present moment.

Again, I opened my eyes and tried to rationally figure out what was actually happening. All I had seen was, like I said, a documentary about my brain tumors, how they started, how they advanced, how I was warned, how I was shown. So I couldn't figure it out. Again, I almost experimentally slowly closed my eyes, and the vision was on again. The movie was on. Then it fast-forwarded, and I saw myself walking about a half a block from the restaurant that I managed on North Broadway. I saw myself walking from behind. I knew it was me because I had an orange jumpsuit that my girlfriend had made for me. The vision was 10 feet behind me walking away from the restaurant, and suddenly my head snapped and twitched and I sort of stopped in my tracks. I shook and fell onto the ground onto the sidewalk. And the voice said to me, "At this point, you will relinquish conscious choice on the Earth plane."

For the first time in my head, I said, "Does that mean I will die?"

And the voice said, "You will relinquish conscious choice on the Earth plane." Then the vision went off. The movie went off. I sat there for just a short period, and I yelled inside of myself, "What do I do?? What do I do??!!"

What I was shown in the next couple minutes was this: "You have to go to the Philippines. Find this man, and he will remove the brain tumors." All of a sudden, I saw a big, big face filling the screen. It was as though he was in my mind or in my consciousness. Looking at me right in the eyes, a big smile on his face, a Filipino man. I recognized immediately to be a man named Tony Agpaoa. I had 2 times in prior years seen Philippines psychic surgery movies. This man was in both of those films. A voice said, "You find this man, Tony Agpaoa, and he will take your tumors out." And again it went off.

I almost instinctively yelled, "I don't know how to get to the Philippines. I don't have money. What do I do?!"

Bingo, the movie was on again. And I saw my dear, dear beloved friend Dr. Bill DeHart, who, at that time, was a podiatrist up in Flint, Michigan. And the voice said to me, "You are to call Dr. Dehart and tell him your situation. He will provide the money for you to go to the Philippines, and you're to tell him that we suggest that he go also."

Then it went off again, and this time I didn't have any questions. I actually pretty quickly bounded off of the rock, ran back to the house, and informed my shocked friend Nancy that I appreciated her help but I had to head back to Chicago.

I had a feeling not to tell anyone anything about what was happening and that I better get to Chicago and get to the Philippines. My friends were very distressed that I was leaving after about 3 days, but I got my other friend in whose car I had come in. The next morning, we left, heading back to Chicago. We drove straight back, he let me off at my house. At this point, I had no trouble with the noise anymore. I had only a clear realization that somehow, I had to do everything that I saw in these visions.

As soon as I got home, I called my friend up in Flint. He was delighted to hear from me, but he was in a rush. He said, "Corky, I can't talk right now. The cab is taking our luggage. Gloria and I are flying to Toronto for me to give a lecture. After Toronto I'll be back in a week. Give me a call then."

I said, "Wait a minute, wait a minute, Bill." He said, "They're beeping in the cab, Corky. I've got to get to the airport."

I heard his wife come in and say, "Come on, Bill!"

I said, "Bill, this is a matter of life and death."

He said, "Are you serious?"

I said, "Yes."

He said, "Okay, okay, wait a minute. I heard him giving instructions to his wife." He told her to get on another phone and call the airport and get the next flight to Toronto.

She's screaming and arguing, and he said, "Just do as I say. Corky's in trouble."

He came back on the phone and said, "Okay, tell me what's going on."

I told him the whole vision; he listened. It probably took 10 to 15 minutes. His first reply was, "How much do you need?"

I said, "I don't know. I'm guessing it will probably cost $1,000 to get a plane ticket to the Philippines." He said, "The money will be sent to you tomorrow. I'll send it on the way to the airport, special delivery overnight."

I said, "What about you? The vision said you should come too."

He said, "I can't. I'm committed. I've got things to do."

He said, "You go, and when you come back, let me know that you're okay. Now I have to get going for this other plane."

The next morning, I got a special delivery letter with $1,500 in it. I knew of a Filipino travel agency on Lincoln Avenue in Chicago. I went there and sat down with the owner, an old Filipino man.

I said, "I have to get to the Philippines as fast as I can."

He said, "Why are you in a hurry?"

I said, "I have to go see healers there."

He said, "Are you talking about the psychic surgeons?"

I said, "Yes."

He said, "I'll get you there. I'll get you there fast. I know exactly what hotel to book you into. I'll make all the arrangements so that when you get to Manilla, they'll expect you. You'll have a room at the hotel, and you'll be able to meet the healers."

The next several days were a whirlwind of me preparing for the trip. I did tell the girlfriend that I was living with the entire story. She said, "Go. Just go. Go fast."

Before I left Chicago to get on the plane to Manila, I had stopped by my mother's house and explained everything to her. She was scared to the core with my story, but she knew me enough and trusted her own faith in Christ and God and she said, "Go son. Go and get healed, and then come back home."

Roughly a week later, maybe 5 days, I flew out of Chicago to San Francisco and then on to Hawaii and on to Manila. When I was going out to the airport, I remembered a man, his name was Frank M. He had shown me the first Philippines movies I had ever seen. Maybe four years prior to then. I remember him saying, "If you ever go to the Philippines, you get in touch with me before you go."

So I had the cab driver pull over, I had his number in my little address book. I called him up, "I told him I was heading for the airport and that I was going to Manila."

He said, "How much time do you have?"

I said, "Oh my flight is three hours away, I have to get there early."

He said, "I'm right by O'Hare airport. Tell the driver to take you to my house." He said, "I've got to give you something." So I told the driver. It was no problem; he knew right where this man's home was.

He came out of his house when we pulled into the driveway. He had a bag, a black bag with a handle. He said, "This is my Super 8 camera, but I don't have any film. You'll have to get film in Manila." He said, "They're just little cartridges, stick one in the camera and shoot as many operations as you can."

I said, "Frank I don't know anything about cameras."

He said, "Figure it out when you get there. Just go."

So now I had a camera with me on my way to Manila.

The plane from San Francisco to Manila was full of people all going to Manila to see psychic surgeons. Probably 180 Americans, most of them had come from a group from Seattle. And all the people on this plane were going in hopes of some form of healing; there were a lot of crippled people, wheelchairs, etc.

So, 26 hours later, the plane arrived in Manila. All the flight over, I questioned and doubted what I was doing. Even with this amazing series of events and with the incredible visions, I had doubt. I doubted that I deserved healing, that even if they could heal a lot of people on that plane, they might not know what to do with brain tumors. I had so many doubts.

When we landed in Manila, there were a number of buses to take everybody to the Bayview Hotel. And when we all checked in, we were told that there would be a dinner that night, a banquet in which the head of the healers' organization would introduce people to 4 or 5 of the healers that would be working on them.

I went to my room and took a nap. I cleaned up, and I went down for the buffet. Basically, the head of the healers' organization was Joaquin Cunanan, a very wealthy, powerful, and influential man in the Philippines, who was also a spiritualist, a yoga student, and a teacher and had much to do with the setting up of accounting of nations when the United Nations opened. He was a multi-multimillionaire accountant in the Philippines. He introduced 4 or 5 healers, up on a stage. None of them were Tony Agpaoa.

They explained that everybody should stay in their rooms and the next day healers would start working on people. There were girls who worked for the travel agency that most of these people came with, they were young office workers. They would go to the person's room, get them, take them to the healing room, and then take them back to their room and get the next person.

So the first day, I wasn't called. I wasn't one of the people to be worked on. I watched the goings–on; it was sort of like a conveyor belt thing from 3 or 4 different healing rooms where one healer would be in each room. He would have an assistant or 2 assistants. The travel agency girls would keep shuffling people back and forth from their rooms. So by the end of the first night, I had met with a few of the healers; I just introduced myself. All of these healers were cut out of the same stone. They were all very simple men; they were all somewhat uneducated. Some of them had come from the mountains. They were all very simple, plain men. But they had in common, every single one of them, a tremendous joy. They always seemed full of joy. 1 or 2 of the healers that I was to meet subsequently were more dour and less enthusiastic. But the original group working at the Bayview Hotel just seemed like they were all brothers or all relatives and all on the same page and all happy. I went out that day and found 10- 50ft cartridges of Super 8 film.

The second day I was called into a room. A young healer, Juni Labo, as I was sitting up, went through my right ear and produced a small tumor, like half the size of my little finger. He pulled it out right through my ear, and it was shocking to me. When he touched my head, my OM sound went on very loudly, my head buzzed, I was sort of elevated in consciousness, but I was wide awake. When he finished, he took the tumor out and threw it in a bucket on water. In all the operations, everything that I witnessed coming out of a body was always put into bowls or dishes or buckets of water. The healers explained that the negativity in what they took out of the body actually had life force, and if they put it in water, it was immediately neutralized. But if they were to throw it in a bucket without water, they believed that the energy could leave the tumor and go looking for another body to live in. So I learned a lot that day. Then I asked some of the healers if it would be possible to take my camera and film what was going on. I had the surgery that Juni Labo did on my ear. I had a man hold my camera and shoot that. They told me they would get back to me; they had to confer with Mr. Cunanan.

In the end I was given permission to film any operations as long as the person or the family involved allowed me to be in the room. So for the next couple days I settled into the pattern of asking people who were scheduled for surgeries if I could shoot their surgeries. I was a complete novice with the camera. I had no idea about how to properly move it or pan it. I would just whisk it from one person to another or one thing I was looking at. It was a very amateur piece of film work that I did.

But as the days went on, I kept looking for Tony Agpaoa. I started asking different healers if they knew him. Of course, every one said, "Do I know him?!"

They essentially talked about him and revered him like a king. He was the king of the healers. He was the first and greatest of this crop of healers. He was adored by these other healers.

But they all told me, "You won't be able to see Tony Agpaoa. He went up in the mountains about 2 weeks ago for a retreat."

I said, "When does that end?"

They said, "Normally if Tony goes into the mountains, he goes for at least 40 days."

That really sunk me because after the initial experience with having the tumor taken out through the ear, there was no more interest from any of these healers to do any more serious work on me. I mentioned to a few of them that I believed that I had tumors down in my brain. They would just sort of go blank, go quiet, make no response. So this continued along for—I believe I had a 15-day visa—and I think this was the 12th day. I wondered in my own head, "How am I going to see the man that I was shown would take the tumors out of my brain? How can I possibly see him?" He was somewhere called Baguio City, out in the mountains. I didn't know what to do.

On the 13th day, I was sitting in the lobby of the hotel. I had by this time filmed probably 30 or 40 different surgeries. A couple of them were pretty minor, and a couple of them were pretty important and I had seen with my eyes a few times when I didn't have my camera. I saw more incredible and more miraculous surgeries that were performed at times that I either I didn't have my camera with me or the power went out in the room after the healer started working.

So now it's the 13th day, and I'm quite dejected. I'm sitting in the hotel lobby, essentially not believing that it was possible that I could be shown that vision, travel to the other side of the planet, and then be told, "You'll never see this man."

I was sitting there with all this woe-is-me stuff going on, and one of the group came rushing in the front door of the hotel, very excited. I saw him immediately. He was looking for someone. he spotted me and ran over and said, "I just saw the most incredible healing down the street at another hotel." I said, "Were they other healers?"

He said, "Yea, this other hotel down the road also brings in healers."

I said, "What did you see?"

He said, "I saw a guy named Tony…"

As soon as he said that my body had goosebumps everywhere. I jumped to my feet.

I said, "You saw a guy named Tony?"

He said, "Yea! He's incredible. They say he's the best of the healers."

I bolted out the front door and sprinted down the street to the other hotel. I went in the lobby and had to ask a half a dozen people. Finally, some-one said, "The healers are up on the 7th floor."

I went up there and knocked on the door and a tall, very distinguished 55- to 60-year-old American woman opened the door and stepped out in the hallway and said, "What can I do for ya?"

I quickly mumbled out my story and said that if Tony Agpaoa was there, I had to see him.

She said, "Are you connected to the healers at the Bayview Hotel?"

I said, "Yes, yes, yes."

She said, "Tony won't see you. Tony has an agreement with the healer organization that most of the Filipino healers belong to."

The name of the organization was The Union Espiritista de Cristiana de Filipinas. The Union of Spiritual Healers of Christ in the Philippines. Tony was not part of that group. And the 2 groups had sometime prior agreed that if a person came over to Manila and came over to stay at one of the 2 hotels, neither group, Tony nor the other group, would work on any-one who had come with the other group. Well, I was just beside myself. I said, "Look, I had this vision in Syracuse last month to be here."

The woman said, "Okay, come inside." It's a waiting room, no open chairs. "Just wait. Don't say anything, don't disturb anybody, and I'll try to get Tony to see you."

So I sat probably for 3 to 4 hours as every person in the waiting room went into the room that Tony was in. This lady, this very wonderful, distin-guished lady was a chiropractor in San Francisco. Her name was Sarah. She kept coming over telling me just be patient, be patient. When the last person was gone out of the waiting room, Tony came out, and I was just electrified as soon as I saw him. He was wiping his hands on a towel. He went over to Sarah and talked about their schedule. Sarah said, "This is the man I've been talking to you about," and pointed to me.

He looked at me from about 10 to 15 feet away and said, "You've been worked on by the other healers?"

I said, "Yes."

He said, "I can see in your aura where they opened your body. I can't help you. I can't break the agreement that we have."

He said, "If you want me to work on you, get on a plane, get back to San Fran, get on another plane, come back to Manila, check into this hotel, and I'll work on you. That is what's required."

He turned around and walked out.

I was just crushed. I couldn't believe what was happening. This woman Sarah said, "I have to get a cup of coffee. Would you go down to the cafeteria with me? I want to hear your whole story."

So I went down, and while she drank coffee, I told her my entire story, beginning to end. She was quite taken in with it and was quite sympathetic.

She said, "I don't know what I can do. I know this agreement with the healers' organization. I know that nobody breaks it, nobody disrespects it." She said, "Can you go back to Frisco and come back?"

I said, "No. I have no money and no time."

She said, "This vision—when do you think your time would be?"

I said, "I'm certain before Christmas. I have no way to go and come back."

So she said, "Okay, let me call you at your hotel in the morning. I'll talk to Tony and see if I can get him to change his mind."

So the next morning, I sat on the edge of the bed next to the phone until it rang, and it was Sarah. She said, "Come over, come to the room and do the exact thing I asked you to do yesterday. He has a full schedule. He is just starting to work." So I went back to the other hotel.

She said, "Come in, sit down against the wall on the floor, and I'll work with him, try to convince him." So the prior day was repeated. There were probably 40 people in the room. And I sat and waited as each one was taken in for their healing with Tony, and they would come and be taken to their hotel room. The same way when the last person got up and went in the room and then came out and left the hotel room, again Tony came walking out, and he said the same thing. He said, "I can't work on you. I'm sorry." And he went off into a side room. I guess it was like his bedroom or something.

Anyways, Sarah again said, "Let me talk to him, and don't give up hope. You just wait here."

She went into the other room. She was in there for 10 minutes, and she said, "He still won't work on you, but I want you to go in and try to convince him. You tell him about the vision."

So unannounced she opened the door and pushed me through the door. Well, Tony was sitting at a table, reading a paper, smoking a Salem cigarette. And I stood there, and he looked up at me and said, "I can't help you."

Sarah then stepped forward and very forcefully said, "Tony I have brought groups to you for years. I have never disagreed with you on anything. But you are making a mistake now. Hear him out."

He stopped, looked at me and immediately everything changed.

I had his attention and I said, "Tony, I had this vision, and in this vision, I was shown your face and the voices said to me that you would be the man to take my brain tumors out. I don't care anything about groups or hotels or about what travel agency brought who over here. I'm not affiliated with either of your groups or any of these arrangements that happened here. I'm affiliated with Spirit, and Spirt has directed me to you."

I saw a shocked look on his face. He quickly stubbed his cigarette out and came and stood real close to me and looked in my eyes real hard. Then he said, "Oh, oh, oh! Okay, let's go."

He went back out into the reception room and 2 of Tony's assistants were still there. He said, "We've got to work on this man immediately. Right now, come on."

In a matter of minutes, I was lying on his table, and he had one of his assistants playing a guitar and singing a Beatles song. Then he changed to singing the Lord's Prayer. The other one was preparing cotton and a bucket of water. Without any further talk or explanation, he rolled my head over to the left, exposing my right side and started putting all 10 of his fingertips together and started massaging my right temple, and when he did that, there was an explosion of high-pitched vibration and intense heat and energy.

It was like burning heat and intense vibration. He rubbed and rubbed, and then all of a sudden, I felt blood running down my cheek, down my neck. He had opened my skull. He put his hand over the open hole, held it open with one hand, and put his other hand open, sort of waved his hand. I could see the movement in my peripheral vision. Then he reached over, and his assistant handed him a hemostat, and—I could feel it go down into my brain. I could feel the cold. Then he was pulling something. I could feel it pulling out of my brain. And then there was a plopping sound, and he immediately moved it in front of my face.

I opened my eyes and saw that on the end of the hemostat, he had what looked like the size of my thumb, a tumor.

It was wiggling like a worm on a hook; it was like alive. It was moving; he had a good hold on it. After he knew I saw it, he put it down in a bucket of water and dropped it in there.

Then he said something in Tagalog, and one of his assistants went and got a mirror and held the mirror up above my head so that at an angle, I could look in the mirror and see my right temple area.

He again rubbed, and in a split second I saw my brain. I saw the folds and the actual liquids; blood was running out, not pouring out, just dripping out. Then he grabbed the hemostat again and put it down into my brain matter and grabbed another tumor. He pulled it out, and it plopped just like the other one. This one was a little bit bigger. He put it in front of my face. I got a clear look at it, and then he put it in a bucket of water. Then they took the mirror away. He put his hands over the area that he was working in, rubbed them in a circle, and then took his hands away. The assistant put the mirror back up. My head was closed, and all the hair on that side of my head was all matted with blood. There was blood running down my cheek and neck.

While this was going on, all I heard was this intense, explosive, loud roaring in my head. I can't put it into words— but the best I can say is I felt joy, ecstasy, and bliss. I felt a tremendous heat on the side of my head, as though someone had taken a hot iron and put it on my head, but there was no pain. I was in an altered place, and when they sat me up, I was very woozy. They got me up on my feet, and I started to get grounded. I stood there for a moment or two while he reached out and grabbed my shoulders. And then he was talking to Sarah. He said, "Sarah, you were right. This was my work. This was supposed to be done by me."

Then he turned to me, and I was sort of back in the room. He pulled me close to him and hugged me. He was shorter than me, and he sort of reached up and put his mouth by my ear and said, "It was by the grace of God and the persistence of your guide that this healing was made possible." And it was done.

Sarah took me out to the front door. She said, "Walk real slow, be careful, go home, and get on your bed immediately. Just get on your bed and give thanks to God."

I did so. I followed her directions. I lay there for a long time, realizing that I had just been given a gift. I had just been given an extension on my life, and I had just been given a divine intervention to prevent a premature leaving of the planet. I had just been blessed, and I was overwhelmed. I just lay there fully, totally understanding what had happened from the moment the visions had started 1 month before.

Early the next morning, Sarah called and told me to come back to the hotel. Tony wanted to say a few words to me. I went back to the hotel, and he almost apologetically tried to explain why he had been so stubborn, why he had stuck to the agreement, which he actually had violated for the first time by working on me. But he said, "Your tumors had my name on them. None of the other healers could have touched them. They might have seen them, they might have known that you have them, but they couldn't have gone in there. When you got my attention and I woke up, I saw that this was my work."

I said to him, "Can I ask a question?"

He said, "Of course."

I said, "Can you tell me what that energy was that came through your hands into my body yesterday?"

He said these exact words: "The best way I can describe what happened yesterday was that Jesus Christ walked through my back, into my body, put his arms down through my arms, and I just watched him do the work." He said, "That's the only way I can explain it to you."

We hugged again, and I profusely thanked him. I didn't have any money to give to him, but he didn't look like he wanted any money. Then he sent me downstairs into the lobby where a friend of his was giving a seminar to that group that he had worked on. They wanted me to sit in on that seminar. I listened to this man; he was a powerful spiritual Filipino man, and his name was Rolando Carbonelle.

I listened to his talk, and then I went back to my room. Two days later, I got on a plane and headed back to Chicago. I actually arrived at O'Hare airport at 9:00 a.m. on Thanksgiving morning.

Marcello Jainar

Of ALL THE HEALERS I MET IN THE PHILIPPINES, Marcello Jainar and I made an incredible connection. He spoke very little English, so we didn't have much talking. But he and I were like 2 long-lost brothers who were meeting. Anyways, we were talking through an interpreter one day and he told me that several years before, a representative of the Japanese government had gotten in touch with the healer organization and Mr. Cunanan. He requested that one of the healers come to Osaka, Japan, to their nuclear energy center so that they could test him. Cunanan picked Marcello Jainar to go.

He told me about it. He said, "I went over there. They took me into this tremendous facility. They kept me several days, and what they were trying to do was measure the energy that came through my body. But they had no success. Then they tried to see if I could heal a person that they brought in. And I was able to heal this person with breast cancer, I took the tumors out."

He said, "Then they wanted me to heal another woman in room lined with lead, and I would be outside the room, not even touching her."

He said, "We have the ability to do that. It's called absent healing. You heal from a distance."

So they put this woman in a room, and Marcello healed her from outside the lead-lined room.

He said finally before he left, they wanted to hook him up to a machine that measured atomic energy. It was a machine that could measure the output of their reactors. It actually measured physical atomic energy. He said, "They felt that if I could even show a reading on that machine then there would be proof of the energy going through."

He said, "So they hooked me up to the machine and turned it on. They said, 'Okay, go into your trance or do whatever you do when you heal.'"

He said, "I immediately contacted my high self and blew the machine out."

He said, "There were sparks everywhere, bells, whistles."

He said, "Everyone was running around in circles. They turned everything off."

He said, "I just ruined their piece of equipment."

I said, "Did they have any way of explaining how the energy that came through you worked?"

The best I remember of what he said was this: "They said that the reason that the energy coming through the healer's hands could separate flesh was that the energy was so strong that it set up a state they called neo-polarization. They said in neo-polarization, there is such a tremendous force introduced that it causes atoms to stop moving in their rotation, in their field, and hang suspended."

They speculated that the energy from the healer's hands caused the atoms in the flesh where they were directing their energy to stop and hang suspended in their movement. And that the fingers would just push the atoms apart, and then when they would take their hands out, and the neo-polarization state would end, all the atoms would go right back in their normal movements. That was, at that time, the best and only scientific explanation that I had ever heard.

On the Road Again

WHEN I GOT BACK TO CHICAGO FROM THE PHILIPPINES, there was a lot of residual joy that I felt. I felt so incredibly privileged and honored. I felt blessed beyond words. I felt literally like I was being gifted with who knows how many years of life. But to this day, I've always felt like from 30 years old, I've been living on borrowed time

In Chicago, I got in touch with my friend Frank, who gave me his Super 8 movie camera. When I got to his house, he asked me, "Where are the films?"

I showed him that I had a bag of 10- 50ft cartridges. I didn't have any of them numbered or dated; they were just 10 unmarked little cartridges. He said, "Let me get these. I know a guy who will develop all of these and put them on one reel for you."

A week later he called me up. I went out to his house, and he gave me the master copy.

I pretty quickly found a Super 8 projector and a small screen and started showing them to my most immediate friends and to people close to me. I would show the film and, at times, put it on pause, to explain what was going on, who was being worked on, what their ailments were, and what the outcome was. So by narrating the film I was able to explain it in a cohesive way that made sense. Other than that, there were just 10 cartridges put together with no order, no connection, etc.

In the first few times I showed the movies, I would narrate, and then after the movie would end, whoever I was showing it to would just have a battery of questions.

By mid-December, I had already shown the films maybe 5 times to small groups of friends. I realized that though to me it was a scrambled mess of poor film work, people got something out of it; people saw something, people were excited, people were amazed.

Later in December, my girlfriend told me that she would like to go back to Syracuse for Christmas; her parents wanted her to come and bring me along. So we decided to head out in an old Chevy panel truck that I had and drive to Syracuse. This was the period of time when Nixon had already signed the paperwork to ration gas. And one of the days of the week, all gas stations in the United States were shut down, and that was on Sunday. So at midnight on Saturday, every gas station in the country, depending on time zone, closed until Monday morning.

So we packed up our stuff, and I took the films and the projector, and we headed to Syracuse. I gave myself one extra day of driving—we left on Friday morning; normally, to drive to Syracuse is about 18 hours for me. Friday evening, we took our time; there was no hurry. Friday evening, I was in Ohio, on Interstate 80, and we were headed up to the Pennsylvania Turnpike to swing up into New York and then over to Syracuse. It was probably 2 or 3 in the morning, Saturday morning, and I think I had just passed Cleveland, not too far from where I got off for the Pennsylvania turnpike. We were driving along, and my girlfriend was in the back of the van. I had built a platform, and she was sleeping in the back of the van.

The roads were perfectly dry, and there was virtually no traffic. I saw very few cars in front or behind me and very little oncoming traffic. And I was going about 75. And this was what I could call divine intervention number 3. In very close proximity to my Philippines intervention. The facts that I am going to give now, I have no doubt that the reader might have trouble understanding, but I have to include this story because it was utterly miraculous.

I'm driving along, both lanes clear, no one near me. All of a sudden, I feel a tremendous wave of impending doom—it is the best way I can say it. Not fear, not paranoia, but the sense of an impending disaster. It hit me so hard that I immediately started saying out loud the Gayatri Mantra that Dr. Mishra had given to me years earlier.

The Gayatri Mantra, according to Dr. Mishra, is the most powerful protection mantra of the whole Sanskrit language, of the whole Hindu religion. I started repeating this mantra out loud, very quickly. It was like what had hit me was truly frightening in a way that my nervous system, my brain, every cell in my body went to work instantly. All I knew was to do this mantra, and I started repeating it forcefully out loud. My girlfriend woke and stuck her head through the curtains dividing the back from the front and said, "What's wrong? What's wrong?"

I said, "Just start praying, just start doing the mantra." And I went back to it.

She realized the urgency in my voice, and she started doing the mantra also. That went on for about one minute. It never occurred to me to pull over and stop. There was no danger in front of me, the road was clear, it was well lit, and there was no reason to think to stop. So we continued doing the mantra for I don't know how long; it might have been a minute or two minutes.

Suddenly, the front right corner of my panel truck seemed to have hit a big hole that I didn't see in the road. It was like my whole front end dipped down, and I guess I thought we were going to flip over. Then a split second later, it was as though with that same tire, we hit a giant rock or big piece of concrete, and I lost control of the truck. It started weaving back and forth, back and forth. I was on the shoulder on the left side, across 2 lanes, and then on the shoulder on the right. I was fighting to get control.

Finally, I got control, put on the brakes, and pulled off to the side of the road.

Both of us just sat there (well, she was lying there). Both of us were in total shock. I don't think we said word to each other for a minute or two. I got out the truck and I started to walk around the front, just as a state trooper flicked his lights on and pulled over behind me. He got out of his car and said, "What the hell happened back there? Did you hit something?"

I told him, "I don't know what happened. I didn't see anything in the road. I thought I drove in a hole, and then I thought I had hit a big piece of concrete. I was losing control, I got control, and just pulled over."

He said, "I saw the whole thing. I was right behind ya. The front end went down, and all I saw was a sheet of sparks, and then you were all over the road."

He said, "I thought you were going to flip. I don't know how you got control."

I said, "I don't know what happened either."

We both walked around to the front of the vehicle; the headlights were still on. I went around and looked at the right tire. It looked fine, and there was no visible sign of any damage. Both of us stood there and couldn't comprehend what I had just experienced driving and what he had experienced following me.

So he said, "A couple miles up the road is a truck stop. Follow me up there. There's a Standard Station. I know the guy who runs it. You better have this thing checked before you try driving anywhere else."

I said, "Okay."

I followed him; he kept his lights on. We pulled off at the exit, but I forget which town it was.

We pulled up into the Standard Station, and the man who ran the Standard Station came walking up toward us. I stopped my panel truck. There was no sign of anything wrong while I drove. There was no pull to the left or the right; everything seemed absolutely perfect.

I pulled up and stopped, and then the trooper stopped behind me. The gas station attendant went back and talked to him for a second. Then he came up to my window and said, "Pull your panel truck right up to the end bay over there, where the tow truck is inside of the bay."

So I pulled up to this glass door, right up close, and turned the ignition off. I got out, and my girlfriend got out. The trooper was trying to explain to this guy what had happened.

The guy was shaking his head. He said, "None of that makes any sense."

He said, "Let me look at the front end."

So he got down on the ground. He looked underneath, but he didn't see anything wrong. As he was getting up, he touched the bumper and he pulled his hand away and said, "Oh my God. Come here, look at this."

I had a big steel bumper. The whole right underside of the bumper was all chewed up, and the whole bumper was still hot. I reached out and touched it, and it burned my fingers. He said, "I don't understand this! This is crazy. This bumper is chewed up like it was dragged along."

And when the trooper said there was a tremendous wall of sparks coming out, the guy was just mystified. He said, "Let me hook the tow truck up to the front of this truck and see what happens."

He went inside, came back, opened the bay door, took a chain, put it under my front bumper, and picked the front end of my truck up off the ground. When the tires were about 2 feet off of the ground, he stopped. When he stopped the truck being lifted, the whole right wheel and tire fell down onto the ground and lay there, spinning in a circle.

This is hard to explain any deeper; I'm not a mechanic. But we stood and stared inside of the brake drum for, I don't know how long. The brakes were all mangled. Inside of the drum, they were all twisted and bent like pretzels. Everything was so hot that steam was coming off of it—steam or smoke. In the middle of the brake drum was the spindle. The spindle is a part of the truck that you put the wheel onto, and then you put the lug nuts on. The whole brake drum was fused inside the tire. Everything had melted and twisted, and the spindle had broken off; half of it was stuck up in the truck, and the other half looked like a piece of taffy that had been twisted until it broke. The spindle—a big long, thick piece of hard steel—had been melted in half, and both ends looked like taffy that had been twisted.

There was such silence, such disbelief. The full impact of what we were looking at was obvious to everybody. This gas station attendant was speechless. The state trooper was speechless. And I, even in my limited understanding of what I was looking at, I knew that what I was looking at was impossible. That I could not have gone through the entire driving experience, lane to lane, flying all over and then pulled up on the side of the road, and then stop my vehicle without any strange feeling on those brakes.

I—and the trooper too—knew that I could not have followed him several miles to the gas station and then have the tow truck lift the front end up and then have the whole wheel fall off onto the ground with the mangled, twisted brakes and a broken spindle. All of us knew what we were looking at. The gas station guy saw me drive up. He said to the state trooper, "I saw this truck drive up here."

The state trooper said, "I saw this truck look like it was going to crash and flip. And then all of a sudden it was fine, and then this kid followed me in here."

We were all just fumbling for words. Finally, the trooper said, "I don't even know how I can report this. There's no one who will even believe it if I write this into a record."

The gas station guy said, "I've been here for 26 years, and nothing like this have I ever seen. I can't even explain what I'm looking at down in that tire. Somehow, the wheel bearings must have gone dry, and somehow the bearings froze, but that should have immediately stopped the truck. There must have been so much heat to cause the spindle to melt. This is all beyond my comprehension."

The trooper said, "Back down the road about 10 miles is an outfit that repairs all the trucks in the area." He asked if when the attendant was done with his shift, could he tow the truck and the wheel down the road to this junkyard repair place to see if there was anything they could do.

Shortly after the trooper took off, this guy's replacement came in for the early shift. The attendant hooked up the truck properly, backed us out, and threw the wheel in the back of his tow truck, and he took us to this place that was just opening up. It was about 6 in the morning, it was just getting light. He pulled into the yard. It looked like an old junkyard, but it was a big, big, big garage. There were broken-down vehicles everywhere. It was like a junkyard and a repair place.

The owner came out with 2 of his mechanics and said, "What have we got here?"

The driver told him, "You're not going to believe this," and he reached up and grabbed the tire from the back of his pickup truck and threw it down on the ground. And it was the same thing with the owner and these 2 mechanics. I looked at their faces; their mouths were hanging open. They were looking at something they had never seen. They were looking at a situation that couldn't have happened.

The tow truck driver explained to the owner that he had seen me drive the truck up to his bay, hooked up the front end, lifted it up, and had the wheel fall off.

The boss said, "What? Are you kidding me? You're trying to pull one over on me? It's impossible that you could have seen this truck drive with this mess in here." The tow truck driver said, "Bill (or whatever the trooper's name was) followed him up in the station. Bill saw the whole thing happen." Well, this went on for some time. None of these 3 men could believe what they were looking at, not even believing their friend who was pleading with them to accept his story. Then one of the other mechanics, who hadn't said anything, said, "Wait a minute! This is too much."

And his boss turned and said, "What's too much?"

He said, "Look over there!" And he pointed about 30 feet away, further down the driveway. There was an exact duplicate of my panel truck. It wasn't the same color, but it was the same year, make, and model.

The owner said, "Oh my God! That's unbelievable."

He said to the tow truck guy, "We took that panel truck in yesterday as junk. That truck has every piece that would be required to fix the front end of this vehicle."

I'll make a long story short now. The owner consulted with his 2 guys; they heard my story about needing to get to Syracuse. They knew that that evening the gas stations would close, and the chances of me getting to Syracuse were actually pretty slim.

So they decided among themselves to put aside all their scheduled work that day, and all 3 of them would change the front end and rebuild my truck from the truck that had come in the day before. They worked all day long; we had no money, and we called my girl's parents. The father reluctantly sent us the bill. They told me that the bill would be—if they were able to fix it by closing time and get us on the road—something like $350.

My girlfriend's father Western Unioned the money to us. It came 15 minutes before the garage closed. They had just completed putting the entire front end from the old junker into my truck. Didn't even have time to road test it.

The owner said, "You know, you're on your own. We think we have everything adjusted, but you drive careful, and if you see any trouble, get to a truck stop."

We paid him, and he closed the doors. We drove off, and with the help of our friends along the way, we actually got to our friends' house in Syracuse the next morning; about 6 hours after the gas stations of the whole state closed.

This was truly a miracle. I don't doubt that the gas station guy and that state trooper and the truck repair guy and his 2 men remember that day for the rest of their lives. I don't doubt that they futilely tried to explain what had happened to friends and coworkers. I don't doubt that they all had a hard time getting anyone to comprehend what had happened on that stretch of road. But when we got to Syracuse on Christmas morning, we truly felt that the hand of God had come into our lives. I had already had it happen a month before that.

But my girlfriend and I were grateful beyond words when we got to our destinations—our friend's house and then my girlfriend's parent's house after that. We told them the story; nobody understood or comprehended it. Nobody probably believed it. But it was truly a miraculous event. I often think back to it as a Christmas gift to us from the universe.

At that point, we did the Christmas celebration with the parents; then we went back to our friends' house, who lived on a lake in a little town called Marcellus, just outside Syracuse. There was a lot of excitement about me having the Philippines movies. My friends, whose house I had gone to do the fasting and had the vision, were absolutely overjoyed because not only was I alive, but I was coming to spend a week or so with them with my girl.

The next night they set up a movie showing. They packed their house—probably 30 people. I did my first movie presentation to a large group of people. I showed them twice more before I headed back to Chicago. I showed them to a psychiatrist and a teacher of psychiatry at the Syracuse Med School. His 3 boys had seen it and asked if I would show it to their father and their friends.

When the movie ended, the oldest boy said, "Well Dad, what do you think of that?"

The father said, "Basically I can't believe any of it."

The other son said, "What do you mean? We all saw it. It was right on the screen."

The father said, "What I mean is that I can't afford to believe any of it. Because if I believe what I just saw, I would have to throw all of my training out the window." I thought that was quite an interesting statement and mind-set for that man.

After my visit to my friends in upstate New York, we went back to Chicago. Already by the time we got back, on our answering machine, we were having requests to show the movie. I felt at that time that I not only wanted to, but I felt it almost a duty to share this information of my whole experience in the Philippines along with the pictures I had taken. I felt like this was my job; this was what I must do.

So I went back to the restaurant that I was working in, and on the side, I started showing the healing movie. At first, I showed several small groups, and then I made a rule that there had to be 8 or more people. I gave a showing to any group, any people in Chicago, who called me and could put a group of 8 together. From the very beginning I felt an incredible fulfillment every time I showed the movies, every time I told the story. The biggest part of all the showings was afterward, I was always bombarded with questions, many of which I had answers to and could explain.

So this pattern started of me showing the movies, sometimes multiple times a week. I started showing them at bigger groups. I showed them at some small churches, and I showed them at consciousness groups. I showed them once to a Silva mind control group. I mention this one because this was the first time that I saw the potential impact of the films on a higher level than just people being amazed or giving people insights into other potentialities. When I showed them at this Silva group, the woman whose house it was went away, and came back into the room with a woman that turned out to be her maid of many years. This was an older Lithuanian woman. The woman looked to me like she was in pain, all doubled over. She sat down and watched the movies for about 15 minutes or so, and then abruptly she got up and walked out of the room and went back to her room. That group was very open, they were very much into metaphysical things, they were very receptive, and it was a very good showing.

The next day the woman called me up. She said, "My maid was afflicted by long-standing pain in her abdomen. It was suspected by a family doctor that her pancreas was giving out, that she might even have pancreatitis or cancer."

So this woman told me this maid's history and said, "She sat and watched the films, and at one point when you were honed in on a pair of hands working on a man's back, she suddenly had some sort of experience. She suddenly felt something. She got up and went to her room and lay in her bed. What she experienced was the hands in the film going into her abdomen and taking away the pain. The next morning, she came out bright and cheery. She told me she had no pain, she wasn't bent over, had no affliction whatsoever. She told her boss, 'The hands on the screen came into my body and healed my pancreas.'"

The woman said, "I'm positive that she is totally healed. She hasn't looked this good in years."

So that one made me realize that above and beyond sharing the films and my whole experience, there was a potential for something else to happen also. So this film-showing pattern continued on for almost 2 years. There were many individual showings that I could talk about where amazing things happened. Amazing exchanges, amazing realizations, etc. I showed my films in the actual operating theatre of Augustana Hospital, where they do neurosurgery, at the invitation of a nurse. The neurological operating team, 15 or 20 people on the staff, were in the room. That turned out to be one of the most bizarre showings because 5 minutes into it, every male doctor ran out of the room.

Of the nurses that were left, some of them began crying, and one of them kept saying, "What are we doing to people??!! What are we doing??!!"

There was so much emotion, and it was so raw. And it *was* Augustana Hospital.

I showed my films once at a Catholic church on the north side of Chicago at the invitation of my grandmother, whose senior citizen group from the church—were more than curious. My grandmother had told some of them about her grandson going to the Philippines and getting healed—asked the priest if they could have a showing in the church. The church actually had a big roll-down projector screen. My grandma asked if I would come and show all her church friends. There were probably 100 to 150 people spread out. I showed the films over the altar of the Catholic church. My grandmother afterward was so proud. All of her friends gathered around, saying, "Mable, Mable, what a wonderful grandson you have!" That was one of my happier film showings.

I took the films on the road too. I showed them in Indiana and Wisconsin. I showed them at University of Colorado at Fort Collins—a man had invited me; he was the head of the Psychology department. I showed them to 2 of his university classes. I showed them all over. I never kept track of what date or who I showed them to. I kept no records whatsoever. I estimate that in 2 years, I showed the movies maybe 200 times to what I'm guessing may have been as many as 10,000 people.

I never got tired of it, but my girlfriend got tired of it, and after a while I wouldn't require her to come along anymore. I never got tired of narrating what I saw or telling what I had experienced. I never got bored or felt like, "Okay, that's enough," or "I shouldn't do this."

Many of my friends thought I was incredibly foolish because from day 1, I never charged a dollar from anybody for any showing. Nor did I take any money from people offered to me. I felt that this was my way of giving back from the gift that I had received. I did it very easily, very smoothly. And I thought that it would just go on.

Then there was an intervention, this time from the US government. My phone rang one day, and I picked it up, and the voice said, "I want to speak to Ralph Matson."

I just thought it was another movie showing, another stranger going to set up another showing.

I said, "Who are you?"

The man said, "I'm a lawyer, and I'm representing the FTC and the FDA."

I said, "How can I help you?"

I already knew what was coming. I had sort of been waiting for this. I was told by many people that sooner or later the government is going to stop you from showing these movies, as had been done already nationwide to different people who had publicly shown Philippine Psychic Surgery movies.

So I was quite cocky. I had had a number of lawyer friends or people I showed movies to tell me that if I ever got in trouble, they would defend me. So I felt pretty cocky. So I said to this guy, "What can I do for ya?"

He said in the clearest voice—words I've never forgotten— "We want you to cease and desist from the transference of information about the Philippines healers. Either by word or in writing, pictures, or film."

Then he was silent.

Then I was really cocky, and I said, "What if I don't want to do that?"

I had already decided long before this phone call, that I would resist any attempt to stop me from showing the movies.

He said, "If you don't cease and desist, we will put you under a federal harassment program."

And I laughed. I said, "Oh, a federal harassment program? And just what does that mean? What are you going to do to me?"

I think he was in deep thought for several seconds. He saw I was ready to take on a fight. He said, "Let me just put it to you like this. We will go into the lives of every person around you. All your friends, everyone you have contact with, we'll go into their lives, and if we find anything, any illegal activities or behaviors, we will immediately come down on them very hard."

When he said that, my blood ran cold. I literally shivered with the realization of what he was telling me. He was telling me essentially that everybody you care about, we'll hurt their lives if they do anything wrong.

Well, too many of the people in my life were engaged in some sort of minor illegal activities, like smoking pot.

As soon as he said that and I got over this chill with the realization of what I was being told, I said to him, "As of this moment, this day, I will cease and desist. I will stop all movie showings, and I will stop any talk of the Philippines healers."

That day I stopped the movie showings. Every request I had for the next several months, I told them the situation and put my films away. For many, many years I never took them out, never showed them again. This was roughly in the middle to the end of 1975.

At that point, I felt very, very fulfilled from the work that I had done, from the teachings that I had been allowed to do in front of these groups. The opening of peoples' minds and consciousness to other potentialities. I found myself often saying during these films, "In Manila, miracles are a dime a dozen." I said, "Miracles for all of us are actually a dime a dozen. If we would just allow them to happen, believe that they could happen, and if they showed up, allow them to happen."

That ended that period of my whole Philippines story and the ramifications afterward.

I'll close by saying that I asked one of the healers one day, "Why is it in the Philippines that this powerful healing is happening?"

He said, "If you take a magnifying glass out into the sunlight and a piece of paper and you focus the point of light through the magnifying glass on the paper, you'll burn right through the paper."

I had done that when I was a little boy.

I said, "Yea, I understand that."

He said, "The Philippines are the point on the piece of paper. And it has something to do with the way the sun and the ocean combine to bring forth the energy of the sun. It is magnified and empowered in the Philippines."

And that's the end of my whole Philippines story.

Uncle Frank

TOWARD THE END OF THE '70S, I did a lot of traveling. In March of '76, I went to Taos, NM, with a friend for a few months and met a lot of incredible people. I made long-lasting friends and got very close with Jan Sultan, my rolfer and now lifelong friend.

I met a woman named Ma Parker, who was the matriarch of Taos's inner society. Ma Parker was a tremendous, powerful woman who was able to telepath with the mineral kingdom. She could telepath with rocks and stones and gems—an amazing woman.

I met so many other wonderful people, artists—Sammy Heaton, a tremendous artist. Anne Merrill, who was a contemporary and very good friend of Georgia O'Keefe. I met a lot of people who had UFO experiences, personally, in the Taos area. Probably 6 to 8 people who had single or multiple UFO experiences. I found Taos to be a truly magical place and in the category of what I would call a rapid-growth area. If you go there, you grow. If you don't want to grow, you leave. Anyways, I really enjoyed that period of time.

I went back to Chicago for a while, and then in February of '77, I took a long road trip with a good friend of mine, Gene. We drove from Chicago to upstate New York. In upstate New York, we stayed with Joe and Nancy Martins; we stayed there for a while. Then we drove down to Fort Lauderdale, where I stayed with other of my Puerto Rican family. My wonderful friends Slim and Lulu Padro. We stayed down there for a while, and then we drove out to LA.

In the time were out in LA, I got very close to Lee and Glen Perry, who were the owners of the Samadhi Tank Company. For a short while, I helped them install tanks. The Samadhi Tank Company was the first to make the Samadhi Isolation Tanks. And they were wonderful folks. I hung out with them for quite a while. They were helped to design and build Samadhi tanks by Dr. John Lilly.

Then probably around the end of April, Gene and I drove down to visit one of my mother's brothers, my uncle Frank, Frank O'Neil. We got down there and spent a day with him. That night, Gene and I stayed at my uncle's house, and my uncle had a bad night. Gene woke me up in the middle of the night and said, "Your uncle is having a lot of trouble."

I went into his bedroom, and he was belching. He couldn't stop belching, and he had 5 or 6 empty packages of Tums. He was eating Tums like candy for hours. He just said, "I'm okay, I'm okay. Let's go tomorrow down to Tijuana for a while."

So in the morning, another uncle of mine, my mother's youngest brother George, showed up, and my uncle Frank said, "George will take you down to Tijuana. I want to rest."

So we got back in the late evening from Tijuana. My uncle Frank was still feeling badly, and he insisted that Gene and I go back up to LA and call him in a few days. So we got back to LA where we were staying, and the next day I got a call from my uncle George to say Uncle Frank had actually had the highest level of severe heart attack. He was in the VA and probably wouldn't live very long.

So I went back down to San Diego the next day. A doctor friend of mine actually helped me get into the VA. They weren't going to let anybody in to see him, even family. But I got to sit with my uncle, and he told me about the night before, when he had had his second heart attack. He was a code blue and he was dying, and then he died.

Then he told me—and this is a very, very straight old Irishman—he said, "I'm going to tell you things, Corky, that you're probably never going to believe, but when I died, I floated up over my body, and I watched this entire team of people trying to revive me, shooting me with paddles, electricity, pounding me on my chest. And then all of a sudden, I was back in my body, and they were all relieved."

He sat there and said, "You can't believe this, can you?"

I said, "Frank, this is not hard for me to believe!"

I assured him, "I know what you're talking about."

He said, "I wasn't hallucinating. I saw them all and what they were doing. I told one of them the next day, 'If you pounded on my chest like that and I was okay, I'd pound on your face.'"

The guy was shocked and said, "How'd you know?"

I said, "Because I was floating above the bed!"

So Frank insisted that I go back up to LA. He said, "I'll be okay. I'll be out of here in a couple days."

The next morning my uncle George called again and said, "Your uncle Frank died last night. He had his 3rd heart attack in 3 days. This time they couldn't get him back."

I was sad, and I was somewhat relieved. My uncle and I had had a disagreement when I was 22 years old. My uncle told me that he didn't like anything about my father and hoped I didn't grow up like my father. I took exception to it, and we had quite a falling-out. Then when my mother knew that I was going out to LA, she made me promise that I'd bury the hatchet with her brother. Which I was very, very grateful to do before he passed.

2 days later I was going to take a dip into the Samadhi tank. I had a very powerful, very profound experience. I went into the tank, which was pitch-black. I got into the salt water and got relaxed. I was very calm. All of a sudden, the entire inside of the tank lit up in a luminescent emerald-green color. It was like someone had a bulb in there and had flipped the bulb on. The whole inside of the tank was lit up. I was quite startled. I sat up in the water right away, and then I heard my uncle Frank's voice in my head.

He said to me, "Corky, I have to give you something."

I out loud said, "Frank, Frank, am I hearing you?"

He said, "Of course. Listen to me. This is important. I have something I have to give you that none of my sons wanted from me and you never got from your father."

I was talking to him out loud. I said, "What? What are you talking about?"

He said, "The only thing my sons wanted from me was my money. And they got all that even before I came to LA. But what I needed to give them was my manhood."

He said, "You, on the other hand, were never even offered your father's manhood. He didn't know how to give it to you. Now, I need to pass my manhood on. And I need you to accept now, from me, my manhood."

I can remember feeling almost electrocuted. I just sat bolt upright and felt this surge of energy through my body. And as soon as that happened, he was gone, the light went out, and I was sitting there in this dark, dark place, just awed.

I had never thought of anything related to manhood from my father. Or that men passed on their manhood to their sons if they were men and able to pass it on. So in that experience, I spent 3 days with my uncle. I watched him, essentially, have 3 heart attacks, and then met him 3 days later in a telepathic communication, where he gifted me his manhood.

I can't honestly say how it impacted me. I can't honestly say that there was any huge noticeable difference in my life. But I have no doubt that from that day on, something good had been added to my consciousness.

The Edgar Cayce Movie Project

AFTER THAT TIME IN **LA,** Gene and I went back to Chicago. Shortly after that, in June, I went back to Syracuse, and I drove my own car this time. I went back to Syracuse for another 2-week convocation with Margaret Coble and Dr. Mishra.

This was maybe the 3rd or 4th one that I had attended. It was very, very interesting. My good, long time doctor friend came. I introduced him to Dr. Mishra, and they became good friends. It was the last time I saw Dr. Mishra or Margaret in this lifetime.

After the convocation in June, I went to nearby Skaneateles, NY the lakes outside of Syracuse where Joe and Nancy had a home. I spent a month or so with them. It was always wonderful to be with Joe and Nancy because they truly loved me in ways that I never felt love from people. Way beyond love from friends. In fact, for me, way beyond the love of most of my blood family. I had a wonderful time with them.

I went back to Chicago very briefly, and then in September, I went down to Indianapolis, where I hung out for several months with Johnny, who I had just traveled to Taos with earlier in the year, or the last summer, the summer of '76 (this trip went much smoother than the first trip). I spent several months with Johnny down in Indianapolis, did a lot of stuff, put on a concert, and had a good time.

Then in January '78, I hitchhiked out to Sky High Ranch in Apple Valley in the desert of Southern California. On January 9th I arrived at Sky High, which was owned by Dr. Brugh Joy. Brugh used to be a very famous, very successful Los Angeles internist. A very conscious, aware, and good man, who began having powerful spiritual experiences a couple years prior to that. He had powerful meditation and dreams and experiences with the light. He abruptly one day quit his entire AMA practice and started teaching spiritual healing. And a system came through him, a new system of how to balance and integrate and heal chakras.

So he bought this Sky High ranch, up in the mountains in the desert, and he would have 14- to 17-day workshops. He'd have people come from all over the country. He had published a book (*Joy's Way*) and was very famous. I attended one of his workshops. Of all similar types of gatherings in my life, this was the most impactful.

Everyone would get up at 6:00 a.m. and start meditating. We would go to bed at roughly 10:00 or 11:00 p.m. We would spend the whole day doing spiritual work. Brugh had many types of programs, techniques, methods, meditations, and visualizations to raise a person's consciousness. His whole program was designed around raising the consciousness of every participant and their healing abilities. He had a bunch of little cabins. I had a cabin with a roommate, an older man named Sanford Drucker.

I didn't know anything about Sandy except for that he lived in LA. But he picked my brain a lot, through the whole workshop. He would ask me at night, "What did we just do all day?" So I was sort of mentoring him, while Brugh was mentoring all of us. I had many altered-state experiences during that workshop; he had us doing ceremonies and rituals out in the desert to clear our past and clear our consciousness. Native American ceremonies.

When the 14 days ended, I would say all 30 of us were profoundly affected, probably for the rest of our lives. On the last day, we had breakfast, and then at noon we were dispersing, and my roommate Sandy asked me, "What are you going to do now?"

I had a suitcase, and I had no money. I was broke. I said, "Sandy, I don't know! I only have a suitcase, no money. I'm going to hitch a ride to LA."

He said, "I'm going to LA. Come with me."

He had a brand-new Corvette. It was a couple hours' drive up to LA. In that time, he asked me if I would join his filmmaking company. He actually said, "I've been looking for you for months."

I said, "What do you mean 'looking for me'?"

He said, "In my group, I'm one of 3 producers that have the rights to make a movie about the life story of Edgar Cayce."

And Edgar Cayce, I knew a lot about. I had talked extensively about Cayce during the gathering.

He said, "You know more about Edgar Cayce than any person I've ever met. You've been to Cayce's center in Virginia Beach. I've carefully questioned you over these weeks, and I realized that you're the person that has to fill one of the slots in the film."

I said, "I don't know what I could do. I don't anything about films or filmmaking."

He said, "That's okay, I do."

He said, "What I want you to do is to fulfill 3 roles. First, I want you to be the technical advisor for all special effects for all things happening to Cayce."

I said, "You mean like when Cayce was a young boy and saw an angel?"

He said, "Yes. I need someone who can understand what that might look like and to be able to guide a special effects team to put that on film."

I said, "Okay."

He said, "I also want you to take on the role of being my advisor on all spiritual aspects of the movie. I've watched you for 2 weeks, and other than Brugh, I think you know more about spirituality than anybody at that workshop."

I said, "I've got some interesting background."

He said, "You know the tarot and the I-Ching as well as anyone in the workshop. I want you to do readings on every person involved with the project."

He said, "I'd like you to go back to Bel Air. I live in a 7-bedroom mansion by myself. I want you to move in with me, immediately and become part of the movie project. In the beginning you can work for room and board, and I'll give you a contract to receive part of the profits of the movie."

Well, that was a dream come true at that moment for me. I was looking at standing out on highways trying to hitchhike to LA with no money. That night I moved into Sanford's gigantic home and became part of the Inner Space Films Movie Production Company.

In the ensuing days I met the other 2 producers. One was a wonderful man that I had a very good relationship with, Henry Gellis. He was just a beautiful wonderful soul. And also a woman named Riyn Ross, a real powerhouse and also a good soul.

I became part of the project. We just called it, "The Project."

The first thing that Sanford asked me to do was to engage each person involved with the movie—the producers, lawyers, accountant, everyone—and do a tarot spread with them and do an I-Ching to decide if they were good combinations for the movie. So for the next couple weeks, I did a lot of that. Sat with a lot of people who looked at me and said, "What is this all about? I'm a lawyer/accountant/etc.…."

But we did it, and there was not one person that I found wanting, or not cohesive with this team. I could talk forever about this movie project and the incredible ups and downs that I experienced and observed and the ultimate failure of the producers to find financing. They had made an agreement with Hugh Lynn Cayce, Edgar Cayce's son, at the Cayce Foundation that by June or July of '78 the movie would go into production or the movie rights would revert back to the Cayce Foundation.

I left the project in May because my mom had a heart attack in Chicago, and my meditations told me that she would not be on the planet very long. I left the project and returned to Chicago. Shortly after that, everything fell apart. They didn't get into production on time, and the rights to the movie were surrendered back to the Cayce Foundation. Since that day to my knowledge, no one has ever been given the rights to make that movie.

I'll throw in here that Edgar Cayce had had several secret readings; they were never made public. They were kept private by the Cayce family. In the '20s, and I believe again in the '30s, he did readings on himself related to a movie. The first reading said that a motion picture would be made of his life story and it would alter the consciousness of everyone who ever saw it. That was the presumption of the 3 producers.

Then in the '30s he did another reading specifying what type of people the movie should be turned over to. I won't give that information right now. It was very sad to see this project that looked just terribly exciting not able to get funding.

Basically, the 5 major studios had told Sanford that they would finance the project totally, but they wanted 90% of the profits. But Sanford would never go for that. So the movie never got made, and sadly, it went under.

While I got very, very deep in meditation when I lived in Sanford's home. We would meditate together every morning, and then I would meditate an hour before bed. And often during the day at any interval that there was time. The man who originally wrote the best seller about Edgar Cayce was a man named Jess Stearn. He wrote a book called *The Sleeping Prophet*, which I had read many years earlier. While on this project, I got to meet Jess. At first, he was sort of standoffish to me. I was just some hippie kid, and he was, I won't even go into it, but a Hollywood hotshot in some ways. At one point, Sanford had told Jess that I had had horse dreams. Sanford had heard that at a conversation at the Brugh Joy workshop.

So Jess called me one day and asked me to come to his house. He lived in a beach house in Malibu. I went to his house. I sat down next to his desk in a wooden chair. And he told me, "The chair you're sitting in, Edgar Cayce's spirit would sit in and dictate to me the exact events that I wrote into the screenplay for the movie." Jess had been paid $ 50,000 and interest in the movie to write the screenplay.

I asked Jess, "So why'd you call me? Is it something about the movie?"

He said, "No. Sanford told me you've had horse dreams."

I laughed and said, "Yea, I've had quite a few of them in my life."

He said, "Have you had one lately?"

I said, "I don't think for a couple years."

He said, "Have you ever requested one?"

I said, "No."

He said, "Could you?"

I said, "I don't know."

He said, "Would you request one tonight?"

And I laughed. I said, "You play the horses?"

He said, "Oh yea, I live out at Santa Anita and Hollywood Park."

I said, "Alright Jess, I'll request one tonight."

So that night in my meditation, I threw up in my head—I had never asked for a horse dream—but I asked, "Could I have a horse dream for Jess Stearn?"

I had one dream that night, and in the dream, I walk into my lawyer's office in Chicago. I had an old lawyer friend who was sort of on retainer for me. He was a Greek man, a wonderful man. His name was Strat Maheras. So in the dream I walk in, and he's sitting behind the desk. I say in the dream, "Strat, what are you doing here?"

He says, "What am I doing here? It's your dream." And it ended.

I woke up the next morning, and I couldn't make head or tail of that.

But at that time, I knew that if I was going to get a horse dream, I was going to have to figure that out.

We lived in Bel Air. Our neighbors on 3 sides were Henry Fonda, Red Skeleton, and across the street was Barry Gordy. I decided to borrow Sanford's car and go down to the UCLA campus and get a newspaper and see who was running that day at Santa Anita. I thought, "Maybe there's a horse called lawyer or friend or something."

So I go down. I get the paper and take it back up to Sandy's house. I'm looking through the entries in the sports section for Santa Anita, and there is in the 8th race a horse named Maheras. Spelled exactly as my lawyer's name.

So I got on the phone. It was probably 10:00 a.m. or so. And I said, "Jess, believe it or not I had a horse dream for ya."

He was so excited, he was jumping through the phone. I told him the horse's name, and he said, "It's running today!!"

I said, "Yea, it's in the 8th race."

He said, "I'll come pick you up."

I said, "No, I've got stuff to do."

He said, "No, you want to bet it too, don't ya?"

I said, "Nah. I've got stuff to do, Jess."

I didn't want to tell him I was broke. I had my false pride intact.

So he said, "I'm going out and betting it. I'll bet $200 to win for ya."

I said, "No, no, no, no."

He said, "Come on, if it wins, you've got a heap of money."

I said, "No, don't worry about it, Jess. This was a gift for you."

He said, "I don't understand you, but I'm going to the track."

That evening, he calls up, almost insane. The horse had won and paid 16 or 17 dollars I think. He had gone out and bet $2,000 to win, I think. He had won a small fortune. And he was beside himself on the phone.

"Do another one! Do another one! You've got to do another one!"

I said, "Jess, I'll be leaving to Chicago soon, but I'll ask once more, and that's all. I'll ask." So he said, "Okay, okay."

That night I asked for another horse. And I saw a big neon sign, and the name on the sign was JO Tobin. I looked in the paper, but there was no JO Tobin.

I said, "Jess, I had a dream, but there's no horse running."

He said, "What's its name??!!"

I said, "It's JO Tobin."

He said, "It's running Saturday at Santa Anita!!!"

I said, "Okay."

He asked me later that day if I wanted to play the horse. I told him no, and we never spoke again.

By Friday, Thursday or Friday, I was on the road to Chicago. Later in Chicago, a month later, I was talking to a horse trainer I knew in Chicago. And I said, "Do you know anything about JO Tobin?"

He said, "A couple weeks ago he won the Santa Anita Handicap."

I said, "Was he favored?"

He said, "Yea, he probably paid $4."

I thought, "Poor Jess, he only doubled his money." If I remember right, this horse went on to win maybe 8 or 10 races in a row.

Then right before leaving, maybe 2 nights before leaving to Chicago, I had a meditation. I was very, very deep into it, my mind had gotten very silent, and I was very relaxed. And in my head, almost like a ticker tape, I heard these words. I call them my 17 words. And the voice in my head said,

Spiritual work must be done
In one's self
On one's self
For one's self
By one's self!

Then it was gone. I scrambled to my ledger and wrote those words down. They would later in my life have more impact. I didn't completely understand what they meant at that time.

Mother's Last Days

So I WENT BACK TO CHICAGO AROUND JUNE. I spent a lot of time that summer with my mom. My mom was a die-hard Cub fan. And we would spend time watching Cub games. At one point, in maybe July or August, she asked me if I would talk to her about dying.

I said, "Mom, don't think like that."

She said, "No, Son, I need to know what I'm facing."

She said, "I've never thought about it."

I asked her, "Are you afraid?"

She said, "No, I'm not afraid. I'm ready. This body is worn out, tired out. I've done my life's work. I've raised my 7 kids. That's all I wanted, but I don't know what's going to happen. Do you know anything about that?"

So, I started bringing over books and reading her various information from various people about dying. I read stuff that Gandhi wrote, I read stuff from Elizabeth Kubler Ross, and I read from Edgar Cayce. Almost every other day I would go over and have another chapter or paragraph.

She started to get an idea of what these various pieces of information might mean to her. And then in August one night, she called me up at my house at about midnight. As soon as I heard her voice, I was afraid. I thought she was in trouble; she had never called me that late in my life.

She said, "Son, I need you to come over right away."

I said, "Mom, are you in trouble?"

She said, "No, no, no. Just come over right away."

So I hotfooted over to the senior building that she was in.

She was in her robe; she never let anyone see her in her robe. She had me sit down next to her on her bed and said, "Son, I just woke up from a dream. In the dream I was standing in front of a long staircase, a white staircase winding up into the clouds. I felt I was supposed to climb it. So I climbed."

She said, "I climbed for a long time. It didn't tire me or anything. Then I got to a point where I saw a man standing at the top, and he was waving at me to come forward. I walked a little further and realized it was my father (she had dearly loved her father)."

She said, "I stood there, maybe 20 stairs away from him, and he was beaming and smiling at me and waving his arm at me to come. Then I woke up. I called you right away."

I said, "Mom, that was a phenomenal, tremendous dream."

She said, "Son, will it be like that?"

I said, "Mom, it will probably be exactly like that."

She took a big sigh, a sigh of relief, and hugged me.

She said, "You go home now. I'm fine. I know what I have to know now."

We had talked the week before she passed, and I asked her if I could be there when she passed. And she said, "No, I don't want any of my kids or anyone else there. I want to die on my easy chair that my mother gave me. I'll recline back in my easy chair, and I'll just let go when it's time."

I said, "Mom, let me be there with you."

She said, "No, Son, I can't gamble."

She said, "I'm afraid that you or any of my kids might panic and call paramedics. The nightmare of my life right now would be to have my death interfered with. To have people cart me to a hospital and stick tubes in me or to die in a strange room with strange people around me."

I said, "Mom, I wouldn't panic. I'd be okay."

She said, "I'll think about it."

I said, "Well, how would you tell me?"

She said, "I don't know."

I said, "Okay, Mom. If you think you're going to pass, you just think about me real hard and want me to be there."

She said, "Okay."

So on September 12 in the afternoon, I'm driving down Lincoln Avenue. I'm in the passenger seat. All of a sudden, I was just in a swoon. I was disoriented, and then I like collapsed against the window. I banged my head on the window. My friend was concerned and pulled over into a bus stop. I was sitting up and was kind of groggy.

He said, "What happened?? What happened?? It looked like you fainted."

I said, "Chuck, I don't know what happened."

I think that was the moment that my mom had reached out to me.

Later that night at about 10:00 p.m., I was going over to a girlfriend's house to go out on a date. When I walked in, she said, "Corky, you better call your Uncle John. Here's his number."

I said, "He called here?"

She said, "Call him right now."

I looked at her and said, "My mom."

She said, "Yes, your mom passed."

So I called my uncle John. He was at the hospital where they had taken her. I went down there, and he told me, "I couldn't get your mom on the phone. So I went to her house. She was sitting back reclined in her easy chair with a big smile on her face."

I knew that my mom had successfully investigated and planned her departure from the planet. Lots more could be said about that night and that day, but I'll skip forward to the mass at Holy Name Cathedral on Clark St.

I had another rather powerful experience. I was sitting in the front row. Her brothers were there, and nieces, nephews, and all my sisters were there along with my brother. She had requested that a certain young priest do her mass because he used to come to the senior building, and in her apartment, he would do communion for her. She liked him. So this young fella is up on the pulpit talking about Mary Matson, talking about what a good woman she was, etc.

All of a sudden, I was angry. I was filled with anger. I was thinking to myself, "How dare he be up here to talk to us about a woman that he could know nothing of! I should have been up there. Why didn't I get to—"

At that moment there was a brilliant flash of light. I have to qualify this experience. It was perceived by me only of all the maybe 100 people there. But there was a brilliant flash of light up near the ceiling. I looked up and saw the sky through the roof of the church. I saw Jesus Christ floating down into the church. I had the most powerful tears of joy, most powerful ecstatic crying going on. It just poured out of me. I stared up and watched the figure of Christ float down and land right next to her coffin while this young priest came down out of the pulpit and stood at the other end of the coffin. He did something with holy water. I just sat there with what felt like honey pouring out of my eyes. All of a sudden, I saw my mom's astral body—I guess I would have to say "astral body;" other people might say ghost or soul or spirit—rise up out of the coffin, and Christ took her by the hand. I watched both of them slowly float up through the opening at the top of the church and then out. And then the light ended, just stopped.

Well, by this time, I had my niece Anama, who was sitting next to me, and on the other side, my kid sister—they were putting their arms around me. They were trying to comfort me. I sort of looked around, and everybody in the church was looking at me. I could hear my uncle George down the aisle say, "He's having a nervous breakdown. He's having a nervous breakdown!!"

Nothing more need be said about that day. From that time on to the rest of my days, till this day, there was never one minute about feeling any kind of worry, any kind of remorse, any kind of negative feeling about my mother, her life, our relationship. I knew she was with Christ. It was something shown to me.

I asked people afterward outside, "Did you see a flash of light??"

Nobody saw anything. But I was gifted to see my mother ascending.

After my mom passed, I didn't go into grieving; I don't think I grieved one minute, I celebrated in my heart her ascension. But the loneliness of not having her there, something I never thought about, became a very big reality.

I sort of moped around, didn't know what to do with myself. I decided to go back to the bars. I needed money. I went back to the 2350 pub, where I had worked on and off 20 years prior, when I'd be in Chicago and need money. The owners loved me, and all I had to do was walk in the door, and I had a job instantly.

So I went to the pub, and one of the owners said, "Could you work for me for 6 weeks? I've got 6 bartenders that each need a week of vacation. Can you spell each one of them, so I can give 'em all a week?"

I said, "Sure."

I was actually trapping myself for years without knowing it.

And as '78 turned into '79, it was like a fog for me. Even in my memory, it's hard to pick out specifics. I sort of fell back into being a workaholic. Being a soldier worker. I worked 6 days a week. When the 6-vacation people were done, they told me to please stay. They didn't want me to leave.

As '79 slipped off of the calendar, I was still in a fog. I was still uncertain of where to go or what to do. For many years it was as though my high self, my spirit guides, the universe had supplied me with one option after another. One adventure after another. One place to be, one job to do. All of a sudden, I didn't feel like I belonged where I was at. But I didn't feel I belonged anyplace else. And so '79 just sort of ended like that.

And the feeling I have now is that unbeknownst to me, right then, I was slipping into darkness without having any idea what was in front of me.

Comments on the '70s

I DO WANT TO EXPLAIN IN A LITTLE MORE DETAIL a few of the mind-sets that I went through about the use of psychedelics. I had an early agreement with Joe Martins, my partner and friend, to learn and experience all we could from every path and way that we encountered but to never stop our quest and our search. In essence to keep climbing the ladder to a place we knew not where. It is still much of my way to this day and has served me well.

After Joe and I began our psychedelic excursions and explorations, I suppose one of my main motivations and drives, after my first trip, was to understand the unknown. To push past the fears of my childhood and my life to that point and overcome the walls of worry and anxiety that I had habitually lived with and built around me. This drive, this search, this desire centered on me moving inward, not outward. I had no wants or needs to climb the highest mountains or delve the deepest oceans outside of myself. But I do very powerfully now and I did very powerfully then desire to move inward and upward and sometimes downward into my own inner worlds and realities. Though I was to seek out people and places in my life to help me understand the mysteries inside, the desire to know the world and physical plane outside never really appealed to me as did the understanding of myself and my other selves by myself.

Though I must admit that in the early '70s and late '60s, I did not clearly comprehend nor plan my life's path in the way I have written above. At these times, it was more of a yearning, a subconscious prompting to follow the path I chose at the time. That, in retrospect, I can now see more clearly and define now and explain now with more clarity.

There was a period in the '70s where I abandoned psychedelics to seek other paths. After much experimentation with mushrooms, peyote, DMT. The need to attain higher altered states by long-accepted spiritual methods and work, including meditation, yoga, fasting, chanting, fasting, nature experiences, etc. That became the path and the reality that I chose later in the '70s and after that.

I want to say a few words about Timothy Leary and Richard Alpert, or Baba Ram Dass. I, as stated in the book, met both of these men at different times. I want to give just a short synopsis of my feelings about them personally. First of all, I'll say that the common denominator for both of these men is that they were both intellectual powerhouses; they both were tremendously energetic, incredibly wise, and they both had tremendous senses of humor. They were both a joy to be in the presence of. One of the ways that they were quite different, in my humble opinion, is that Tim was an intellectual genius of psychedelic science. He related his psychedelic experiences into psychedelic knowledge, verbiage, explanations, and understandings. Tim was an incredibly fast mind and a fast thinker and had little patience for any kind of low-level or surface verbiage or talk of any kind. He was a very serious man who always wanted to talk about higher consciousness—raising the consciousness of the whole planet and raising higher consciousness out into the cosmos.

Baba Ram Dass, on the other hand, was an intellectual spiritual genius, related to the psychedelics and beyond. He was really a spiritual powerhouse who had vast knowledge and understanding of the many paths of Buddhism, yoga, as well as many other religious and spiritual paths. He understood all the different schools. He was a brilliant spiritual teacher. When he was working with people, he had infinite patience. He could listen to any person's questions and stories and dissect them and replay them back in profound spiritual teachings. I never saw these 2 men together; they never spoke of each other in my presence, but they were both incredibly powerful spiritual men—a spiritual psychedelic master and a scientific psychedelic master. In their own ways they used psychedelics and interpreted their own experiences scientifically or spiritually, but with profound understanding and profound insight. They were wonderful, wonderful teachers.

I stayed remotely connected with Tim right to his final days. I e-mailed his wife in the last days of his life, and she made it clear that he was ready to let go and leave the Earth plane. He was a joyous, powerful genius. And Ram Dass, I haven't seen him for 20 years. I used to talk to him when he moved out to Hawaii.

But both of these men as leaders in the psychedelic movement were so clean in their purpose, their intentionality. They were both spiritual, intellectual powerhouses, and both were wonderful friends.

I'd like to add on to that some of my own personal feelings about psychedelics. In general, I believe in the '60s, our government made a wrong turn and a wrong decision in banning, outlawing, and creating fear and loathing in the public's mind about psychedelics. I would just like to say that an intellectual understanding of mind-altering substances, be they natural and grown worldwide by Mother Earth, or synthesized in a laboratory, a general intellectual understanding does not make one an authority or give more than intellectual substance. Only by experimentation and exploration does one become knowledgeable of the said substances, both intellectually and experientially. In my opinion, this is irrefutable logic.

Ralph "Swede" Matson (Corky's Father *late 1930s) left*.
Mary Matson (Corky's Mother *early 1940*s) *right*.

Left to right - Mike Matson (Corky's brother) and Corky. *1966*

Corky's longtime friend, Joe Martins. *1967*

Dr. Mishra and Margaret Coble. *1967*

Left to right (standing) - **Corky, Bob and Carol with others at Woodstock.** *1968*

Corky. *1970*

Left to right - **Mabel Schaefer (Corky's Grandmother), Corky and Chloe (Corky's Great Aunt).** *Mid 1970s*

The Wang Family:
Left to right - Susie, Sharon, Woody, Pa, Sheila,
and Sandy at Sheila's wedding. *1979*

Corky and Sharon at midnight on their wedding day. *1999*

Corky and Nancy on their Valentine's Day wedding. *2018*

Left to right - Corky's nephew John Kessenich, Jasmin Iskandar (John's Partner), Nancy and Corky. *2018*

'80s

Back to the Bars

So, AS I ENTER THE DECADE OF THE '80s, I'm back in Chicago, back in the bar business, working at the 2350 Pub. Back on old streets, old turf, with old friends, old acquaintances, old patterns, old influences. After what was 10 to 15 years of pretty exciting movement through my life on an almost continuous basis, I was back in the bar business. I guess I would have to describe 1980–1981 as sort of falling into old routines and patterns of workaholic mentality. I was very good at what I did in the bar business. In fact, when I finally ended my stay at this 2350 Pub, I was talking to one of the owners, and I said, "I started by committing to you for 6 weeks, and now it's been many years, but I have to leave. It's time to move on."

He said to me, "Oh, it's been fine with me. I got a bar manager all that time for the price of a bartender."

And we laughed. So what happened, especially in '80–'81, was 6 days of between 8, 10, or 12 hours a day of working in a very popular, very busy, very fast-paced restaurant and pub in a very busy nightclub/restaurant area of Lincoln Avenue in Chicago. I just threw myself into it. I didn't have too many outside interests because the bar work took up most of my days, but I fell back into a pattern of playing the horses a lot, gambling with bookies— all of that was part of the pub atmosphere that I worked in. If I worked a day shift, I might go to the harness track at night and then go home and sleep and get up and start all over. If I worked night shift, I'd go home, get up, maybe go out to the racetrack, Arlington or Sportsman's, during the day. It was a considerably automatic-type lifestyle for me. I fell into it. I never really abandoned at any time my spiritual quest. I still read books. I still did some meditating, but mostly I fell out of consciously, with awareness, every day doing spiritual work, and I fell into consciously, every day doing bar work and gambling.

I'll briefly say at this point a little bit about my romantic life, which isn't the focal point of this book in any way, but in those years I had significant others. I never played around too much. When I was a young man, I would go for casual relationships, casual sex. The older I got, the more discriminative I got, and I was less interested in anything related to conquest. I had in these years a number of very sweet, very loving relationships with very good women. I've always felt my whole life I was really blessed with being able to find compatible good friends, good lovers. During this period I had a couple girlfriends that were very near and dear to me who, like me, had very busy lifestyles of their own, or busy careers, so we were able to fit together our time and our relationships without either one of us needing any kind of serious commitment. So this was my pattern during the early '80s into late '82, early '83.

Different Results

RELATED TO MY EARLIER GAMBLING AND HORSE STUFF, as time went on, either the symbology or dreams related to horses, or actual events outside in waking time got harder and harder to interpret. It was like I was being told, "You had an easy ride in the beginning but now you've gotta work. You've really gotta work hard to figure things out. And if you work hard, the abundance will still be there; if you don't, you won't have the abundance." So at one point, the tried and true perfect dream events took a turn and they began not working. I can't remember exactly when it started, but all of a sudden, there was something that in a dream led me to a horse and I went out and bet it and it didn't win. And I was shocked, I didn't know how to interpret that. I was like, "Wait a minute, what just happened here."

Another dream, I wouldn't quite get the numbers right. I'd have a good dream and the horses would run at the top, but in the wrong order, and I'd lose. And then I had an event that in many ways ended the free ride of dreams that were always true and profitable. I had a dream once of seeing a harness horse win. And the horse's name was "Ramblin Shorty." And in my dream, Ramblin Shorty was the #8 horse. And I was standing watching the horses coming into the beginning of the race, down into the stretch and I looked up at the tote board and Rambling Shorty was like 39:1. And in the dream, the horse ran last all the way around and then in the stretch ran by the field and paid a giant longshot price. So I looked the next morning and out at Hawthorne Park, at the harness track, in the eighth hole, was Ramblin Shorty. And I said, "Oh! Here's a good one, here's a payoff." I didn't have a lot of money, so I think I bet 50 to win and place on it.

I was standing in the area of the fence that I was at in the dream and the horses were coming down the stretch to start the race. And I looked up at the tote board and Ramblin Shorty was 18 to 1, but in the dream, he was 39:1 and I went, "Uh Oh!"

Well Ramblin Shorty ran last all the way around for the entire race. And I stood there and I could not believe that the dream was so clear and that I was a loser. I threw my tickets on the ground and left.

At that point I felt like, "Maybe I'm making mistakes in my life. Maybe I'm not thinking positive, maybe I'm not helping enough people, maybe I'm hurting myself too much with negativity, behavior and thoughts." I was trying to figure out why I would be tricked by a dream. I didn't get an answer.

Anyways, about a whole year later, I'm at the same track, I've already made a bet on some horse, I'm standing in the same place that I used to like to be, the horses are coming around the turn and the announcer says, "And the last into position is Ramblin Shorty!" And my head just snapped back. I grabbed my program and looked at it. The number eight horse was Ramblin Shorty. My heart was literally pounding, I looked up on the tote board, 39:1. Rambling Shorty ran last the whole race until the stretch, circled the field, blew by the field and paid $84 to win. So one year later, the dream that I had a year earlier comes true exactly as I'd dreamt it. I realized at that point that there is some disconnect now with my consciousness and my higher consciousness.

I pretty much felt that it was my lifestyle. I was not doing a lot of spiritual work. I was doing a lot of abusive bar behavior and I just realized, "You've got to step back because your lifestyle is interfering with your cosmic connection in such a way as to become a potentially losing situation."

Even after that I didn't have a dream for a long time. Those were years that I wasn't especially productive or creative or living a good spiritual life. And all of my earlier easy gifts sort of ran out. And then I entered into a quagmire of not being able to see clear symbology. Not being able to have good dreams coinciding with being destructive, eating bad food, drinking too much. Sort of losing my way, so to speak. So even though the gifts that were given to me were actually very cosmic, very pure, very clean, they didn't go on automatically forever and came to somewhat of an abrupt halt as I entered a period of my life of more self-destructive behavior and less conscious awareness.

Down into Darkness ✕

AFTER THIS TIME, my life took a turn into what I can only best describe as darkness. Much of my early childhood was very dark and my teenage years I consider to be very dark. Then I broke loose in my early 20s and then sought after the light, people who knew about light, teachers, pathways, books. I was engrossed with the desire for spiritual knowledge, teaching, experience. In the latter part of '83, it was the elements of the street that I was working on; the more negative elements, the more I connected with them. Though I had in my lifetime experimented with and experienced many street drugs, many psychedelics, and a lot of alcohol in my early Rush St. days, at this point I just sort of slid into drinking a lot and then started doing cocaine. This was a period of my life that, as I look back and have looked back at many times, I'm sort of in awe; it was as though I let go of the steering wheel, as though I just stopped my vigilance, my conscious aware- ness, and I went down this pathway forming new "friendships" with people who were deeper into drug addiction and alcohol addiction than I had ever experienced. And I just went willingly. I went not from any coercion from outside or any need from inside; I just sort of went unconscious and let go of the reins. By '84, I was doing serious amounts of alcohol and cocaine. I was playing with people who were very addicted; they called themselves junkies. I maintained my semblance, my working consciousness. I was able to do that in the bar as I became more involved with addiction than I ever had in my life.

I've often wondered, in looking back at those years, how the transition from a life focused on and many times filled with light or very positive, pow- erful, strong feelings had degenerated into what, by the end of 1984, was addiction, ignorance, and darkness. At one point, in 1984, I made a decision to quit the bar. I had a pretty good amount of money saved. For the first time in my life I had money saved, I had a good vehicle that I drove, and I had a lot of things that I collected. I decided to get into this cocaine addic- tion with my new friends to the point that I was not able to function in the bar business at my normal level of functioning. I could see on people's faces I worked with, with the owners, they were all seeing what was happening to me, and I decided to vacate the bar business. When I did that, I started daily use of cocaine that I had never experienced before. I began to run through my money. I was very frugal and very careful with spending my money. I was never into partying with cocaine. I sat with people who were trapped in addiction. Those people don't go out and snort lines in bathrooms of nightclubs; those are casual players. I played with people. We sat behind locked doors and imbibed in our addiction and somewhat inane, useless repertoire dialogues. It was so unlike how I lived my life, and yet I was in it, and I was continuously going deeper.

So I was careful with my money. There were a lot of people in this crowd that I was in that would gladly share their stash with me if I didn't have anything on hand just to have me around. I was very well liked in this crowd of very unhappy, very hurt people. I seemed to be able to handle the dark side of it better than most of the people around with me. If I would walk into a room of 4 or 5 of these addicted junkies (I was one too), I would lift them up. They would be happy to see me. I always had more of a positive influence than a negative influence. So there were a lot of times when I would be able to spend a whole night with a group of people, and just to have me around, they would be glad to pay for my habit.

But before long, my good savings I had was gone, and then I got to a point that I realized the only way I could continue would be to sell my vehicle. I had a very good vehicle, and I put it out in the paper and sold it in 1 day for $5,000. And then I was back for another long run into 1985 now. Then when that money went, I started selling off everything I had. I sold a tremendous power saw for which maybe I paid $500 in Colorado and I sold it for $100. I was liquidating everything around me. And while all that happened in my life, I stayed clear of my old friends, my serious friends. I sort of vacated all of the healthy relationships I had in Chicago, which was quite an amount of good, loving friendships. I vacated any communication with those people. I stopped going out with any of my girlfriends or lovers. I was becoming a hermit, a junkie hermit. While I was in that darkness, I wasn't able to see how I was spiraling down or to put the brakes on it until I got to a point when I sold everything I could. Then what I started doing was going to people who cared about me and borrowing money. I just started borrowing money left and right from anybody who would give it to me, $20, $50, $100, $500, to keep my habit going.

Then after the summer of '85, the day came when there was no one else I could borrow money from. The word had gone out on Lincoln Avenue, and my friends, everybody knew what was happening to me. Some people tried to pull me out of this.

I have to backtrack here and tell the actual exact time when this addiction to cocaine started. I was still working at the restaurant. I was walking down Lincoln Avenue one day, and I saw a man who was a good friend. We were not really that close, but we always had a warm handshake and a hug for each other. He was a friend of friends. We were always very, very respectful and sort of honored each other. I saw this man walking down the street, and he looked terrible to me. I could sense that he was in a terrible, terrible place. I caught up with him and asked him what was going on, and he brushed me off. He had never done that. He brushed me off and said, "Nothing, just leave me alone."

I trailed him down the street, pleading with him, "There is something wrong. I know there is something wrong. You gotta tell me." So after a couple blocks, in annoyance, he turned around and told me he was going to Lincoln Park to commit suicide.

He told me he had been to a doctor that day who examined his throat, told him he had throat cancer, and had taken tests to confirm it, and was going to tell him the next day. But she was sure he had throat cancer. He told me, "I can't go through it. I won't go through it. I won't put my mother through it. I'm going to go to Lincoln Park, rent a boat, go out in the water, and then go over the side."

I just grabbed hold of him, and I said, "Wait a minute. Wait a minute. You aren't going to do anything like that." I just muscled him and told him, "This is crazy. You don't even know for sure."

He said, "Oh no, I know she's right."

I said, "You don't know. I'm not leaving you. If you are going to Lincoln Park, I'm going with you. If you are going out in the water, I'm going with you."

We kept walking and talking, and finally he said, "Okay, maybe you are right. I'll wait until tomorrow until I see the doctor."

I told him, "I'm not leaving you. I'm staying with you."

He said, "No. I'll go home right now."

I said, "I don't trust you. I don't believe you. I'll just stay with you. Let me come to your house, and I'll sleep on your couch."

He said, "No, I do things at home that I don't want you involved with." And I said, "What are you doing at home that I can't be involved with?" He said, "I have a habit, and I don't want you to see what I'm doing."

I said, "That is BS. I'm staying with you."

He said, "I wouldn't feel comfortable having you there watching me unless you were doing it."

I said, "What the hell are you talking about?"

He said, "I do cocaine."

I had done cocaine before recreationally, you know, at parties and things. I said, "So what, I'll do it. I've got a pocketful of money."

So I actually went home with this man, 12:30 in the morning and did cocaine all night with him. And by 7 in the morning, he went to bed, and I left. When I drove away, I had an inkling that I had just stepped over a boundary, had just stepped over a line, but I didn't think anything about it. I went home and slept for a while.

At 5 in the evening I went back to his house. He hugged me, and he said, "I'm so glad. You are right. The doctor said that from smoking I had burnt my vocal cords, but there was no cancer." He was just so happy, and I was so happy. Then we celebrated. He brought out a whole bag of cocaine and said, "Come on, let's do some lines." That's how it started; that's how the serious level of surrendering my consciousness, my body, my health, my awareness started, and then it just cascaded from there.

Fast forwarding back to the end of 1985, I got to a point, one day in October, where I was desperate, and I thought in my mind, "The only way I can continue my addiction is, I've got to go get myself a pistol and start robbing stores or gas stations." When I thought those thoughts, for the first time in the last 2 or more years, I realized the trouble I was in. For the first time I saw: "Oh my God. I'm thinking of taking things away from people, and maybe even harming people to keep my addiction going." I started *trying* to quit, and now there were only a few places left that there was enough abundance of cocaine where people would give me freebies.

I was broke. I had nothing. There was a particular day in November, and it was a day that a friend of mine needed medication (he was one of the junkie friends of mine). He needed medication desperately, and he asked me to go to a drugstore nearby to buy his medication. He gave me $100 to cover it. I went into this drugstore, went back to this pharmacy which was over in the corner, and there was an old Pakistani or Indian woman in front of me. She was talking to the pharmacist. He said, "Okay, I'll go in the back. It will take me 10 to 15 minutes." Then he told her what it would cost, and he turned and went in the back. She laid out on the counter 5- $100 bills, and then she walked away over to a magazine rack and started going through magazines.

I stood there and looked at that money. The pharmacist was completely out of sight, the woman was 30 to 40 feet away with her back to me, there were no customers near me, and I thought, "That money is mine. That money is mine." I stood there, and something in my consciousness said, "You can't do it. If you do it, either this woman won't get her medications or that pharmacist will have to…" And I wrestled—it was like a war going on inside of me, between my middle self and my low self, between my consciousness and my addiction, between my desire to take that money and run for the door and my conscience feeling not to put other people in a terrible position.

While I'm getting ready to grab the money, all of a sudden, the woman turns and walks back to the counter. I look up and see the pharmacist is walking into the room, and I just let go of it. He had her prescription, he took the money, they did their transaction, she left, and he asked me what I wanted. I gave him the information on my friend's meds. He went and got them. He gave them to me, and I headed for the door.

As I got to the door, over on a platform just to the left of the door, I saw a young security guard, a young black man, and he was frightened to death. He had his hand on his gun and was staring at me, and I could see his hand was shaking; his whole body was shaking. I walked past him and out the door, and as I walked out the door, all of a sudden in my mind's eye, I saw myself running out the door, and this kid coming out, pointing the gun, and shooting me in the back of the head. I saw myself go face down on the sidewalk and my hat rolling down the curb and into a puddle of water. It was a perfectly clear inner vision I stood out in the street. I must have stood there frozen for 10 minutes. It was so clear. There was no question, no doubt, I had just literally, not figuratively, but actually I had ducked a bullet and avoided a catastrophe.

I went on to my friend's house and gave him his meds. I hung out there all afternoon and in the evening. Toward the later part of the evening there was a knock on his door. He opened the door, and this big Irishman burst by him and walked into the living room where I was sitting against the opposite wall. This was, at that time, the only person on the planet that I considered an enemy. He was the only person in my life that I had near hatred for. I won't say I hated him, but I knew who he was and knew what he did with people's lives. This was a very bad man. When he stormed in, he was all hyped up and crazed, and he knew from prior verbal encounters we had had what I felt about him.

My friend, whose house it was, closed the front door and got back quickly between us because he knew our history. This Irishman said some very ugly things pointed at me. And I came up off the couch. I was going for him.

As I advanced on him very quickly, my friend got between us and forcibly pushed me back to the couch and said, "Corky, sit down. I'll get rid of him, just sit down." We turned, and this guy was standing with a gun in his hand. He had a gun in his waistband, and he pulled it and had it pointed at me. My friend got in between the line of fire and said, "You can't do this. You can't do this; this is my house." He started pushing the man, oblivious to having a gun pointed at him, and he literally pushed the guy back to the doorway. They talked for a minute or so; then he opened the door, and the guy left.

I was in a state of mind that I had never been in in my life. It was as though a different reality had taken over my life. It was as though I didn't even know who I was or what was happening. I can't even describe the impact of the full awareness that in a day's time, I had just almost lost my life 2 times to violence. My buddy sat down with me and said, "You are crazy. You should know he always packs. He's always carrying. What were you thinking of? What you were going to go after him for?" I didn't know how to answer. I was deflated. I was emotionally just wiped out, destroyed. I just sat there like a lump.

There was another knock on the door, and he went and let in a woman friend of ours, a very wonderful, good friend of ours. My friend told her at the door what had just happened, and she came over and tried to talk to me. I don't even remember what was happening. They started doing lines. I don't even think I did any. I didn't want any. I was in a fog, in a daze. Then at one point she said, "Corky, come on upstairs, go to Billy's bedroom and go to sleep." She took me up into this bedroom, I got in bed, she sat by me in the bed for a while, and she said these words. I don't know how she could have known to say them, but she said, "Think of some wonderful place that you have been in the water. Think of the most wonderful water you have ever been in, and just think about that place and go to sleep." She got up and left. I immediately flashed down to one time in the '60s I was in Key West, FL. I went out in the Caribbean in the afternoon, put my legs in a full lotus—which made it impossible to sink, and lay for 2 to 3 hours just bobbing up and down in the warm water. It was like being in heaven. I started thinking about that and went to sleep. When I awoke…

Re-Rebirth

THESE ARE DIRECT WORDS FROM MY JOURNAL I wrote the next morning, November 16th.

The Re-rebirth

On the morning of 11-15-85, after 2 close encounters with death and deep decrees of the day before, the following experience happened. After my lady friend suggested at 3 AM that morning that I lay down and clear my mind and think of blue water, I fell into deep sleep. At exactly 6:08 AM I awoke. I looked at the clock and had an urgent need to meditate in the next room. I got up and went into the next room naked and sat down in meditation. In a matter of moments, tears began flowing freely and I can only say that the spirit of the Holy Ghost descended upon me. For the next 30-40 minutes, I cried deeply and freely. In that time, I was made aware, I was shown internally that I am a blessed being, that I am well thought of by my gods and guides. I knew of the tremendous love and concern that many beings have for me. I made a verbal declaration to unite myself with Christ and truth. I felt my soul being cleansed and purified. I declared at one point out loud,

"Woe be it unto any motherfucker that crosses my path and tries to force me into untruth and lies."

Then after a while, being concerned with disturbing the others in the house, I got up and went to the bathroom, still crying. I looked at the mirror and felt strong and straight. Then my lady friend came in and with worry and concern, she threw a blanket around me. In an attempt to relieve her concern, I quelled the tears and the release, and I said to her with gut wrenching truth, "This man has just gotten straight with his soul."

That was, in my understanding of my life, a spiritual intervention of high order. What happened to me for the rest of that day was I felt alive and full of light. I felt free. I had just actually been freed of my cocaine addiction and the years of spiraling down into darkness. I walked almost all day. I walked through the streets of the north side of Chicago. I was in an altered state that I can only describe as blissful, ecstatic, and joyous. I was in such a state of peace of mind and peace in my soul and peace in my consciousness. I had somehow for years allowed myself to go deeper into darkness, and then it almost culminated into my untimely and undignified death in this life. But I got through those final challenges. I slept a period of hours, and I woke up to my release from darkness. I woke up to maybe one of the most powerful experiences of my life, in the regard that the forces that came through me (the forces that I have called the Holy Ghost, I have later thought of as the Holy Spirit or my High Self) were so powerful that they cleansed every cell and every atom, molecule, and electron of my consciousness. That day, as the bliss carried on, I was amazed that my life meant enough to intervene and pull me out of darkness, when in truth in those days, I felt essentially that I had wasted my whole life. I had worried that I had neutralized or blown everything that I had ever accomplished or experienced. I was clearly shown that none of that was the truth.

I didn't fully understand the ramifications as much as I do today of what that event and those years were about. It was almost comical, as if I had had so many years of wonderful loving experience that I manifested an imbalance and had to go into this period of time in the early '80s. It wasn't actually that I had to. It was what I had manifested in my unconscious and my conscious mind. Then when the intervention came and pulled me out of it, I walked that day in a state of altered grace. I literally felt that I was in a state of grace. I won't go into much detail, but the next day when I awoke, I was in the same place. It was no different. I more or less expected to wake up with like a hangover from the events of the prior day. But when I woke up, I was in the same state. Everything looked different; everything was lighter and brighter. These were very dark and gloomy days in Chicago, but as I headed out that day, I had no purpose, I had no intent. I had no plan; I had no idea. I was walking as though I was walking on clouds. I had such peace of mind that I had little or no thought coming through my mind. I didn't think, "Go here," or "Go there," or, "Go see this person." None of that was even in my consciousness. I was in a virtual perpetual experience of the grace that now followed me into a second day.

As I walked down Lincoln Avenue, at one point, probably early afternoon, I went into the restaurant that I had worked at for all those years. One of the waitresses that I knew quite well for years came up to me, and I could see in her face a look of amazement. She was in awe of whatever I looked like. Whatever she was looking at, she looked dumbstruck. She came over to me and very gently put her hands on my arm and said, "Corky, are you alright? Are you alright? What happened?"

I don't even remember answering her. I think I mumbled that I was okay. And she said, "Can I get you anything?"

I realized that I had a ravishing thirst. And I said, "Yea, could you get me a pint of ice water?"

I had rarely drunk a pint of ice water in my life.

She said, "You don't drink ice water. Do you want a Coke? You want a pint of Coke?"

I said, "No. I want an ice water."

She brought it to me, and I drank it in one drink. And she stood there with the amazed look on her face.

I handed the glass back to her and said, "Another one!"

She went back and got another one, and I drank almost all of it instantly again.

I handed it back to her again and said, "Fill it."

She came back with a 3rd and said, "You look like something happened to you."

I said, "I can't talk about anything right now."

I sat down at a booth in there. She said, "Can I bring you a bowl of soup?"

I said, "I have no money."

She said, "Oh, don't worry about money. I'll get you some soup!"

She went away and came back with a big bowl of chicken soup and a loaf of bread. I ate ravenously although I had no hunger. I drank the water that she gave me, I thanked her, and I left. This became a pattern. For the next, at least 2 whole weeks—in my memory I can't exactly say how long, but between 2 and 4 weeks—this went on. For this time, I walked the streets of Chicago. I had a place to sleep. I slept, got up, put on my clothes, and walked.

Not thinking, not planning, not any conscious decision making about what to do or what I should get involved with. I just walked and marveled at what I saw. At people, at plants, at the sky. It was almost every day gray and gloomy. I remember walking into one restaurant, and a waitress there who knew me came up to me and said, "Aren't these dark and gloomy days?"

And I said something to her like, "Despite the dark and gloom inside, the sun is shining brightly in this man's heart."

That is almost the best way I can describe the period for 2 to 4 weeks after I had my Re-Rebirth, my visit from the Holy Ghost or Holy Spirit. My divine intervention that was—unlike the near truck-accident, when my truck's front end melted apart—an intervention before the fact. This intervention, I had to go through that day and those dangerous situations and survive on my own before I was delivered from the darkness that I had fallen into.

In this 2- to 4-week-period of being in grace and bliss, there was another thing I did every day. Pretty much from the time I got out of bed in the morning, I would pretty much just walk the streets. But when nightfall would approach, even the very first day, I would go to one of the houses that I knew my prior friends and addicts would be doing what they did every night, what I had done every night with them for years. I would go in and sit with these guys and not do any cocaine. They would offer it to me, and I would say, "No, I don't do that anymore."

I would sit with them and talk with them. I would listen to them. I would exchange. I would be back into the environment and with the exact people doing the drugs that had almost swallowed up my life, only, I was completely impervious to the entire environment. There was no temptation; there was no danger. There was no chance on any level that, for any reason, I was going to involve my body with anymore cocaine. Some of these people had become very dear to me. Even in our distorted and crippled and twisted mind-sets and behavior, my empathy was still alive, my caring was still alive. Now that I was free from this addiction, I felt it was almost messianic. If I were talking to shrinks at that point, they would have told me I had a messiah complex and I was trying to share my revelation. Well, I didn't do that quite that way, but I did sit with them and talk spiritual talk. Not biblical talk. I didn't proselytize. I didn't try to guilt trip. I didn't try to, in any way, make them feel bad. It was more like witnessing or testifying to the light. I found myself, in those days, in those nights, often repeating the same statement.

I used to say, "I have traded meditation for masturbation, and I have traded white light for white powder." I had become free of those illusions, and I would never walk that path again. Some people understood what I was saying, many of them didn't. Some actually started becoming ill-at-ease when I would come into their rooms. Some of them became very insistent that I would do the drug and would tell me that they weren't comfortable having me around without doing the drug.

But for the period that I was able to do it, I would go to a different one of these places each night. If there was no one doing anything, I would just leave. If there were 2 or more doing drugs, I would sit, and sometimes I would be silent for hours. I would just be like a mirror. I don't feel in those times that I ever judged any of them. I had incredible compassion in my heart for their plights. That ended at one point. I'm not sure if it coincided with my whole blissful experience ending, but at one point, I had sort of worn out my welcome. I realized that I had done what I could do. I know for a fact that at least 2 or 3 of these men, possibly because of my influence, had gotten strong enough to kick the habit and get out of that environment by themselves.

That was pretty much what I did day and night during my periods of bliss. I do know that there was one common denominator with the cocaine junkies I was with, or my bar friends, or my acquaintances and friends that I would meet in those days. The common denominator that none of them talked about, but I was very aware that none of them could look me in the eyes for more than a few seconds without diverting their gaze. I, on the other hand, would be fixated on looking everybody in the eyes. I've been in the situation in my life where I looked at people who were in, what I consider, spiritual rapture, and there would be so much light in their eyes that I would divert my attention or my vision from looking in their eyes. This happened to me every day, whether I was walking the streets, or at night if I was sitting with some of my lost friends. Nobody would look me in the eyes for very long. So that began a change wherein, when the end of this bliss came, I don't remember it real clearly, but I remember waking up one morning and feeling "normal." I remember instantly knowing "It's done. This period of grace, of walking in grace, is done."

Back to Life

I REALIZED THAT MORNING that it was time to go back to living and time to put my feet back on a spiritual path. Start cleaning up the mess and debris that I had left all around the north side of Chicago. I struggled for quite a while. I had a friend who had watched me go through the whole routine. And he offered to let me stay at his house with him. I gratefully agreed. I had no car, no money, and no job. I had essentially little to nothing, and I didn't know exactly what to do.

He said, "Go back to the 2350 Pub. They'll take you back in a heartbeat."

But I knew I couldn't go backward. I stayed with him for months, much of the time staying home all day. He was a salesman. When he came home, he would take me out and buy me dinner. I was reading. This man had a fairly good-sized spiritual library. He was a devotee of Rudolf Steiner. And so, I was reading deep spiritual material again for the first time in years. And I was slowly getting some sort of strength back in my body. The addiction period had absolutely devastated my body. At one point in the winter of '86, I was a year free from cocaine. I had picked up a little bit of money here and there doing odd things. I actually did a few massages on a few people. I was starting to get myself together. Then that winter I got very sick with what looked like a flu. But it was much more ravaging than a flu. It went on the whole winter. I stayed in this poorly-heated apartment on the floor. My friend would come home in the evening and bring me food.

This continued all winter. In the spring, I was in such bad shape, I was having some of my friends tell me things like they were giving my name to spiritual prayer groups. I realized that I was in my 40s, but my friends thought that I was dying. I didn't feel I was anywhere near death or anywhere near the danger of death, but I was very sick and very weak. Out of nowhere one day, one of my most beloved friends in Chicago, Bob Zagone—whom I had known from high school and then we had just fused ourselves together in friendship—came to my place and said, "Do you have a bag and some clothes?"

I said, "I have a little bag with a few clothes."

He said, "Get it and come out to my car. I'm taking you somewhere."

I said, "Where are you taking me?"

He said, "Don't ask any questions, just come with me."

I had nothing to lose. I could hardly walk or stand. I was sick as a dog. I put my meager things together in this little gym bag I had and got in his car, and we were off for Michigan.

4 or 5 hours later, we pulled into a little town called Coldwater. He told me on the way, "I'm taking you to an Ann Wigmore wheatgrass center." I had heard of Ann Wigmore, and I knew all about her raw food diet and drinking wheatgrass, and I knew it was a cleansing, healing place. I just easily surrendered to that.

I said, "This must cost money."

He said, "Yea, it costs a lot of money."

I said, "Well, I don't have any money, Bob. I don't have anything."

He said, "You don't have to worry. I've arranged for us to stay."

I believe it was for 2 weeks—10 days or 2 weeks.

He said, "I've already talked to the owner. I've taken care of our stay."

They welcomed me, in the sick, decrepit condition I was in. The people who ran the place were good, loving, kindhearted people. From day 1 they started filling my body with good, live food and green drinks and juices. I drank this awful-tasting wheatgrass juice all day. Within 2 or 3 days, I felt stronger than I had been since my rebirth experience. In a week's time, I was out taking mile walks down these country roads. By the time our stay came to an end, they had so revitalized me, I was back on my feet, I felt strong again, and I thanked everybody. The couple who ran the place, Ken and Jeannete, gave me a big bottle of green capsules. They said, "Start taking these every day, take 6 or 8 a day."

My friend Bob dropped me back at my salesman buddy's house in Chicago. I started, in my mind, trying to put together a game plan. Trying to figure out what I was going to do. I knew I couldn't make money the way I was used to. I ate these 6 or 8 capsules from this big bottle every day. They seemed to give me a lot of energy and a lot of enthusiasm.

I got near the end of this bottle in about a month's time. When the bottle was empty, I threw it in a garbage can and thought that was great, whatever those things were. The next day when I didn't take them, I felt less energy. The day after I felt much less energy. I realized there was something in that stuff.

I called my friend Bob back. I said, "I gotta get more of that stuff."

He said, "Well, we'll have to go out to Denver."

I said, "To Denver?"

He said, "Yea, the people who ran the Wigmore center, they left a few weeks ago, left Michigan and moved to Denver."

I said, "What? How? There's got to be another way to get it."

He said, "What you were eating is blue-green algae, and it's not sold in health-food stores. It's only sold by multilevel marketing."

I didn't know what that was.

He said, "You have to become a distributor and sign a paper to be able to buy it from the company directly at wholesale price. So if you want to eat more of that, you literally need to become a distributor."

I said, "Bob, I think I need that stuff desperately."

He laughed. He said, "What are you doing tomorrow?"

I said, "I'm not doing anything. I just sit home and read."

He said, "I'll be over to pick you up at 10:00 a.m."

He came over, I got in his car, and we got on the expressway.

I said, "Where are we going?"

He said, "We're going to Denver."

The next morning at about 8:00 a.m., we drove into Denver and went to the house of the 2 people who had given me that first bottle. We switched driving all night. Each one of us would take a nap, and the other one would drive. We drove all day and all night. We knocked on their door, and the 2 of them came to the door and said, "Bob! Corky! What are you 2 doing here?"

We hadn't even called them.

I said, "We need more of that algae."

They said, "You didn't need to come here. We would have sent it to you. We could have put it in the mail."

I said, "I don't have any time for that. I need it right now."

They actually took me in their kitchen and went and got a bottle of the powder they had and gave me a big tablespoon.

I said, "What do I do with that?"

They said, "Put it in your mouth and swallow it."

I had a whole mouthful my teeth turned green. They gave me some water, and I washed it down. And in the next half hour, I signed the paperwork. My friend Bob gave them $20, my distributor fee. And I was a distributor of blue-green algae from Klamath Lake.

We left. We didn't even stay overnight. They offered.

Bob said, "No, I gotta get back to Chicago."

We left. Again we traded sleeping and driving and eventually got back to Chicago. Bob had bought me another big bottle of capsules, and I had my answer to the question of what I was going to do—start a business and start making money.

Patty Robles and the Beginning of Algae

SHORTLY AFTER, THIS WAS NOW INTO **1987,** somebody, I don't even remember who, but one of my friends said, "There is a spiritual teacher. She is giving an all-day free seminar in one of the hotels outside of Chicago in one of the suburbs." I wasn't interested in any of that. I had a long history of hunting down gurus and being with enlightened teachers.

But whoever it was that directed me was insistent. I had borrowed $100 from another friend for pocket money. I said, "I can't afford to pay."

They said, "NO, no, no. This is free. This woman doesn't charge."

I said, "If she doesn't charge, she must not be worth much."

I believe it was on a Sunday, this free seminar. I borrowed a car from one of my bar friends that I knew. I drove out to the suburb. I went out to this big room; there were maybe a couple hundred people sitting around this podium. I sat in the back because I had pretty much already decided that this was going to be boring. If it was boring, I would just slip out the door.

Well, this woman came out on the stage; her name was Patricia Diane Cota Robles. Patty Robles. She came out on the stage. There were big pots of flowers on either side of a podium. She got behind the podium. She had a brilliant smile. She said hello to everybody. Everyone said, "Hello."

She started talking. I don't remember any content that she was talking about. I was sort of in my own mind and my own place, sort of planning the drive back to Chicago. Then she said something that caught my attention, and I, for the first time, put my attention on her. And I just gasped. I literally gaped. Because when I first really looked at her, I saw her aura. And I saw her aura very, very prominently.

Maybe once or twice in my life had I seen someone's glow around their head and shoulders, very slight. I looked at this woman, and she was radiant. The aura around her body was 12 to 24 inches out from the surface of her body. It was a halo of golden light. For the rest of that entire day, I sat there mesmerized. This woman's talk was pure, spiritual, high-level truth. No negativity, no emphasis on any negativity. She was talking as though from an angelic viewpoint. In a matter of minutes, I realized that this was a truly enlightened woman. I realized that I was in the presence of one equal to, or vibrationally more powerful than, my dear beloved Margaret Coble that I had spent so many years around. At the end of the seminar, she left the stage and I was one of the last people to leave the room. I drove back to Chicago, and I realized that I had my connection back. I had witnessed this woman and her aura the entire day. It never lessened. I would look around the room at other people—no aura, no nothing. I would look back at Patty and see that brilliant aura. I realized, "I still am blessed, I still am in the game," so to speak. I was uplifted, I was charged, I went back to Chicago, and I went back to a man that I knew in the cocaine world. He wasn't a junkie or addict, but I knew him from there. We were just acquaintances.

I went to him and boldly asked him for a loan of $1,500. He said, "What are you going to do, buy cocaine?"

I said, "No, I'm going to buy blue-green algae and start pedaling it on the streets."

He thought I was crazy. I showed him the algae. I showed him some of the literature I had.

I said, "I'm gonna start a business. I'm gonna pull my life together by helping people with this powerful nutritional food. I'm going to change my life from the darkness of when you knew me in the cocaine world. I'm going to start helping people and getting my life back together."

I was almost knocked off my seat when he said, "You know, I wouldn't do this for anyone in the world, especially an ex-cocaine junkie, but there's something about what you're saying that makes me feel I've gotta trust you."

He went in his pocket and pulled out a wad of money. He counted out fifteen 100-dollar bills and handed it to me.

He said, "When are you going to pay me?"

I said, "I don't know when I can pay you."

He said, "Then give me the money back."

I said, "No, I'll pay you!"

He said, "No, I need to know when you're going to pay me and the day you're going to pay me, and if you're not paid up that day, I'm gonna come lookin' for ya."

He was a concrete worker. And he was like the hulk.

I said, "Dick, I can't tell you when I'll pay you."

He said, "You tell me, or give me the money back."

I said, "Okay, how about 6 months?"

He said, "Too long."

I said, "Okay, how about 3 months?"

He said, "You have 3 months from today, and I want every penny back. I don't want any interest. I don't want anything. Maybe you can give me a bottle of that algae. But in 3 months, I want that money."

I went to work real hard and real fast.

I found that I could convince people about the algae, especially people I knew that were bodyworkers, yoga teachers, people who were into health, vegetarians.

I started signing up people as distributors. I think in the first month I made a bonus check in my sales of like $170 or something, and the next month I think it was like $700. But the 3rd month I got a big enough check, and on the day that my debt was due, I went to a bar that I knew the guy would be hanging out in. I walked in, and he was ready to pound on me because he hadn't heard from me. He said, "You better not have a story."

And I pulled out fifteen 100-dollar bills. I said, "I don't have a story. I have your $1,500 and a big bottle of algae."

He became an algae eater.

That quickly, I started putting my life back together. I found that helping people with this incredible powerful nutrition was very rewarding. At least half of the people that I sold the algae to had very dramatic experiences. From 2 to 3 days into eating it, almost everyone universally saw better energy. And for other people, whatever symptomology they had started disappearing. The algae seemed to be able to help anything wrong with almost anybody I sold it to. And I went on building my business. I left the terrible cold-water apartment that I stayed in with my salesman friend in.

I rented an apartment up on the north shore in the Sovereign Hotel. It had a swimming pool and steam room and health club in the building. I started swimming laps every day. They closed one day, but I swam laps six days a week. I swam laps like a furious man. I did steam baths every day. I was preparing all my own food. I started going to a jogging track at Loyola University.

By the middle of 1989, towards the ending of 1989, I had become very fit, very strong, very healthy, and I was making more money than I had imagined that I could have made. I was giving two to three seminars or lectures a month, sometimes I would rent the Holiday Inn. I was building a team of algae distributors. Everything was turning around and becoming alive again. My life in this decade had gone from darkness into an abysmal pit of nightmare, fear and loathing. And by the grace of God, I was lifted out of the darkness and then I slowly stumbled and struggled until I had gotten my life back. I had begun serving people again. I was meditating, I was back on the spiritual path. I looked back at the end of '89, and was truly amazed at how one person could experience the depths of darkness that I went through and also the heights and brilliance of the light and the new way of living that I then had taken command of and ownership of. And that's how the 80's ended.

Christ Dream

To END THE 80's, I want to share a dream. On April 30th, 1988, I had the most amazing dream of my lifetime by dimensions. I'm going to read it out of my dream journal.

Most amazing and puzzling dream last night. First many events that were completely clouded out by this one. There was a tomb with the likeness of Christ chiseled on the outside cover. Then I was in a different room doing something when I heard my mom call out loud in an alarmed voice, "Corky, son, come here!"

I ran back into the room with a tomb and she was raising the lid of tomb off. I knelt next to her to see that in the tomb was Christ. I was shocked in amazement to see him stirring into wakefulness. He was young, looked like early 20's, short, thin, and with a goatee. His eyes opened and he looked bewildered. After some short time, he stood up and stepped out of the tomb. I was shocked when he stood next to me in a short white loincloth. I went to my knees and he stood looking down at me. Then I felt compelled to kiss his feet. I did so, kissing his right foot by brushing my lips over it. Then went to the left one and kissed it in several places, then returned to the right one, kissing it in several places, as I now felt no hesitation or strangeness. I, at that moment was in deep reverence and aware that both Christ and my mother stood there, watching my supplication in a non-judgmental, patient manner. I could not see mom, but the image of Christ was unmistakable. After kissing his feet, I woke up and replayed the dream in my mind before returning to sleep. I awoke later and had clear replay. Especially of his face, upon awakening and the purity of white light. I felt in the dream and after awakening that I was humbled and honored and amazed by his youthful appearance. I believe this was the first dream of my beloved Christ that I ever had. Even now I feel amazed and humbled and somewhat mystified at this event. I love my mother both earthly and heavenly and my dear Lord and brother Christ. Please God, help me know what this dream means exactly.

'90s

Algae: Food Cohort, Friend

As the '90s began, my life was stabilizing, becoming more cohesive, more grounded. My algae business was taking off. The rewards, not just financially, but in every other way were having a very positive effect on my life. The business was turning into a way to show sharing and caring. I put together a team of people, 6 people; we called ourselves the "Energy for Life Team." They were 6 of my best distributors. We met weekly, and we planned out our seminars, our presentations, where we would rent our rooms, who would give each part of our seminar. Everything was working very well. My days at the Sovereign Hotel were very rewarding. I had a good place to live, a good environment, a good building, a good pool, and a good steam room every day. In this period of time, in trying to promote the algae, I asked the president of the company for permission to try to get him on *The Oprah Winfrey Show*. He said, "Go ahead, do what you can do."

So I began courting Oprah's producers, trying to explain to them by phone what the algae was about, what Klamath Lake was about. I didn't get too far. They weren't terribly interested, but I started breaking through into her world. Later, I actually did have an opportunity to meet Oprah and discuss the algae. In the same meeting, I was able to introduce her to one of my very, very close friends, a man named Ralph Metcalfe Jr., whose father was a state senator. He was, I believe, an alderman in Chicago and then became a state senator. He was also an Olympic gold medal winner in the '36 Olympics in Berlin. In many ways, Ralph Metcalfe Sr. was a mentor for Jesse Owens, who received the most notoriety in that Olympics, but Ralph

Metcalfe Sr. was maybe the backbone and true star of the team. His son and I were introduced through the algae, and we became very good friends.

Then Oprah announced that she was having a restaurant built near the north side of Chicago. The restaurant was to be named "Eccentrics," and I had been invited to the grand opening. I had been invited by a girl I was dating, who was one of the restaurant designers and I was also invited by the guy who built the restaurant, Rich Melman, a wonderful man and friend. I got to go to the grand opening, which was full of the elite of Chicago and Illinois politicians, media people, rich-and-famous people, newspaper people; all the people that associated in Oprah's world were there.

During that opening, I actually had the opportunity to do a very great service for Oprah that day.

About a week later, Ralph Metcalfe Jr. and I went to the restaurant, and shortly after we got a table, Oprah came in. I asked the maître d' to let her know we were there and could she come and visit with us. She was extremely happy to meet Ralph Metcalfe Jr. They had quite an intimate and warm connection; they spoke about Ralph's father for a bit.

Not too long after that, I presented my case to do a television show on the blue-green algae in Klamath Lake to one of Oprah's producers. She talked it over with Oprah, and it was decided that they would have the president of the algae company come on and explain to the public through the Oprah Winfrey show what blue-green algae was about. Shortly after that, it was discovered by Oprah's people that this man also had designs on running for president. He was an independent from Oregon that was trying to get together the backing to run for president. At that time, the show had to be canceled because the producer explained to me that if he was a candidate for president and they gave him an hour's show, then they would have to, by law, give every other candidate an hour's show. So the algae never got to be presented to the American public like I had hoped. But my algae business continued on.

My Wifey

ON **T**UESDAY, **J**ANUARY **15, 1991,** the Desert Storm conflict began. On that very same day, I had planned the beginning of a 40-day fast. I completed my 40-day fast, coincidentally, with the ending of the Desert Storm conflict. During that 40-day period, I began talking with a woman I had known for many years, socially in Chicago, when our paths crossed. She lived in California, and we did quite a bit of talking, and a romance started. Her name was Sharon Wang.

At this time, I would like to make a general statement about the good fortune that I had had up to that point with relationships with women. From my teen years on into my 20s, 30s, and 40s, I had many wonderful, wonderful relationships and love affairs with good, loving women. Women who loved me very much, who allowed me to love them very much. Most of them, I remained friends with, even after we parted ways after 1 year or 2 years. One woman I was with for 6 years.

I won't go into detail about each relationship or give the names of these women. But I was truly blessed by more good, loving opportunities with good women than most men could ever hope or dream for. The woman that I had the romance with during the Desert Storm period was the one I had known in Chicago for maybe 10 years. We always had eyes for each other.

I had always been attracted to her and found out later that she had always been attracted to me. I always felt that I was not in her league. She was a very intellectually brilliant woman. She was very beautiful. I never really thought she could be interested in me. Later, I found out that she also didn't think that I would ever see her as the beautiful creature that I did. So we began talking from Chicago to California with outrageous long-distance telephone bills.

After Desert Storm, our talks became very intense, and it became clear to me that I felt differently about this woman than any woman I had ever been with. I had felt the same kind of love, but there was something else stirring in me that I had never felt.

So in mid-March, she decided to get on a plane and fly to Chicago and find out what our long-distance romance would be about in person. She came for several weeks; in that time, we visited a property that her mom owned part of and later gave to friends, up in Watervliet, Michigan. We spent some days there; she had a lot of childhood memories of hanging out there. I met her sister Sheila and her husband and their 3 incredible kids, Paul, May Lin, and John John.

I was very enamored with what I saw to be a cohesive, loving family that I didn't personally know in my own life experience. I was awed, especially by the kids, by their ability to love and care for each other and play and just feel joy with each other. I was so taken aback by it. I'll never forget the realization that I felt at that point that this family, this family of Sharon "Gaia" Wang, was going to be a big part of my life in the future.

On April 7, 1991, just before Sharon was going to return to California, I proposed to her. I had never thought of marrying any woman I had been with in my entire life. I had never desired to be in a marriage. I had been in committed relationships, but I never thought of marrying any woman. When we woke up that morning, I found myself blurting out to her a proposal. She was ecstatic and immediately accepted it, and the next day I put her on a plane back to California. About 2 weeks later, she told me that her father, who lived in Colorado Springs, would be in Chicago and staying at the Palmer House. He had some legal business to do. I asked her if I could have his room number. I wanted to meet him. She readily gave it to me.

I called him up and talked to him on the phone and asked him if we could have lunch the next day. He agreed to that. I picked him up out in front of the Palmer House, and I drove up to Rogers Park to a restaurant called The Tao, which little did I know at the time, was a most appropriate place to pick for lunch.

After we gave our orders for lunch, with carefully chosen words, I asked him for his blessings to make his eldest daughter my wife. He responded with what I can only say was a smile that was like looking at the sun at noon. He was overjoyed. He was extremely happy and in no uncertain terms, told me very rapidly, "Yes! Yes! Yes!"

I began to start thinking in terms of my life turning from a monad into a dyad. I had never lived any other way than as a single person really. Even if I was in a relationship, I always felt myself individual and free. I was moving in to a dyad, a combination, 2 people. The next couple months, Sharon and I, over the phone, we were actually spending $500 a month each on telephone bills. That's what it cost at that time for our long talks every day.

In that time, I started preparing myself to leave Chicago and to move out to California. She lived in Northern California in a small town called Cotati. By fall, I was ready to leave Chicago. I packed up all my goods and rented a U-Haul trailer. And in my station wagon, I believe it was October, mid-October maybe, I took off from Chicago to join my soon-to-be wife.

When I got there, we were both literally ecstatic with each other. We couldn't get enough of each other; our mutual happiness was just off the wall. We spent every minute of every day together. Our friends and family wanted us to have a big wedding, but she and I felt differently. Not only did we not want a big wedding, we actually wanted a very private wedding. We decided to marry in Lake Tahoe on New Year's Eve, as close to midnight as we could.

It was the late hours of December 31, 1991. We found Reverend Love, who agreed to marry us right before the stroke of midnight. Our marriage was consummated beautifully. That night, I remember having such an overpowering sense of happiness that my face actually hurt from the smile that was plastered on it all night and through our ceremony. Not too long after that, we began a 3-week Hawaiian vacation, which her father gifted to us as a wedding present. We decided to spend a week on the Big Island of Hawaii, a week on Oahu, a week on Maui, and a week on Kauai.

When we were on the Big Island, the second day, we were staying up on a volcano. I forget the name of the volcano, but it was an active volcano. The fumes from the volcano were everywhere. The second day we were there, we both became incredibly sick. One of the maids said, "This happens to people all the time up here. With all the winds blowing volcanic emissions and smoke and gasses toward the resort."

We spent 3 or 4 days so sick in bed, we had the maids go out and buy us food and water. We felt that Pele, the god of the volcano, was essentially not happy with our presence and kicked our asses all over the place.

When we left there, we went to Maui, then to Kauai. When we were in Maui, Sharon discovered a lump on her left breast, rather large from one day to the next. We both surmised that it couldn't be a tumor because it couldn't have grown that fast. It continued to grow.

But from that day on, Sharon went on a juice diet. Through our whole time in Maui and Kauai, this growth became larger and larger. By the time we went back for the last few days on Honolulu, we decided to go to a hospital. The doctor we talked to in the ER room didn't know what to do with it. He couldn't diagnose it. He said he wanted to do a mammogram. While he was out of the room, Sharon was very vocal about not wanting to do a mammogram; she felt that was a terrible idea. I got on the phone and called a doctor friend of mine, who immediately said, "You can't do a mammogram. If it is some kind of infection, a mammogram would spread it, send it systemic, and she could be in terrible trouble. Get out of that hospital."

We quickly hung up the phone and left. Somebody tried to grab us in the hallway, and we just brushed them off and told them we'd be back tomorrow. We went back to the United States, back to our home, our rented apartment in Cotati. And this growth became bigger and bigger. Sharon had me prepare juices for her every day. Raw, organic, vegetable juices. But the abscess got so big that at one point she had to start carrying her breast around in the crook of her arm. It got, first, as big as an orange. It wasn't a growth on her breast, as much as it filled her breast. Her breast became as big as a cantaloupe.

As a month went by, she wouldn't consider doctors, no matter what I or anybody else said. She said, "I am not going to be involved with doctors." She felt if she stayed on a juice fast, it would end it.

In the second full month of this growth, or whatever was going on, her breast had become the size of a small round watermelon, weighing many pounds. We were both completely in a state of unreality as to the danger she was in. We were both in such denial, we were certain that medical intervention would be trouble, and we couldn't go that route.

One day the phone rang, and it was a woman named Hilda Toranado. She introduced herself and told me, "I'm Slim Padro's sister." Slim was part of my Puerto Rican family who lived down in Fort Lauderdale with his wife Lulu.

Slim had given his sister my phone number and suggested that she call me and that we get together. I told her very quickly, "This is a bad time. Call me another time."

She said, "There's trouble, isn't there?"

I said, "Yes. We've got big trouble."

She said, "What is it?"

I said, "This isn't a time for me to talk about."

She said, "Tell me. What's going on?"

I gave her a brief, just short explanation.

She said, "I have to go talk to my guides. I'll call you back."

I was trying to explain that to Sharon when the phone rang. I picked it up.

Hilda said, "I have a spiritual guide who is an old American shaman, medicine man. And he said that she needs to see a doctor immediately."

And I said, "Hilda, neither one of us trusts doctors. We don't think that is the answer. We'll talk again."

She said, "I'll go talk to my guides again."

And she hung up.

Ten minutes later she called back and said, "Do you have a pencil?"

I said, "Yea, I've got a pencil."

She said, "Write this name down."

She gave me the name of a woman doctor in Concord, California, which was about a 2- or 2 ½-hour drive from where we were.

I wrote down the number and said, "Are you telling me that some spirit guide gave you this woman's number for us to call?"

She said, "Call right away, right now. Don't waste time."

She hung up.

So without even talking to Sharon, I called, thinking that I was going to get a receptionist and they'd tell me to get an appointment in a month or something like that. Well, this doctor answered this phone herself.

I said, "You're not going to believe this, but a clairvoyant woman's spiritual guide just gave me your number and said, I've got to bring my wife to ya."

She said, "What's going on?"

I explained to her. She said, "Get her here right now."

I said, "Right NOW?"

She said, "Yea."

She told me how to get there. I explained it all to Sharon and said, "We better go. This is not something we can ignore." I made a bed in the back of the station wagon and got Sharon comfortable, and we took off for Concord.

We went into this woman's office; she was in a private practice. Her nurse immediately took us into her workroom. Sharon took off her shirt, and the woman was absolutely shocked. She said, "How could this have happened? How could you let this grow to this point? This has been going on for months."

I said, "Yea about 3 or 4 months."

She said, "This could only happen in a Third-World country. This couldn't happen here."

I said, "Well, what do you think?"

She said, "Well, it's obviously an abscess. This whole breast is full of poison. I have to do a needle aspiration immediately and see if I can relieve this pressure."

I left the room for a few minutes and came back. She had inserted a needle into Sharon's breast and filled a whole curved metal tray with brown fluid and then took the needle out. The breast size hadn't even changed.

And then she said, "I have got to do a surgery."

Sharon started balking, and she said to Sharon, "I'll do this right. I won't hurt you. Nothing bad will happen. But I have to get this poison out of you."

So the very next day, I drove back early in the morning, and she met us at a local hospital, and she did a surgery, where she took out 4 liters of poison.

When I took Sharon home, the doctor had left a tube in her to drain. She had explained to me how to clean the tube every day, what to do with it, and to come back in a week. The tube drained continuously the excess fluid that was left. We went back in a week, and the tube was taken out. In a few days the wound healed, and her breast was normal.

The doctor had very carefully cut an incision in a circle around the areola, and it wasn't even obvious, unless you looked very closely, that she had had a surgery.

This incredible health challenge from the beginning of the honey-moon until, I believe, the end of April or early May that she finally had that terrible infection taken out of her—this was the beginning of our marriage. It didn't look good to either one of us. We felt that from Pele on, the hand-writing on the wall was not pretty.

Not too long after that, Sharon had very, very bad teeth problems. She had a lot of decayed teeth. She had a very bad situation with her teeth, which was very bizarre because her father was a dentist. But she apparently didn't take care of her teeth very well. Within a month of getting out of one health crisis, Sharon started having abscesses in her mouth, and at my strong suggestion, we went to a dentist in a nearby town. He took one look at her mouth and said, "You could spend $50,000 trying to save those teeth, but I strongly recommend getting them all pulled out and have dentures made."

I encouraged Sharon to do just that. I believed that that was easily the best route to take, having had a long history of infected and bad teeth myself. So we began going to this dentist and having 3 or 4 teeth pulled every day. Finally, all the teeth came out. We waited a couple of weeks. This dentist made her a brand-new set of teeth. It took 2 or 3 weeks before she got used to them, but for the rest of our time, she had the ability to smile without hiding herself or feeling ashamed of her teeth trouble.

So again, we got through another health crisis. This dentist explained, "There is so much toxic poison going into your bloodstream every day with these teeth that it is amazing that it doesn't make you sick." And of course, he knew nothing of what we had just gone through.

So that brought us into the late summer of '92.

A New Home

SHARON AND I, at that point, decided that living in California, which was very expensive, was not the best idea. We both felt we should find another place to live. We decided to take a road trip in her little Hyundai and go around to some of the places that we would consider relocating to. We drove around for several weeks. We went to Chicago, where we were both born. We went to Michigan; we went through Kentucky, Indiana. We went to a number of different locations that we thought we might like to relocate to. We didn't have a good feeling about any of the places we visited.

So we decided to head back to California, and Sharon said, "Would you mind if we travel back through Colorado Springs? I'd like to see how my dad is doing."

I, of course, agreed.

We went to Colorado Springs and got a motel. We spent several days with her dad. In those days, Sharon clearly and strongly felt that the companion that her father had was not capable of taking care of him if his health got any worse. This woman used to be one of his nurses in Chicago at one of the hospitals that he did surgeries. As it was, he had a leg brace on. He walked with a very big limp. He was extremely healthy, but Sharon had a feeling that he wouldn't be taken care of properly by this woman.

Before leaving the Springs, Sharon asked me, "Would you mind moving back here in case I ever need to take care of my dad?"

I quickly said, "Of course Not." I thought Colorado Springs was a nice quiet town and knew it would make Sharon happy.

The next day Sharon talked it over with her dad and it was a go. We called ahead to Cotati's Hertz Rentals to reserve a truck and were told it might be months of wait, as there was a mass exodus from California at that time. So we rented a big Hertz truck in the Springs, left her car at her dad's and drove to Cotati. We packed in a matter of a few days and, at Sharon's insistence that she drive the truck back, we were off to Colorado Springs with me following in my station wagon.

At this point, I'd like to just say a little bit about Pa and the Wang family. Sharon had a brother named Woody, whom I had met in Chicago, when she came to visit to me and when I proposed to her. I liked him very much. He was a very jovial, friendly, good-natured, college professor at the time. I had met her sister Sheila up in Watervliet. When I got to Colorado Springs, I met her younger sister Sandy, who was a CPA, living in Colorado Springs. Later I would meet her sister Susie, who lived out in Seattle with her second husband and her kids.

When I met all of Sharon's siblings, they all opened up to me in such a way, I was so touched. I actually felt the warmth of a family that, in truth, I never really felt with my own family. I had 5 sisters and a brother that were never close. We all struggled through our childhoods, and it was very difficult living. We all fought like cats and dogs. We were civil to each other in our adulthood, but coming into this Wang family was sort of mind-numbing to me because they were all so loving; all the children that I met were loving. They cared about each other, and they were amazingly sane and sound and joyous people (the Wang family was actually very much like my Puerto Rican family of Joe and Nancy Martin, close-knit and loving).

I asked Dr. Wang early on if I could call him "Pa." He agreed. I didn't want to call him Dr. Wang, so I always called him "Pa."

He was a rather incredible man. Shortly after arriving in Colorado Springs, he proved to be the purest, most authentic humanitarian I had ever met in my entire life. It turned out that he was not a religious man, nor a spiritual man. He was a Taoist. A Taoist, as I understand, is a person who essentially does not read books about their life path or go to buildings to worship some form of deity or God. A Taoist is a person who lives impeccably in their inner life and then mirrors that into their outer life. The yin-yang symbol is the symbol of the inner and outer lives.

Dr. Wang was a pure Taoist. He lived an impeccable life internally, and then he manifested that impeccability in his daily living. I'll talk more about him later in the book, but he was truly, truly the most evolved humanitarian, unconditionally generous, and beneficent man that I had ever encountered in my life.

China

ONE OF THE WONDERFUL THINGS ABOUT DR. WANG, other than him just being an incredible human being and an incredible father, was that every year he would take the entire family on a family vacation. Sometimes he would take a lot of friends of the family along. Not long after we were married, the first family vacation that I remember was to Michigan. Roughly a 2-week stay in Watervliet.

Camp Renora in Watervliet was originally owned by Lonny Myers Wang, Dr. Wang's wife and the mother of all the siblings—Sharon's mom. She gave it over to 2 friends of hers, who updated it and would rent it out for a 1-week- or 2-week-long seminars for every kind of group and organization that wanted to have a beautiful setting for their seminars or conferences. So we went there for our family vacation where I got to meet all of the Wang children and all of Dr. Wang's grandkids.

Later, we went on family vacations in Westcliffe, in the mountains in Colorado; other times we went to Seattle, Vancouver, etc. These vacations were usually 10 days to 2 weeks. In 1994, Dr. Wang had Sharon plan and organize a vacation for 20-odd people—all his children and his wife—

although at that time they were separated, as well as several college professors from the university in Colorado Springs where he attended classes into his late 70s. The generosity of Dr. Wang knew no limitations. He had brought along these college professors and their entire families, their spouses and children. We all went to China for a whole month—his kids, their spouses, and grandkids.

This was an amazing vacation because we started out in Shanghai, and we took planes, buses, trains, cruises and traveled through a good portion of China. From Shanghai, we went to Dr. Wang's hometown in Wuxi. He had always told me about Wuxi as a small town in China. When we got there, it was a city of 9 million people. We went to Wuhan; we went to Xian, where the Terracotta warriors were. We landed in Xian on an old Russian transport plane, a propeller plane. It had been a Russian mail plane, and then it was given to the Chinese, and they turned it into a passenger plane. We flew into the town of Xian, and the plane was rattling all over the place. I remember we were all very nervous. When it finally touched ground, we all applauded. The very next day, that plane was given a complete inspection because, apparently the crew had complained about the safety of the plane. The morning after, I picked up a newspaper in the hotel, and it showed the tail end of that plane full of people. It had taken off from Xian and had crashed in a field, 15 miles outside of town, killing everyone on board. We had been the last group of people to survive that plane's lifetime.

We went from Xian to Beijing and toured all the wonderful places in Beijing: the emperor's palace, the Great Wall, etc. The Great Wall was spectacular.

In this stay in China, I remember personally going through a culture shock. I don't know if anyone else had had a similar experience, but I had been brought up from the time I was 4 or 5 years old to believe that the Chinese communists, the Red Chinese, were mortal enemies. Along with the Russians, they were the most dangerous, uncivilized people on the planet.

In the time I spent in China with our group, I had so many culture shocks. The night we arrived by plane into our hotel in Shanghai, our man who was assigned to us as a tour group leader for our entire China stay, Mr. Li, he told us on the bus from the airport to the hotel, "While you're in China, you don't have to be afraid of anyone bothering you or stealing. You don't have to lock your hotel room doors. You don't have to worry about your possessions. If in the middle of the night you can't sleep and you want to go out and wander the streets of Shanghai, take along some money and a business card from the hotel lobby. In case you get lost, you can grab a cab, and they'll take you back to the hotel. But you don't have to worry about being mugged or harassed or robbed in any way."

I remember snickering inside thinking, "Well, this is some kind of strange propaganda." Well, it turned out to be the exact truth. In all the places we stayed, in all the places we traveled, wherever our luggage went, there was never a time when one person even lost a bobby pin in 30 days. The kids would run out of their hotel rooms to the swimming pool or whatever and leave the doors wide open, money on dressers, cameras everywhere, and nobody lost anything. Nobody was ever harassed; nobody was ever bothered. For me, one of the great shocks was encountering the friendliness of these people in every single place we went; openness, smiling, friendship. On many of the real old people, I could see in their faces what I thought to be hangovers from wars, but the young people were exuberant; they were excited. So many of them spoke English. They would come up to our group and ask very politely, "Could we practice our English? Would you take pictures with us??"

It was as though I had been transported into another world where everybody seemed to be open and friendly and honest. There are many, many examples that I could give of heart-touching experiences that happened, interactions that happened between our group and the people of China. What became very clear to me after the first day or so, was that these people weren't anybody's enemies. They were industrious, they were educated, they were sane, they were conscious, they were aware. Even people that I met who were in the military. Sharon and I one night met 2 friends of Mr. Li, 2 of his college friends. One was a major, and one was a Colonel in the Chinese army. We were in Wuhan, which was the Chinese military center.

At first these men were both very cold to Sharon and me, but as we communicated with them, talked to them, they became warm and friendly. I saw the potential for the strength of the Chinese people if they were challenged or they were misused. I saw that they would be formidable opponents to anybody on this planet if they were pushed into any kind of confrontation. But the average people on the streets and in the parks and in the public places we went were openhearted, beautiful wonderful people. I can't say that I've ever been in a country in my life that had such a mass of easygoing, happy, easy-to-interact with people. I've never seen anything like it before that trip or after. Another amazing thing was the health of the Chinese people. I don't think I saw one obese Chinese person. With my own eyes in the places we were at, I must have looked at a million peoples' bodies. Masses of people, I don't think I saw one obese person. I never saw a confrontation among citizens. I never saw anybody even beep a horn or yell an insult at anyone. These are things that if you walked the streets of Manhattan, you'd be bombarded with continuously. I never saw one incident in our entire China trip of a Chinese person angrily confronting or assaulting another person. This was an amazing thing for me to experience.

I could talk for a long time about the incredible experiences in China. But a memory that I have that stands out so powerfully is that when we flew back to LAX, as I walked out the walkway onto the concourse, there were a group of young Hispanic girls who were waiting for a teacher who was someplace behind me. They were all excited; there were maybe 8 or 10 of them, and they were all probably 15 or 16 years old. Every single one of them had to be 50 to 100 pounds overweight. I remember stopping in my tracks, looking at these girls, and realizing that I had just traveled all through China and had not seen 1 teenager that was 10 pounds overweight, much less 100 pounds.

The health of the people was amazing. On a cruise ship on the Yangtze River, I had occasion to spend a couple hours with the cruise ship doctor, and I picked his brain quite a bit. I asked him about the health of the people in China. He essentially told me that in China, up to that period, that doctors were hired by families to keep the family healthy. That if someone in the family got sick, the doctor would likely lose his job. I asked him specifically, because I don't know if I saw a waistline of even 30 on 1 Chinese person.

I went into a store one day. I saw white silk pants in the window and thought I'd like a pair; it was on a side street in Shanghai. I went into the store, and 3 or 4 teenage salespeople crowded around me. They all spoke English, and they asked how they could help me. I pointed to the pants and said, "I'd like a pair of pants like that."

And they were all excited about helping me and said, "Who are you buying for?"

I said, "For me."

And they all got quiet

One of them said, "What is your waist size?"

I said, "36."

They were all dumbstruck. Finally, one of the young girls said, "We only have up to size 29."

She said, "Maybe we can have them made for you."

I laughed. 29??? Maybe if I were 12 years old.

But back to the doctor. I asked him about obesity.

He said it's very rare in China. He said people were starting to become obese because since '78 the American diet had been filtering in. I asked him about constipation.

I said, "Do you have to deal with constipation?"

He said, "I've rarely had a constipated patient in all of my practice."

I knew that almost everybody in the United States is constipated, whether they know it or not.

He told me that he was certain that the health of the people of the country would degenerate in the next generations with the inclusion of Western behavior, habits, and foods.

One other thing I want to talk about quickly is that during a bus trip in Beijing, our bus was caught in traffic, and Mr. Li was near me. I had noticed a parking lot of teenage kids not doing anything, just sort of standing around.

I said, "What are all those kids doing?"

He said, "That's a smoking club."

I said, "What do you mean a smoking club?"

He said, "That building that they're all waiting by the entranceway, that's a smoking building."

I said, "I don't understand. Explain it to me."

He said, "Every American cigarette manufacturer has smoking clubs all through China in the big cities."

I said, "What do they do?"

He said, "For 30 days, they'll allow any kid to come in and smoke. They keep track of names and days. After 30 days the same kid can't come in anymore. In the time during the first month, if they stay an hour or 2 or 3 or 4, they get free cigarettes. Then if 5 kids leave, they let 5 of the kids in the parking lot go in. For 30 days they get free cigarettes, and after that they aren't allowed in."

I was astounded at the arrogance and the obvious conspiracy to addict kids to cigarettes. And how they were doing it do flagrantly. I said, "Why does the government allow this?"

He said, "I can't comment on that."

The doctor on the cruise ship told me clearly, "I worry for the health of my country. In 1978, we did not have one cancer clinic in the country, but now they're sprouting up in every city. In 1978, we had no heart disease, now hospitals are full of heart patients. The introduction of the Western lifestyle will wreak havoc on the health of this country. I can only hope that the government allows in for some period of time and then will cut back and not allow the abuse of our people the way it's going on now."

When we were in Beijing, we went to what was at that time, the single-biggest McDonald's on the planet. We saw the joy of the Chinese people in eating Big Macs and fries.

The Chinese vacation was, as I said, a true culture shock. It told me more about how I was programmed as a young kid. It made me realize the insidious nature of mass propaganda. It showed me the depth and the beauty of the Chinese people, especially in all the rural areas that we went to. It made me realize that these people, though they are joked about and laughed about as backward people in the American media, and especially in American economic circles, these people are no fools. They are industrious, intelligent, and physically more fit and stronger than any people I've encountered in any country I've ever been to. This was truly an amazing family vacation.

The Generous Heart of Dr. Wang

DR. WANG was not only a truly amazing man in his Taoist lifestyle, which he never talked about yet lived every day, his humanitarian side was also profound. Sharon's stories about Dr. Wang's generosity and humanitarian outreach were amazing to me.

One of the stories was when she was in her early teens. Other than being probably one of the world's premier maxillofacial plastic surgeons, he was also a highly accredited oral surgeon and dentist. Sharon told me that in her early teens, he would come from either full shifts in 1 hospital, sometimes 2 hospitals, come home in the evening, and then, around 8:00 p.m. they would go to another office he had in Hyde Park. It was a dental office, and he would give free dental treatments to anyone who walked in the door. They were mostly older African American people. But it didn't matter who walked in the door that had bad dental issues; he would treat them completely through whatever their issues were, and he would never take a dollar from anybody. All of his dental work was done for free.

Sharon said they would be in his office until at least midnight. Anyone who was there would get treated. He never charged anybody, never asked for insurance or anything. It was completely a service he felt he had to do for poor people.

He was also beyond generous with his medical practice. He was able to reconstruct faces in ways that he developed himself, he created himself, which were not even in the textbooks. He could look at situations, and his genius would lead him into doing things that were near to impossible to do. He would take on the most severe cases of facial destruction. I remember seeing slides of a man who had put a double-barrel shotgun under his chin and blown his whole face off. Pa reconstructed this man's face. I don't know how many surgeries were involved, must have been an incredible amount. All he needed was a picture of what a person looked like originally, and he could reconstruct a face, using that person's body parts, or using bone from cadavers. He was so far beyond the ability of the great plastic surgeons that the referrals that came to him were always impossible situations. People who had put their faces through windshields, or people whose faces were chewed up by pit bulls. Just the worst kind of situations. And often in those cases, if people didn't have money to pay for it, he would just do the work and not worry about the money.

Anybody who ever came to him if they had insurance or money, he would charge his fees, but for people who were in terrible trouble, he would just put the money aside and take care of them. I know one French woman that I met several times, she had a horrible disfiguration, I don't remember exactly what it was. He told her, "Just get to Chicago. I'll take care of you."

She came from France, and he did a long, long series of surgeries on her and put her back, looking absolutely normal. From what I understand, he charged no money. She had no place to stay, so he moved her into his home in Hyde Park with his family, where she stayed for months on end while he did the surgeries. His ability to overlook required fees was like something I've never heard of or encountered before. He was so far ahead with some of his thinking that if he knew he had to do a lot of blood transfusions on people while working, he would start collecting their own blood and keep it in a blood bank, so that when it was time for him to work on them, he would actually return their own blood to their bodies. This was well before any fears about AIDS or anything like that. He just knew that it would be easier for a person's body to receive their own blood.

His generosity and humanitarian abilities, skills and practices, actually put him in a different dimension from the average surgeon. He was truly, in my lifetime for certain, by far the most kind, gentle, openhearted humanitarian that I've ever met or, in fact, ever heard of.

Hard Times for Pa

THE EARLY YEARS OF LIVING IN COLORADO SPRINGS, '93 TO '95, were the best years for Sharon and I, of our whole marriage. We settled into living in the house that her father had very generously paid for when we moved there. He had a meeting with Sharon, and they worked out some sort of payment plan in which they didn't include me. I actually never knew what it was. But we had a wonderful home, 6 blocks away from his home. So we were able to be close to him. We would have dinner with him and the woman he lived with (the one who used to be a nurse that worked with him in Chicago). We would have dinner several times a week.

Sharon and I, in those days, we had our gift we had our time together. We were absolutely, joyously happy. We were past Sharon's health issues and challenges; we left them in California. She was very strong and healthy. She loved our new house; she loved the land around our house; she planted flower gardens and vegetable gardens.

With each other, we had what neither one of us had ever really had with another person in our whole lives. We had a joyous loving, incredibly intimate, incredibly communicative relationship which was literally idyllic. Every day from the time we got up to the time we went to bed, we were with each other. For several years we were literally with each other 24 hours a day, except for a few week-long trips I made to Chicago to support my algae business. In these years, I tried to make a go of the algae business in the Springs. It wasn't too successful. It wasn't a very open place to the ideas of health and the kind of product that I represented. I also took a job selling telephone time for a telephone company located in California. Sharon did a few little daycare jobs, but mostly we were virtually hedonistic with each other. Couldn't share enough. Every hour of every day we were together. We were so happy. We would get into arguments over who loved each other the most. We would go back and forth and declare that our love was bigger for the other than theirs was for each of us. It was rather incredible.

Sharon used to like to say to me, and she wrote it in many cards—I probably have 50 to 100 cards that she wrote this in; it was her favorite saying, "The only thing better than loving you is being loved by you."

She would say that almost daily. We had little rituals we did on a daily basis. She loved to have her feet rubbed. I would give her foot rubs every night before we went to bed. We just literally engulfed each other with care and attention. Sharon was a magnificent bodyworker, and we would share treatments on each other. We would go out to have dinner a few days a week with Pa. Sometimes Woody or Sandy would join.

Pa loved eating at the Chinese restaurants. He knew every Chinese restaurant in town. When he would come to the Chinese restaurants, the owners would always come and speak Chinese with him. He would always order for the whole table. If there were 4 of us, he'd order 8 dinners. If there were 10 of us, he'd order 20 dishes. He never ever let anyone touch a check. He paid for every dinner I ever saw for 15 years. And everyone would take leftovers home with them.

His generosity knew no bounds. His benevolent, loving presence and beingness influenced everybody that he ever met. I believe everyone he met fell in love with him. So in those days, Sharon and I had our best and most intimate and deepest and closest times. Everything in those years was pretty smooth probably up until later 1995.

Pa walked with a limp. I asked him about it one day. He told me this: He was a doctor in Chicago, he was driving his car. He came up to a light in the middle of winter, stopped on ice, and the car behind him went into a slide and rear-ended him. It wasn't a bad accident. He said he thought nothing of it, let the person go, didn't make an issue of it. But the next day at the hospital, he was rubbing his neck where it was sore. One of his colleagues insisted that he allow this other doctor to look at his neck. If I remember right, I think there was an X-ray. Then this doctor convinced Pa to let him to do a surgery on his cervical spine. The surgery was totally botched. The man accidentally cut a nerve in Pa's neck, which made it impossible to lift his right leg. I think they called it a dropped foot. From that time on, to the present (1995), Pa had to wear a thick knee brace that connected the top and lower part of his leg so that he could walk with a cane. With this brace he could lift his foot up.

So this is how he was when I first met him, walking with these knee braces and with a cane. Well, at one point, I think it was the middle of '95, he had Sharon take him to a neurologist, a specialist. At this point Pa was having a lot of pain, not in his leg or anything to do with his foot, but in his neck and his upper back. This man assured Pa that if he could do a surgery on him, he could go in and clean up all of his trouble and that he would be able to walk better than he had since his other surgery. He said it would be no problem and virtually guaranteed good results.

Sharon and Sandy both had strong reservations about it, but Pa wanted to do it. Sharon and I took Pa to the hospital for the surgery. I parked the car at the front door; he and Sharon got out and walked into the hospital. I went and parked the car. The surgery was a nightmare. It was again a botched surgery. From the time Pa woke up, he was in intense pain. He had to be put on very heavy painkillers. The first night in the hospital, he tried to get out of the bed to go to the bathroom, and he fell. It was a long time before anybody came in his room and found him. He called Sharon the next day and demanded that we get him out of there.

It was that day or the next, we took him home. He had walked into that hospital hoping to have relief from his pain. We took him home in a wheelchair, and he spent the rest of his life in a wheelchair. He never walked again.

Thus began a very, very hard time. The woman that Pa was with was not taking care of him well. He started calling Sharon several times a day for help with meds, with food. The woman seemed like a good woman, and she was a nurse, but she didn't seem to have any awareness of how to take care of him. She had her own issues going on; she had trouble with her family. Then at one point, Pa called in the middle of the night. Sharon drove over immediately to his house. This woman had had a stroke. A pretty bad stroke. Half of her face and body were paralyzed.

Shortly after that, the woman moved out. From that time on, Sharon became the primary health provider and care worker for Pa. Going into '96,

Sharon was on call; he would usually call her at 4 or 5 in the morning and tell her to come over right away. He would need meds or help with something. She would get out of bed and go over. I would stay in bed and sleep. Then when I woke up, I'd go over.

Sharon went into another mind-set, into a level of devotion to him that was remarkable for me to watch. Everything else in her life became secondary. His care, his feeding, his comfort, the dispensing of his meds—she took it all over. She worked with his doctors on how to properly medicate him. He was on a lot of medications at this time. She dressed him, and she picked him up out of bed. Every day she put him in his wheelchair. We bought a vehicle that had a front passenger seat that would swing around and down so she could transfer him from the wheelchair into the front seat.

He didn't want to be homebound; he didn't want to be trapped in bed. He wanted to go out 4 or 5 nights a week to Chinese restaurants. He wanted Sharon to take him out driving sometimes; she would often take him up to the mountains. Sandy would come out and help as much as she could, but she was somewhat limited because of the heavy workload that she had. Woody would come down on the weekends from Denver to give Sharon some respite.

Pa became so dependent on Sharon that there was never a period of more than 8 to 12 hours that she could be away from him. The days we didn't go out, she cooked all his food. She would have me juice for him. I bought a big industrial juicer. She would try to get at least 2 quarts of fresh juice in him. He loved drinking melon juices, so I would make cantaloupe and honeydew melon and watermelon juices. Sharon did every single thing possible to make him more comfortable and to make his life easier. As we went on into the later '90s, it was this steady pattern of Sharon up on his first phone call, 4:00 or 5:00 a.m. And then she would usually spend the entire day there. She would usually get him to sleep between 10 and 11 at night. She would come home and be totally exhausted and fall in bed for what we hoped to be 4 to 5 hours. And then he would call, and the routine would continue.

In that time, I was completely committed to helping her in every way possible. I did every single thing that he or she asked of me. No matter what I did, I always felt that I was doing maybe 5% of his care and she was doing 95%. There were certain things that between them, only Sharon could provide. Sharon would ask me to sit with him while she had to run errands. Most days, I'd sit with him maybe 4 to 5 hours. He watched television. We bought a big TV for his bedroom and had a friend of mine—my good friend Dave Cartee—build a holder for the television up into the ceiling so Pa could lie flat in bed and watch it easily. And he loved watching television.

But most everything was nonsense to him except the Discovery Channel, the History Channel, and NOVA. We hooked up the VCR, and we had a tremendous number of nature videos. He loved anything about nature or wildlife. So I would sit with Pa, and we would watch that stuff and talk about it. I remember one observation that he made one day that was striking to me. We were watching how minnows were eaten by bigger fish and those fish eaten by bigger fish and finally sharks eating the big fish. He laughed and said, "Everything on the planet Earth eats something else. Everything eats everything!"

So in those years, Sharon had a level of commitment and a level of loving care for her dad that just humbled me by the day. In all those years, she never one time, not one minute, complained. No matter what the workload was, no matter what was required of her, there was not one sentence of complaint in all those years. She was committed beyond belief to making him as comfortable and peaceful as possible.

There was a period earlier before his surgery where he had trouble with his bowel movements. We had taken him to a couple of colon therapists for colonics, colonic irrigation. He didn't like it at all. We tried a couple, and then we didn't do that anymore.

In these years it became harder and harder for Sharon to get him from his bed into his wheelchair and then into a bathroom and then to lift him up and put him on the toilet. Then come back and transfer him back to the wheelchair and back to the bed. He was having constipation caused by the medications. He was having more and more bowel trouble and discomfort, finally moving into pain, where he would have to struggle to force out a bowel movement. Things were very bad at that time. I suggested to Sharon that I build a colonic unit into his bathroom. I had done this in the past, when I was a young man. I had lived with a colon therapist and built into our bathroom a whole colonic irrigation system, so I knew how to do it. She thought that was a great idea; he thought that was a great idea.

My friend Dave and I got together and designed a platform for him to lay on, and when he was finished, we could pick the platform up and hook it back to the bathroom wall so there was still access to the toilet and to the rest of the room. Dave designed it all, and we bought all the necessary supplies. Dave hooked up all the plumbing. I already had old stainless-steel speculums that I had carried with me for years. We found a supplier for hoses, so that we could dispose of the hoses after every colonic. In 2 days, we had a solution to his bowel blockages.

In those days, he had much less discomfort and he seemed to be in much better spirits. So for the last several years of his life, Sharon probably gave him an average of 2 colonics per day, every day. He felt that this was making him healthier. At one point, he told me he believed that the colonics would add years to his life.

So as we went into '96, '97, '98, everything in Sharon's life was a routine. Getting up early every single morning, going to his house, attending to his needs. She would, in the later years, start hiring people to come in and help and sit with him. Caregivers who would be on 8-hour shifts during the day, that would give her some time to come home in the afternoon and give her a little bit of space away from attending to him 24 hours a day.

I would sit with him a lot. I found out a lot about this man in the days that I sat with him or that we would be by each other. He liked to be in silence, so I didn't poke him with any kind of unnecessary conversation. But if I asked him a serious question, he would be glad to engage in conversation. I remember I asked him once about Taoism.

He essentially said Taoism isn't something you read about, it's something you live. Well, already by that time, I had been around him for almost 10 years, and I had seen what a Taoist was. This man was a true Taoist. But in trying to explain it, he had very few words. One of the things he told me was, a Taoist does not fight. He said, "I've never fought anybody in my whole life."

I thought he was referring to a fist fight, a street fist fight. And I said, "Oh, you've never had a battle?"

He said, "No, I don't fight at all. Physically nor mentally. I've never had a fight in my life."

That was sort of stunning to hear from a man already in his 80s. I probed him a little more about that and got down to where I realized that he never argued. He said he never argued. There was no arguing in his consciousness. He was like a mental martial artist. He was like an aikido master. Anything that came up, he turned his shoulder away and never had the need to strike back. Then talking to Sharon about it, she confirmed that even though his wife (Sharon's mother) was very combative when they were kids, a very feisty, hard-fighting woman, she had never seen Pa raise his voice or engage in an argument. He would defer to her on almost every single issue that came up. He would defer to business partners, defer to doctors, defer to anyone. He would not engage in fighting.

So in those times and conversations, I realized the depth of his Taoist abilities. He was at a level of peace in his consciousness that he allowed no one to take away from him. He lived it in his consciousness so powerfully that it played out into his life and his world. I saw that all of his children, they all had that same quality. Some of them to higher or lower degrees. They had the ability of their mother to stand up for themselves and to be very strong, but they also had his ability to be at peace with their world or their environment, with their relationships.

As I grew closer and closer with his family, I realized that the kids were all, in their own way, amazing. Of any family with children that I ever engaged with in my life, they were the most astounding. Their moral character, of each of the 5 of them was truly amazing. Their morality, their character, and their integrity were all just of the highest caliber. Each in their own way were amazing human beings to me. Being part of this family became a growing joy.

Sharon made me a better man every day from the day I joined her. She made me a more integrous man. She made me a more conscious man. Not by pointing out errors and flaws in my personality or behavior, but by living at such a high moral standard that I could do nothing but improve myself by just being in her presence. In the Chinese world, she was the older sister, the "jie jie." The "jie jie" of Chinese families had the responsibility of taking care of all of the younger ones, and she was that figure for her brother and for her 3 sisters. She was the leader and she was the "jie jie." She took that responsibility seriously. The kids had their differences at times. They had disagreements, but they were a tight unit of loving kids that I had never witnessed before. Sheila and Susie's kids really emulated that.

It was something where I got to watch 3 generations of Wang kids and grandkids. I got to see 3 generations of very high-character and high-integrity people.

I once asked Pa about his parents. He told me that his mother had lived to be 113 years old and his father 107. And that night at home I told this to Sharon, and she said, "That couldn't be... Well, he's on a lot of meds."

I said, "Yea, but I don't think that's why he said that."

Well, the next day as I sat with him, I brought it up again and said, "Pa, are you sure of all those ages?" He directed me to a bookcase to a small pamphlet thing. I gave it to him. It was in Chinese, and he read to me that his father had lived to be 107 and his mother 113. It was recorded in this book that he had gotten while he was in China. I suppose some family record or a record from the town of Wuxi. Anyways, the realization that his parents had lived to those ages made me understand how he could have been so healthy all of his life. Apparently, he knew virtually no sickness through his entire medical career. Only after becoming bedridden did he show any signs of colds or flus or anything.

This man, in our times together, he exemplified to me what a true Taoist is. He lived with his discomfort and his bad fortune. He did admit that after the surgery he had felt rare anger at the surgeon who had promised to do such a good job. He didn't feel anger about the surgeon 30- or 40-years prior who cut the nerve in his neck that crippled him. I had asked him about that man. He said, "Oh, he just made a mistake."

He had forgiven him immediately; it was no issue. But this last surgeon who put him in a wheelchair for the rest of his days, he did have some anger for a short time. Then he told me one day, "I have no more anger for that man."

Those days of watching the interaction between Sharon and her dad, it was pretty amazing, pretty incredible. All of his kids would come and see him. Susie would come often, bringing her family from Seattle whenever she could get off work. Sheila would come whenever she could, bringing her kids. They were all so committed to him and loved him so dearly, and I could always feel his inner difficulty in having people see him in that condition, being bedridden. When there would be kids or grandkids, he would always have Sharon get him up early and get him dressed; he preferred being in the wheelchair rather than in his bed. It was just amazing to watch the devotion and love between Sharon and her dad.

He called me over one day. Sharon and I were both at home. He called her up and told her to send me over. He wanted to talk to me. This was probably in early 1999. He had me sit down in the chair I always sat in, next to his bed. He said, "I want you to do something." He was very serious and bordering on stern, which I rarely ever saw.

I said, "Sure Pa, what do you want?"

He said, "I want you to force Sharon to quit smoking."

And that took me aback, and I didn't say anything for a minute.

He said, "Did you hear me? I want you to force Sharon to quit smoking."

The memory of that conversation has not been easy for me to live with. I've thought of it 100 times.

I told him, "Pa, I don't force anybody to do anything."

He said, "No! I want you to FORCE Sharon to quit smoking."

I said, "Pa I don't force anybody to do anything."

He said, "You have to! You're the only one. No one else can do this. You have to force her to quit smoking."

I said, "Pa, I'm not going to force her to quit smoking."

He got real silent for a minute and pointed to the door and said, "Get out. Get out right now."

It was the only time in all the years together that we had any kind of trouble between each other. I got up and left, and I went home and told Sharon. "He wants me to force you to quit smoking."

She said, "What did you say?"

I said, "I told him I wouldn't do it."

She said, "And?"

I said, "He pointed to the door and said, 'Get out.'"

Sharon had smoked since she was 14 years old. Even in our marriage, she had many, many times tried to quit. She described her addiction to cigarettes as greater than heroin addiction. Every time she would quit, she would last a week, maybe 2 weeks. By 2 weeks she would be almost impossible to live with. She would be just a bear. She would be angry and short-tempered. So every attempt that she had already made hadn't worked, and she hid her smoking from her father. She would use gum and mouthwash and perfume. She would only smoke at home. She wouldn't smoke near him or in his house; she would hide it. But every once in a while, she would get careless; she would reach down and pick him up out of the wheelchair, and he could smell the cigarettes. He would get very, very unhappy. I won't say angry, but he would scold her about her health.

So this was the only time that Pa and I had ever had a hardship. By that night, he had let it go. He didn't ever bring it up to me again. We never talked about it. By the next day, everything was back to normal between us. As '99 progressed, his health started noticeably deteriorating. He had more pain, more difficulty, and was on more meds. By the summer of '99, his doctors told Sharon that they could not continue to write prescriptions for as much pain medication as he was taking. They said, "You're going to get a hospice involved because we're in jeopardy supplying this much narcotics to a man." At one point in the summer of '99, Sharon conferred with all the doctors and the hospice people, and we brought hospice into his situation. Not so much because it looked like his death was imminent, but much more because hospice could supply enough morphine to keep him out of pain. He had somewhat become impervious to the pain meds. He was in terrible pain all the time. So the hospice people came in, and they showed Sharon how to medicate him with morphine. Sharon hired a nurse to sit with him all night at that point so that she could try to get more sleep. We would have the hospice people come in regularly to check on him. But he just looked like it was time to let go. I had engaged him in conversations about death and dying. He had a belief system that there was no afterlife. That when you took your last breath, that was just the end. I never tried to dissuade him from that.

Pa's Death

As we went into **A**ugust, his ability to stay conscious began to evaporate. The morphine was doing the job of keeping him out of pain. But it also rendered him more and more unconscious. All of his kids came, and I can only say, in their own ways they said their goodbyes to him. It was a very, very sad time. Then he got a bad infection in his mouth. When this infection hit, he couldn't eat anymore. He had no desire to eat too much anyways, but now he couldn't eat at all. Sharon would try to get him to drink fresh juices out of a straw.

At the end I was sitting with him. Mostly he would be unconscious, but he woke up at one point and said to me, "Did you see her?"

I said, "See who, Pa?" I thought he meant Sharon or one of the nurses.

He said, "Did you see her at the end of the bed?"

I said, "See who?"

He said, "My mother, my mother was at the end of the bed."

He turned his head over and was back to sleep. I knew then it was very close to time.

Then I had to go up to Denver one night. Woody had come down from Denver and was with Sharon and Pa. Driving back from Denver, there was a full moon. I guess they call it the autumn moon. I was struck by how gigantic it looked in the sky. By how orange it was. It was so rare to see the moon look like that.

When Pa was born in China, they didn't keep track of birthdays by days, they kept track by the month and the moon. Well Pa had been born on the autumn moon all those years ago in China.

I got back to Pa's house about 10 p.m.; he was unconscious. Woody said, "Why don't you guys go home and try to get to sleep?" We went home and went to bed. Sometime after midnight, Woody called, and Sharon answered the phone. And then immediately hung up and jumped out of bed.

She said, "Get dressed. We gotta go over there right now."

I said, "Is there a problem?"

She said, "Woody said he's passed."

We went over there, and the hospice nurse verified that he had passed.

Sharon and I both sat for hours, crying. Woody would come in and out. He'd share our grief. We were all just devastated. Sharon had informed the hospice people, and because there was a nurse present, the coroner was not required to come in. I can't remember if police came or not. But Sharon had made it clear that following Chinese custom, he would be allowed to stay in his bed for 3 days. In those 3 days Sharon and I would sit with him. The funeral home people that she had made arrangements with told her very clearly that it wasn't a good idea to have him stay in bed. They essentially, very pointedly, said, "If he stays in this room for 3 days, his body will decompose, and it will be very, very ugly."

Sharon said, "That's not any of your concern. We're going to keep him here for 3 days, and you come back on the morning of the 4th day and take him for cremation."

So she put the air-conditioning on in his room. For 3 days, she and I took turns reading out of the *Tibetan Book of the Dead* to him. The last several days that he lived, she and I had started doing this practice of reading the *Tibetan Book of the Dead*. Then we continued to read it. The *Tibetan Book of the Dead* is essentially words to help guide the spirit of a person who was near death or after death into the next world. So we did that every day for 3 days. His body showed no decomposition whatsoever. The funeral people said he would turn all black and blotchy with sores. None of that happened. The 3rd day, he looked like he was just sleeping. His skin was like silk, or like velvet. He didn't seem to show any kind of decomposition at all.

The 4th morning, when the funeral home brought their people, they brought in a gurney. They had gloves on and masks on. The one guy, before he got to Pa's bedroom, he said, "This isn't going to be pleasant."

Sharon said, "There isn't anything wrong with him."

There were two men that went in, and I could see on their faces—they were both completely shocked. They lifted him up and put him on the gurney. His body didn't even seem to have gone into rigor mortis. His skin was still soft. There was no odor; there was no discoloration. They took him and cremated him. This happened in August 1999.

This was the beginning of probably the hardest grieving I had ever seen anyone go through in my life. Sharon went through it all up until the beginning of 2000. There were times that I felt, with all the talk about Y2K and computers going down and food stores being empty and nationwide chaos, he might have departed because he didn't want to see what Y2K might actually be about.

Anyways, the days and months after Pa died were very difficult for all of the Wang children. I could see it in the face of each one of them; they had their own level of difficulty and their own level of suffering and grieving. The loss of this incredible Patriarch. The emptying out of his house and the selling of his house became the major chore in September and October and November. Sharon lost herself in that work, and I believe before the end of the year, his house had been emptied out and sold. That's how the '90s ended for us. Very, very unhappy. Very difficult. I had hoped that when Pa did pass, Sharon would have some relief from the tremendous burden of the last 4 or 5 years. But sad to say, her difficulty was just beginning.

Mike's Death

As MORE OR LESS A FOOTNOTE, the only other very important event that happened in the '90s was in 1996. My kid brother Mike was at that time 50 years old. He met a very undignified and very questionable end to his life. This could be a whole book in itself. And in fact, he did write his account of these events before he died. But he was killed by FBI sharpshooters in a standoff down in Texas with a group he was involved with, called The Republic of Texas. This happened in 1996, and for many, many months, it was a tremendous hardship and a very difficult period of my life. Though I would like to talk about it, this really isn't the place for it. And to do it justice, it would take quite a long time to explain all the events that led up to it. So perhaps there will be another book at another time where I could openly and freely talk about my brother's untimely and undignified departure from the planet Earth.

'00s

A Twist of Fates

THE BEGINNING OF 2000 — new century and Y2K meltdown that never happened—was the period when Sharon and the other kids wrapped up most of Pa's business. They settled his estate, and his house was sold. Sharon, who was always a self-proclaimed pack rat, had terrible difficulty in letting go of so many of her dad's possessions. All of her family was invited into the home to take anything and everything of his personal possessions. When all the kids had taken the things that they were interested in, we literally filled our entire house with boxes. There were rooms in our big house where you could only walk through the walls of boxes. She wouldn't give anything to Salvation Army. I tried so hard to get her to let go of things, and she just would not do it.

So as we went into the '00s with our house bursting at the seams with this man's life, Sharon started going into not just grieving, but overt depression. The grieving was very tangible and deep-seated. But the depression that came on that year, was something that she did not know how to deal with. At one point she was taking antidepressants and taking every natural herbal formula that we could find. But she felt that she had made a terrible mistake in all those years of caring for him, smoking in secret and hiding it and sometimes denying it. This started eating at her, and I was just beside myself with not being able to say the right words.

All through our marriage I had been able to say the right words, I could help her out of her anxiety. She had major abandonment issues when we were married. She told me when we were married that this would be a big problem. It took me several years, but I got her to where there was no more abandonment issue. I always had a sense that I could help her with anything. But when she went into this depression, the more she talked about it, the more she revealed a deep-seated guilt for this smoking stuff, which often brought me back into the conversation when he had me come over and told me to force her to quit and I had refused to do it. I wished that I had listened to him. Because he was right. I could have made such an issue out of it that she would have had to quit.

But anyways, her guilt was so deep. She felt that, as she was still smoking, he was up in heaven watching her. No matter how I talked or what I explained, I could not get her off of believing that her father was in a celestial place sitting and watching her and judging her every time she smoked a cigarette. These were such hard times for us. It made no sense to her when I explained that once a person leaves their body and goes into the next level of life, there is no judgment, no pain, no suffering, and no misery. No matter what I read to her from a dozen books, she held on to that feeling that he was still watching her and still angry at her for smoking.

As 2000 finished and we went into 2001 and 2002, it was almost like we were walking in a fog. I was in my fog with this helpless feeling. She wouldn't seek out any professional help; she was a professional mental healer herself. She was an amazing therapist. She could help anybody with any physical or mental problem, but she couldn't turn it around and work with it on herself. She would not even allow me to recommend that she find professional help. She cried so much. I'd walk into a room, and she'd just be sitting there crying. I'd hold her and finally get her to talk, and it would always be the same thing. Her guilt about things with her dad. It just went on and on. At one point, the feeling of our joyous happiness that we had when we moved into that house was so distant and so far removed; there were periods that I felt we were both zombie-like.

Still the house was full of his possessions, I methodically would get rid of one box at a time. I was pretty sneaky about it, but I started thinning out some of the things, feeling that if I got some of that stuff out of there, it might help her. But our sense of happiness had just disappeared. We both tried to recover it. We would go places and do things. Any time she was with any of her family, she would change her whole demeanor; she would brighten up. Then the minute we were back home, she would be back in that self-imposed misery and prison that she put herself in. I, no matter what I tried and how I prayed, I couldn't pull her out of it. We went on vacations; we went to Jamaica right after he passed. We took a vacation to Mexico and Guatemala. She seemed to lighten up when she got near the ocean and in the sunshine and was away from Colorado Springs. Things would start getting better, and then our 2-week time would end, and we would be back in it again.

At one point, in late 2003, we sat down and decided that we had to leave, not just that house, but Colorado Springs. We started looking for places not in the United States. She was very strong about wanting to go someplace that she hadn't lived before. So we started looking at international places. We thought we could be very happy in Vancouver, British Columbia. We were so sure that could be a good move that she contacted Canadian immigration and essentially found out that they didn't want us. Then we decided on New Zealand, we were sure that New Zealand would be the perfect place for us to live. She contacted the New Zealand immigration people. Again we were told that we were too old. I was well over 50, and she was just turning 50. We were told that we wouldn't be welcomed to live there. Same held true for Australia. The Australians were very candid. They said, "We do not want to start a welfare society." Sharon explained that we had money and were very healthy, but they weren't interested. They said sooner or later our health would break down, and they'd be responsible for us.

Then at some point we both fell into agreement about Panama. We both had read a lot about Panama, and we were getting excited about that. This was the end of 2003 or early 2004.

Suddenly 1 day I had gotten up early. I was in the kitchen, and I heard her screaming for me. She was screaming wildly; it scared the life out of me.

I tore through the house and into the bedroom. She was in an absolute panic. She was holding the back of her neck and her forehead and telling me that they were exploding. She was in intense unbearable pain. I immediately thought to call an ambulance. She stopped me cold and told me, "No, no, don't you dare!"

This went on for an hour or so, and I didn't know what to do. I tried rubbing her neck and her head. She was describing symptomology that I had never heard. She was seeing shooting lights, and the pain was radiating through her neck, all up through her head, over her head, down her face. She was in agony. At one point, after maybe an hour of this, she said, "Go and get some of Pa's meds."

We had a lot of his medications that we had tried to give to the hospice people, but they wouldn't take them. I went and grabbed a bunch of his meds. She said, "Read what's in there." So I read. A lot of them were pain-killers, tranquilizers, sleeping pills.

I said, "This one is Oxycontin."

She said, "That, give me that!"

I gave her 1. She said, "Give me another one."

I gave her another one. She took 2 of them, and after about 15 to 20 minutes she quieted down and then went to sleep.

I was so worried I was going to call for help, but I knew she would be furious with me. So I waited maybe 4 or 5 hours until she woke up. The pain was still intense, she was in literal agony. Every kind of terrible pain that I've ever described she was talking about. She wanted more of the drugs. I gave her more; she slept more. This went on for 2 days. Every time she woke up in this terrible pain, she would tell me to give her more drugs. I would give her more, they would knock her out, and she would sleep 4 or 5 hours. Nobody knew about it. None of our friends, none of her family. No one knew what she was going through. Then when she was sleeping, I called a doctor friend of mine on the East Coast. He couldn't make head or tail of anything I was saying and he gave me a number of a medical intuitive man in Maryland. This man was a psychic and a clairvoyant and could diagnose people at a distance. So I called this man—got him on the phone.

He said, "I'll do a reading on her. You have to agree to send me $50."

I said, "Of course. Of course."

He gave her a reading over the phone and said that one of her body-workers—she had a number of people she went to regularly for different body treatments such as massage therapy, reiki, chiropractors, etc.—had made a terrible error and had misaligned her upper vertebrae, and something was pressing directly on her spinal cord. He said, "You've got to get her to a cranial–sacral expert. Not just a practitioner, a cranial–sacral expert."

I said, "Is that it? That's all? I shouldn't take her to a hospital or neurosurgeon?"

He said, "No, no, she just needs a cranial–sacral expert."

So I hung up the phone from him and got the telephone book. I found a cranial–sacral therapist. There were 6 or 8 listed. I called probably all of them. One of them was also a chiropractor and a woman, and she seemed to be able to grasp what I was talking about. She said, "Get your wife in here tomorrow," and gave me a time.

So the next time Sharon woke up, I told her all that had transpired. She agreed. She took the drugs to knock her out again until the next day.

So the next day, she took less of the medication so that she could function. I got her to this woman's office. The woman worked on her for 2 hours, almost furiously, working very deeply into her cervicals and the top cervicals, doing adjustments on her spinal column. After this long period of having this woman work on her, Sharon had some relief for the first time in 3 days. The woman told her, "You have to come back here every single day. You have to come back. What's going on, I haven't even figured out yet, but I have to keep treating you." So we went back to this woman every day for about 2 weeks.

In that time, all the pain and all the agony stopped, and Sharon stopped taking the pain pills. But the woman still wanted to work on Sharon. She said, "I want you in here at least once a week. I've gotta stay after that area of your spine to make sure it doesn't put you in the same trouble."

So we went once a week for several months. In that time, Sharon would often get into coughing spells, not too bad, but what Sharon and I referred to as smoker's cough. The woman suggested a chest X-ray. Sharon refused. But as one week after another went on, this lady chiropractor became absolutely insistent. So Sharon finally allowed her to write a prescription for an X-ray technician who worked out of his own home. Sharon wouldn't go to a hospital for it. So the chiropractor knew a man who worked out of his own home, a radiologist. We went and had the chest X-ray. He came out of the room after developing the picture, and he became almost overbearing and belligerent. He showed us the picture up on the lightbox on the wall. He pointed to her lung, her left lung. He said, "You see this big spot? You get to Memorial Hospital right now."

She said, "I'm not going to any hospital."

He started screaming at her. And Sharon's reaction was almost violent. She ripped into him; she tore him up. Screaming at him, that he had no right to try to order her. She told me, "Come on, we're getting out of here." He followed us down the hallway and out the door, yelling at her that she had better get to a hospital.

We got in the car, and she turned and looked at me. She was raging mad. She said, "I don't want to hear 1 word from you, not 1 word. You don't dare say a word to me about doctors or hospitals. You keep quiet about this."

I said, "He saw something that scared the hell out of him."

She said, "I don't care what he said. You keep quiet about this. You don't say anything to anybody, and you don't bring it up. I don't want to hear anything about this."

I said, "I'll agree to that if you agree to change your entire diet and start going on raw food, juices. Start cleaning your body up."

She said, "Okay, I'll agree to that."

I said, "No more meat."

She said, "I'll agree to that."

So we went on month after month with me doing all the shopping and most of the food preparation, feeling that whatever was wrong with her, if we got her body in very healthy condition, this problem would be behind us. This went on up into November 2004. In that time, we agreed that we should make a long trip to Panama and find a place, maybe even buy a place to live. She found a tour out of Texas. This tour was to go to every gated community in all of Panama. It was especially for foreigners, Americans, Canadians, and some Europeans. It was to last a month; we were going to be shown every gated community where we could go in and have safety, as well as virtually every area of Panama that we could meet with local realtors. We were both very excited about this. I went into denial with her about what the X-ray showed. I was in complete agreement as long as she was cleaning up her body. She lost a lot of weight. She was feeling better, she was looking better, and her mind was clearing up some.

We went on this Panama trip; it was in January 2005. We spent that month going all through Panama. We both fell in love with the country. We met some incredible people. We met a man who absolutely fell in love with Sharon. A man named Felix, who was one of the political leaders in the whole country. He was also one of the major realtors. He said, "I will find you folks the most incredible deals, the most wonderful places." He took us to absolute paradise places.

By the time our tour to Panama was up, the last morning before we flew out of Panama City, we were having breakfast in our hotel out on the veranda. She said, "Let's do this. Corky, let's do this. Let's start a new life. Let's go home and go to work hard on our house, get rid of everything, sell our house, and within 3 to 6 months, come back here, buy a new home, and live our life here. Buy a big enough home with enough property that we can have our friends and loved ones and family come if they want to live with us." This had always been a dream of ours. So we agreed before getting on the plane that morning that the end of our Colorado Springs life started the next day, when we would start cleaning out the house.

We got into the Springs, and we walked out toward our car. We were talking, and I was so excited. We were both carrying luggage; she could always carry more than I could. We walked about 100 feet, and I realized I was talking to myself. I turned around, and she was standing 20 to 30 feet behind me, her luggage all lying on the ground around her. I put mine down and went back and said, "What happened?" I thought maybe she twisted her ankle or something. She was gasping for breath. I stood there and looked at her, and she had her hand on her chest and was sucking in deep, deep lungsful of air. She couldn't talk. I just stood there for a minute or two watching her, and she said, "I don't know what happened. All of a sudden I couldn't breathe."

She relaxed. I took as much of her baggage as I could, and we got to the car. She was still breathing hard. She had shortness of breath, which from that moment on, just got worse. It got worse by the day.

She had actually quit smoking back in November, mostly due to the influence of her cranial–sacral therapist. But 1 day, she just told me, "I'm not smoking anymore." So she hadn't smoked a cigarette in months.

As the days went on, I did every kind of bodywork I could, every kind of therapy we could. We gave her colonics, and she was on juice only, but no matter what we did, her shortness of breath prevailed. We never even started cleaning out the house. Things got worse and worse. By the end of February, she couldn't sleep. Because she couldn't lie down. If she lay down, she couldn't breathe. So, she started making bed areas where she could sleep breathing and sitting up. All of this, of course, alarmed me no end. But the strict rule was that no matter what, I could tell no one, nobody in the family. I could tell none of our friends, and I could not seek medical help.

She had moved downstairs to be away from me so at least I could sleep. We had a bedroom downstairs. In the middle of the night one evening in

March, she woke me up, gasping for breath. What seemed to help her was to get her into a hot tub. I filled the tub up, and she got into it, sitting up. I worked on her back and her neck, and finally she was able to breathe better. She told me, "Go back up and go to sleep." I went back upstairs and fell asleep. Then probably at 8 in the morning, I opened my eyes, and she was standing next to the bed. She was fully clothed. She had on boots and her heavy coat, her hat, and her scarf. As soon as I opened my eyes, she said, "You better take me to one of those emergicare places."

I scrambled into my clothes and said, "How about just going to a hospital?"

She said, "No, no, an emergicare."

We knew one where we had been to when I had had a couple small accidents. I took her there, they saw her distressed breathing, and they took her in a room immediately. An old white-haired doctor came in. He sprayed something into her throat, which helped her breathe a little easier. He said, "I need to take a chest X-ray." She didn't argue, surprising to me; she didn't resist.

He went in and did the X-ray, and we sat out in the waiting room. He came out about 15 minutes later. And it was a terrible, terrible thing. He walked out of the room, and he had tears running down his face. He was crying. It was so hard. We both knew. He just said, "I've called Memorial Hospital. They're waiting for you." He said to me, "Get your wife over there right now," as the tears ran down his face.

Doom, Hope and Darkness

THE DOCTOR'S FACE SAID IT ALL TO BOTH OF US. We left immediately and went to the hospital. They were waiting for Sharon. She was having a very difficult time breathing. They got an inhalation therapist to make her breathing a little easier. They took her for X-rays. They did some other tests. We waited out in the ER room for a long time. From the drive to the hospital, neither one of us really talked. It was like there was nothing to say. We both knew that our ability to be in denial and avoid the realities had come to an abrupt halt with the doctor's tears rolling down his face. So we sat pretty late into the evening before they could find her room and a pulmonary doctor. Finally, at 9:00 or 10:00 p.m., the doctor came in. He told her that one of her lungs were full of fluid and that he had to do a needle aspiration immediately or she would never be able to rest; she'd never be able to sleep. He asked me if I would assist him because all his normal helpers were busy.

He injected a very long, thin needle between the ribs from the back. I held this big bag and the tubing. He put the needle into her lung sack and filled the bag up. It was a 1-liter bag with brown fluid. He told her, "We can give you a bed now." She said, "What's the diagnosis, right now?"

He said, "Well, I haven't gotten the results of all the tests, but it looks like you have a cancerous malignant tumor in your left lung." He said, "Are you a smoker?"

She said, "I quit in November."

He very dryly said, "You quit 4 years too late."

After all the fluid was out of her, they took her up to a room. I stayed with her until about 1 in the morning. They gave her sleeping medication, afterwards, I went home.

It's hard to talk about it, even having been so long ago. But that began a fight for a miracle that we engaged in.

This was on Friday. On Saturday, they really didn't have any answers. On Saturday there was a tremendous snowstorm that paralyzed the city. Sunday morning, I woke up to what looked like impossible driving conditions. On the news, they told everyone to stay off the streets, as they were not drivable. At about 1 in the afternoon, she called and told me that they had just told her that they had to do an emergency surgery to remove fluid out of her heart sack. She called when the doctor was there. I immediately felt, "No, don't do this." I told her that. She asked the doctor, "What will happen if I don't have this surgery?" She put the phone out so I could hear his answer.

He very loudly said, "Your chances of living through the night are very poor. If we don't get the fluid out with an emergency surgery today, if you went into cardiac arrest tonight, there would be no one in the hospital tonight to even save you. Because of the weather, no doctors or nurses are getting here. The staff that is here is overworked. Most of them will be leaving by 6. You have to have the surgery." I told her I'd get there somehow. I went out and shoveled a path for my 2 wheels out to the street. It was probably 16 inches of snow. I drove as fast as I could down the driveway, turned the car down the hill, and, fortunately, was able to get through the snow down the hill. I got out onto a street that hadn't been plowed, but had emergency vehicles drive down it. I got to the hospital; there was almost no traffic whatsoever.

I got to her room. They had frightened her, and they had frightened me over the phone. We requested that the doctor come back. It was about 2 in the afternoon. He came back about 5. He repeated to us that they had 1 surgeon who had been doing surgery all day the day before, during the night, and all day Sunday but he was leaving at 6 (if he didn't do the surgery on Sharon). If we didn't agree to the surgery immediately, she would have to take her chances on staying alive through the night. Both Sharon and I went sort of brain dead with fear. I didn't think rationally. My gut and my heart said, "No." But I couldn't say it in words. Then she told the doctor, "Okay, go ahead."

They took her immediately to be prepped; an hour later they took her into the surgery room. The surgeon told us before they wheeled her in, "This will be very routine. There will be a 1- to 2-inch incision below the rib cage. The surgery should take no more than 20 to 25 minutes. We are just emptying out your heart sac."

They told me to go wait in the waiting room, and they had a TV monitor that kept us updated. I had her code number up on the screen, and it would announce to me when the surgery was finished. It was supposed to be finished by 6:30. At 7:15, there was still no notification of the surgery ending. I knew in my heart that something bad was going on. At about 7:30, an extremely beleaguered, beaten-down-looking surgeon came down the hall. I went out to meet him. This man was exhausted beyond words. He looked just beaten to death.

I said, "It took longer than expected?"

He said, "Everything is fine. She's up in the recovery room. You can go up there. They'll tell you when you can see her."

At about 8:30 p.m., they let me see her; she was in the ICU. She was a terrible mess. She was in terrible pain. She was begging me, she was crying, she was begging me to get them to give her pain medication. I immediately got the nurse, and she took me aside and said, "Your wife's blood pressure is so low that if we gave her any pain medication, she wouldn't wake up. As soon as her blood pressure gets higher, we'll give her some pain meds."

I sat with her and held her hand. She was just in terrible pain. She had a 6-inch incision under her breast bone. I knew they had done something wrong. Every 15 minutes, I would plead with another nurse to give her something to help her. They just wouldn't do it. At 2:00 a.m. I was sort of wiped out, and they suggested that I go home. The nurses said, "There's nothing you can do here. Until her blood pressure is higher, we can't help her. By morning she should be able to get some pain meds."

Sharon waved for me to go. She knew what I was feeling. I didn't want to go, but I was crippled. I couldn't handle seeing her like that, so I went home and passed out with all my clothes on, on the bed. I was just exhausted. I had parked my vehicle on the bottom of the hill; I could have never gotten up the hill through the snow.

As soon as I woke up in the morning, about 7:00 a.m., I got back down into my vehicle and got back to the hospital. She was awake, but they had given her pain meds an hour before. So at least she wasn't in a bad shape. I stayed with her all day and all night. They put her back out of the ICU into a regular room and gave her a sleeping pill at night. When she went to sleep, they told me to go home. I went home. I came back early the next morning. For the first time, we saw this doctor who had admitted her. The pulmonary doctor. He had apparently taken off Friday, left town for the weekend, and couldn't get back til Tuesday. He came walking in and said something to the effect of, "I'm really sorry."

Sharon said, "What are you sorry about?"

He said, "We can't do anything for you."

She said, "What do you mean you can't do anything?"

He said, "Hasn't anyone given you the diagnosis over the weekend?"

No one had said a word to her about what they had found. She said, "No, no one has said anything. All they did is give me this terrible surgery."

This doctor looked at us, and I could see the frustration on his face. He said, "You're in 4th stage, end stage. You're way beyond anything we can do. There's no surgery or radiation we can do. You've got 2 weeks to live. There's nothing we can do." That was the first we heard since we came into the hospital of how short of a period we would have together.

Without going into all the grim details, he said to me, "Take your wife out of here. Get her out of here. She's going to be required to see a chemotherapy doctor before she leaves. That doctor is going to try to put her on chemotherapy." He said, "Don't do it, don't take anything. Nothing is going to help you. She's got 2 weeks to live, a month if you're very lucky." He said to me, "Do you know any place in the sun by a beach that you could take her?"

I had a friend down in Sarasota, who had already told me that if anything bad happened I could bring her down there. I said, "Yea, I've got a friend in Florida."

He said, "Get on a plane immediately. Get her out of here. Don't let the chemo doctor talk her into anything." He said, "Walk along the beach. You 2 don't have much time together. You won't have much time left."

We left that day. They had a lot of meds to give her. We began frantically praying and talking to everybody we knew. I talked to the medical people I knew. We began looking for a miracle. There was a long-shot hope that might change her condition if we could get her into a certain type of therapy that was going on around the country. We made all the arrangements, all the connections, and airline reservations. 3 days later we flew down to Sarasota. My friend was there to meet us at the airport. We went to his house, we connected with a doctor down there, and we began this therapy. She started to get better; she started to get stronger. We had her on massive amounts of supplements and organic fruits and vegetables and juices. She was feeling better and better. The 2-week period that we had together turned into 4 weeks, then turned into 6 weeks, and then 8 weeks, as we were doing this therapy. We had lab work done almost daily. She was also told that she was in congestive heart failure. Into the middle of May, some of the lab work was starting to come back, reporting that the tumor size was decreasing. We got our hopes very high. We thought that we had manifested a potential miracle. Then, at the end of May, in a period of 3 or 4 short days, everything started coming apart. If I were to give all the details of what we were doing and how we were doing it, it would be a very long, sad reading. So I'm going to skip all that and go right to May 30.

It was Sunday afternoon before Memorial Day. That day, I just had such terrible, terrible feelings that everything was coming apart. She was sitting in a chair, and I was sitting on the floor at her feet. She looked at me and said, "You think I'm going to die, don't you?"

I just started crying.

She hadn't at that point been able to sleep 1 minute for 3 days. Her breathing had become laborious to gasping and struggling. That night she couldn't sleep again, for the 4th day in a row. I sat up with her all night. Early in the morning, she said, "I want to start talking to the kids (her siblings)."

She said the only one who would be awake now was Sheila, who was on the East Coast. We called Sheila, and Sharon talked to her. Sheila got on the phone with me and said, "Tell me what her condition is."

I said, "She is rapidly bloating up. She hasn't had any kind of bowel movement or urination, her legs are swelling, and her abdomen is swelling by the hour."

Sheila said, "Get a nurse. Get a nurse in there to try to get a tube in her to empty her bladder. Call me back later, but get a nurse."

We had nurses. I called a nurse, and she got there a few hours later. Meanwhile I talked to 2 of the doctors. One of them, I had tried to get to give her a sleeping med for days. He said, "No, it's too dangerous." But now hearing her condition this Monday morning, he called the other doctor and ordered Valium for her. The nurse came, put a catheter in her, and started draining fluid out of her. It was just thick brown syrup. The nurse's expression told me there wasn't much time left. My friend went out and filled the script and came back. I opened the bottle of Valium and took 1 pill out.

Sharon said, "Give me 2."

I said, "No baby, I'll just give you 1."

She said, "Give me 2!"

I said, "No," and I handed her 1 pill. She took it immediately, and I gave her some water. The catheterization was still going on. I was helping the nurse empty a pan and put another pan in, and I noticed Sharon was very still. She was propped up, almost sitting straight up. I climbed up by her. Her head was on her other shoulder. I turned her face, and she was turning purple. I turned to the nurse and said, "Does this mean…?"

And she just shook her head yes.

I held her in my arms. She took a deep breath, and then she rattled, sort of shook. Then I lost it. The nurse said to me, "She's gone." I screamed so loud. I could probably be heard by all the neighbors. I screamed for Jesus to come and be with her. I screamed for her ancestors. I screamed for my mother to come be with her.

After that it was all just hard stuff. The nurse called the police. A paramedic team was in the room in no time. Police were there asking me questions. I was a basket case. The nurse pushed me aside; she talked to them and told them the story. They asked if it was an expected death, and the nurse said, "Yes." They said they didn't have to call the coroner then. Somebody called the funeral home, and then an hour or so later, somebody came in with a gurney and took her away. I felt like I had had a cannonball shot through my chest. I felt a hole through my chest.

The next couple days were sort of a blur. I cried almost continuously. I made arrangements for her cremation that she had chosen. A week or so later, I flew back to Colorado Springs with her ashes on the seat next to me. In her last hours, she had told me very clearly twice, "You can't come with me. And you can't follow me. You have to go home and clean up my mess and empty our house and sell it and get out of Colorado Springs. Go find a place in paradise. Find another woman. And get on with your life." I believe, if she had not told me that, I wouldn't have lived 24 hours. I wouldn't have committed suicide or anything, but I couldn't have lived.

When I got home, I sat in the living room. I felt that I could just sit there and close my eyes and leave my body. But her words rang in my ears repeatedly. You can't come with me, and you can't follow me. So I started a process the next day of doing exactly what she told me. I started emptying out this house. I couldn't even imagine giving away anything that was valuable to her to any stranger. I couldn't throw it away; I couldn't give it to Salvation Army. What she couldn't do with her dad, I couldn't do with her.

Some of the kids came right away. They tried to console me, offered to help. A niece of mine in California said, "Let me come out and help you." I let her come. I began a process of going through everything that my self-described pack rat wife had collected her whole lifetime. All her treasures, everything that was special to her, her clothes, her books, her collections from all over the world. I wanted to find homes for everything. I had her phone book. I knew who all her girlfriends were all over the country. Before I left, the day that she passed, about 4 hours after she passed, I sat down and wrote an e-mail and directed it to all the people in her mailing list. All her friends and her family. I told them what had happened, that she was with her ancestors. So I used that list and began calling all of her old girlfriends, many of whom I had met over the years. I asked them if they wanted any of her things. Most of them didn't know what to say; all of them agreed to let me send them something. My first priority was collecting all of her treasures as she called them and finding them homes. For the first 2 or 3 weeks, I did nothing but box up large boxes of clothes and scarves and jewelry and books, everything that meant something to her. I would pick out who I thought would be glad to have those things. I kept the receipts in one pocket from UPS and the post office. I went to one of those stores every day with my van full of boxes. In 3 weeks, I sent over a hundred boxes, $1,785 worth of postage. I dispersed all of the things that were of value. Prior to that, of course, I had all of her sisters come, and they went through all of her things, taking anything that meant something to them. Anything that the family wanted, they had first priority. Then I still had a giant house full of things, and I started giving everything away that I could.

We planned a memorial for her in late June. Her family came. The siblings, all the kids came. We had an incredibly wonderful memorial service for her. Again, I invited everybody to take anything in the building that they wanted. Artwork, everything and anything. When that ended, I got down to sorting out what I might want, what I might need to start another house. Then I found people all over. People from Boulder to Pueblo, friends we knew, who needed furniture or decorations. She had given me the phone number of a girlfriend before she passed. She said, "If I should leave, this lady will help you sell the house."

At that time, the housing market in the Springs was absolutely crushed. It was horrible. Nobody could sell anything. I called this lady, and she said, "Give me a few days. I'll find a buyer." She wasn't actually a realtor.

I had yard sales. I took just everything out of the building. There were tons of cars lined up, and all day long people came and took things. After a few days, her friend called and said, "I'm bringing a man over tomorrow." She came over with this man and introduced us. She said, "He's moving here from San Diego. He'll buy the house." He came several times over the next week or so, and he finally made me an offer. He asked me what I wanted. He made me an offer for $25,000 less than that. I took it immediately. By now it was into September. My friend in Florida had invited me to come back and spend some time with him.

It was getting close to October by the time the house deal went through. It dragged on and on because this man had trouble getting financing. But finally, it went through. The house was sold. I got a pod and had it put in my driveway. I put everything I needed to start another house, all my things and all of Sharon's that I wanted to hold on to. I filled this large pod and put it into storage. Then I filled my vehicle. I think it was about the first of October when I drove out the driveway, tears flowing freely, and I headed for Florida.

When I got to Sarasota, my friend said, "Just stay here as long as you want." I was numb… It had taken about 4 months to complete the emptying of the house and the selling and leaving Colorado Springs. What happened after that down in Florida is that I became somewhat of a robot. I fell into my friend's routine. He was an early riser. We'd go somewhere and have breakfast. We'd watch TV in the afternoon, watch the news. He would go to bed early. I would go to my room and just watch television. I felt literally as though I had nothing in me. I felt just empty. I stayed in Sarasota for 6 to 8 months. Then I decided to go back to Colorado Springs. I had the pod with all my goods in it. I had unfinished business. I decided I had been a burden on my friend for long enough. I went back to Colorado Springs. I stayed in a motel for a few weeks, and then I rented a house. The house was furnished, so I kept all my goods in the pod.

In 2006, I hardly remember anything. I was back in the Springs, but I was zombie-like. All my friends, especially all the Wang kids, they were all so loving to me. They did everything they could to cheer me up. There was no cheering me up. I don't call what I went through grief. I used to be a hospice volunteer. They saw the ad about Sharon's passing in the paper. They called me and offered me grief counseling. I didn't take it. I didn't want to hear anything. I didn't want to be cheered up. Nobody could say anything that meant anything. I didn't feel like I was grieving. I felt like I was dead inside.

A Trip to Teotihuacan with Miguel Ruiz

In 2007, I got an e-mail from a site that Sharon had plugged me into years before. It was from the site of Miguel Ruiz, who had written a book called *The Four Agreements*, which had somewhat swept the country. Sharon had read all of his books, and had gotten me to read *The Four Agreements*. When I was leaving Sarasota with her ashes, I saw the book at the airport. I remembered that she had me read it. I bought the book and read the entire book on the plane.

One day I got an e-mail, and it was Miguel Ruiz inviting people to go to Teotihuacan, the Toltec pyramid site outside of Mexico City. For some reason I felt, this would be good for me. I should do this. So before Easter of 2007, I flew out to Mexico City and was bussed out to the pyramid site. I was still in the same condition in my mind. That day, I was sitting in the hotel restaurant, finishing my breakfast. I hadn't really talked with any of the group of people. I saw across the room that Miguel Ruiz had finished his breakfast. Then I watched as a half a dozen people brought books and had him sign them. They talked, gabbed with him, but then all of a sudden, he was just by himself. I was sitting across the room by myself. He looked right at me, and we made eye contact. I got up and walked over to him. He was a beautiful, beautiful man. I was struck immediately when I got close to him. I had seen him do 2 or 3 talks, but I always sat at the back of the room. I had never been close to him until that moment. He smiled broadly at me, and I think I might have smiled for the first time in years. He looked at me, motioned for me to sit down next to him, and said, "I have something for you."

I didn't know what he meant. I didn't say anything.

He said, "You're suffering inside." And he was certainly right about that. He said, "I have something for you."

I said, "What do you have for me?"

He said, "I have words for you to say when you feel the way you feel now. When you feel the way you feel, I want you to take in deep breaths, and I want you to say to yourself, 'I breathe in love to remove all past pain and suffering.'" I just sat there.

He said, "Do it right now. Close your eyes, take some deep breaths, and say, 'I breathe in love to remove all past pain and suffering.'" I closed my eyes and did it. He said, "Keep doing it." I did it for 3 or 4 minutes and stopped.

He said, "No, keep doing it." I must have sat there 10 minutes; then I opened my eyes, and I actually felt relieved. Just a tiny bit, but for the first time in almost 2 years I felt some relief from the hole in my chest.

He said, "I want you to say this every time you remember, every time you think, every time you feel what you've been living with. No matter where you are, take deep breaths and repeat those words." I started doing it, and within 24 hours I felt tremendous burden off of me.

I had brought along to Mexico a whole bunch of Sharon's little shells and crystals and a baggy of her ashes. I went out among the pyramids the next day and I found different places. There were places that were explained to us that were special places for the Toltec women priests and shamans. I went to all these places and I did little ceremonies. I dug up the ground, and I put in her flowers and things. I went all over the sites, burying her stuff all around the pyramids. By the time I left, I was greatly relieved of this burden. Within 30 days, I felt I was 90% to 95% free of what I had felt from the moment she took her last breath. After that, I was back in the Springs. I still tried meditating. I still read spiritual books almost every day. Through the 5 months of emptying out the house, I had meditated every night, journaled every night, written to her in a journal every night, written to my low self, my high self, and cried every day for that entire period. I continued to do those things, trying to make sense of what I was left with. Sharon and I had planned our life. We had committed to each other to essentially always be together and even to leave the planet together. The night before she passed, she apologized to me. I said, "What are you apologizing for?" With tears, she said, "I'm breaking our agreement. I'm leaving you alone."

Botulism

SEVERAL YEARS LATER, I was able to start thinking clearly for the first time. But I had no direction. I had no real desire to do anything. I essentially got trapped in the Springs. I sort of found a new group of friends that I met at the racetrack. I would spend my days at the racetrack, mostly sitting by myself. I just allowed 2008 to disappear. I did a little bit of traveling. I went to Chicago, visited friends in Michigan, saw my sisters in Wisconsin and friends in Kentucky, and went out to the West Coast. I engaged in some of the Wang family gatherings. We had a gathering in Hawaii after Sharon had passed. The next year we did a family vacation. I put on a brave face whenever I was around people, but I was always empty inside. When 2009 came, my sister-in-law Sheila's oldest son Paul was to be married in Michigan. She encouraged me to come. I told her, "Of course I'll come." I prepared for the trip. I was going to extend it from the Michigan wedding, at least another month. I would see all my Midwest friends, go down to Florida, see my friend down there, and go out to California. I packed my vehicle for my month on the road and I bought a brand-new suit to wear to the wedding.

I planned to leave at 5:00 a.m. and drive straight through to Michigan. The night before, as I would normally do before a road trip, I had a cooler full of ice and I decided to make sandwiches. I was going to make 4 tuna sandwiches to eat on the road. I couldn't find any tuna, but I found an old, big can of salmon. My little voice said, "Be careful." I knew the can was old, but I opened it up and smelled it, and it smelled fine. I made a big bowl of salmon salad with mayonnaise and chopped onions and pickles and olives. I made 4 big sandwiches, wrapped them up, took them out to the car, and put them in the cooler. That was the last thing I had to do before carrying out bottles of water. In cleaning up, I had probably a tablespoon or two left in the bowl, and I just scooped it out and ate it. I cleaned out the kitchen. I would be ready to leave at 5:00 a.m.

At about 4:00 a.m., I woke up in a frightful condition; the room was spinning. I sat up in my bed, and the room was just swirling, and there were sounds like waves. There were strange colored lights. I felt like I had to get to the bathroom immediately. I tried to stand up, but I just fell on the floor. I crawled to the bathroom, lifted the toilet seat, and projectile-vomited like I never had in my life before. It was so violent that I almost couldn't believe that my body was experiencing what I felt. I vomited and vomited and vomited. It went on and on and on. I had probably 4 gallons of water in bottles on the floor in the bathroom. When I finally stopped vomiting, I grabbed one of the bottles, took a big drink of it, and tried to get to my feet. I couldn't get up and started vomiting again. I did that until about noon. For at least 7 to 8 hours, I didn't move from the toilet. I kept drinking water and projectile-vomiting. There was this voice in my head—it wasn't my consciousness; it was a voice that I have heard occasionally through my whole life and sounds like it comes from outside. The voice said, "You have botulism." Botulism didn't really mean much to me except that I vaguely remembered when I was a little boy that people would sometimes get botulism from eating canned goods.

At about noon the vomiting stopped. I tried to get on my feet, but I couldn't. I crawled back into bed. I fell asleep. I slept maybe 3 to 4 hours. When I woke up, the room was still spinning in circles. I tried to get up, I couldn't, and I crawled back to the toilet and started all over again. This round ended in 2 or 3 hours. Eventually, I crawled into my living room to my phone. In all this time, I never thought of asking for help, not for one minute. There was nobody in Colorado Springs who would have come to my house because everybody that knew me, knew I was gone that day for a month. I got to my phone and pulled myself together enough to call my sister-in-law and tell her what had happened. I'm not sure if it was the day of the wedding or the day before. I told her I was deathly sick. I hung up the phone and crawled back into the bathroom. More of the same ensued. I was now filling bottles of water in the bathtub and drinking and vomiting repeatedly.

Finally, at 10:00 or 11:00 p.m., I was able to crawl back again to my bed. I slept all night until almost noon the next day. When I woke up, I was still terribly sick. I was so weak, I couldn't even believe it. I looked at myself in the mirror, and I looked emaciated. I could stand, and, holding onto the walls, I could walk to the kitchen. I had bottled water in the refrigerator. I started drinking that. I looked over at it and weighed myself. And in the 2 days I had been vomiting, I lost something like 20 pounds. 20 pounds off my body. I lost all my biceps; my buttocks were gone. I still had some leg muscles, but my chest was gone too.

Somehow I survived that. I had just stayed home. I didn't tell anyone in town. After 3 or 4 days, I could get into my car. I started eating again. I called my rolfer friend down in Santa Fe. I started telling him what happened to me, what I was experiencing. He interrupted at one point and said, "You had botulism poisoning." I hadn't mentioned botulism, just my symptoms.

I said, "How did you know that?"

He said, "I've dealt with it before, and it's exactly what you went through. It's amazing you're alive. If you had someone there who called 911, you wouldn't have lived. They would have stopped your vomiting right away, and the botulism would have killed you. The body fought off the toxin the only way it knew how—blowing it out of you, every time it could. Every time you took another drink, more botulism was expelled from you. You've gotta get down here as fast as you can because I've got to work on you."

I went down the next day. He explained to me that botulism is like a neurotoxin. It's like being bitten by a poisonous snake. He said, "Botulism attacks the respiratory system." He had me on his table and said he could feel between my ribs, the tissue hardening. He had me put my fingers there and feel it; it felt like beef jerky. He said, "I've got to dig all that out. That's the botulism still in you. You may never be able to get it all out of you, but

I've got to get all of it out of your ribs that will essentially impair your breathing for your life."

So he dug into my rib cage, front and back for a long time. When he finished, he said, "Are you going back home now?"

I said, "Yea. I'm going directly home." He said, "When you get in your car, don't stop for anything, don't eat, get home as fast as you can."

I didn't ask him why. I got in my car, and 5 hours later I was in Colorado Springs.

It was nighttime, and I went to bed. At about midnight, I woke up, and the room was spinning again. I felt exactly as I did that first night; only, I could walk to the bathroom. I put my head over the toilet, but there was no vomiting. There was nothing coming out of me. I realized he had broken loose stuff that was now back in my bloodstream. I realized that I was feeling the effects of the botulism, but it had lost its potency. The next day, I went back to bed, went to sleep, woke up the next day, and I was okay. I called him and told him what happened. He said, "I knew that would happen. That's why I told you to get home."

Ending the 2000s

I WAS RAVAGED BY THE BOTULISM in such a way that it took months for my body to start recovering. I pretty much stayed by myself. Every time it rained, I would sit out on the porch and breathe in deeply the rain energy. I would pray furiously for my body to recover. That's essentially all that happened from the time I was on top of the great pyramid in Teotihuacan, watching the sun come up on Easter morning, after Miguel Ruiz had given me his gift, then the rest of the year was just trying to keep my body alive.

And that took me through the winter of 2009. In retrospect, it was amazing that I lived through that. It gave me a sense of almost miraculous things. There was no divine intervention there. I went through hell in those days and the months after recovering. But I can only say that my memories of that decade were very, very sad. The whole decade was a very rough time.

I'll close with these thoughts that I had written down about Sharon's passing. They were sort of an insight for me. I wrote down: "The greatest of griefs are above words and testimonials. They are incomprehensible to friends and foes alike. So also are the greatest of joys and happiness beyond words or descriptions."

There was nothing in my life that weakened my mind like the grief of Sharon's sudden departure, nor depressed me like the aloneness that followed. From the point that Sharon passed until the end of the decade was a 5-year period that, as I look back, I can hardly remember. I only remember that no matter what happened to me, I experienced it as totally as I could. After Sharon's passing, I had friends that wanted me to go out drinking with them. I had people wanting to give me drugs. I refused all of that. I wanted to feel what I was feeling, even though it was nightmarish. And for the rest of the time after her passing, the only good thing that I did was that I allowed myself to experience the incredible level of sadness and misery, pain and suffering. Somehow, in someplace in me, I knew that this was something I had to do. Not hide it, not obliterate it with alcohol or drugs, but feel everything. And some part of me said, "This too will be a lesson for you that you'll learn from." Maybe it was that strange little philosophical voice in the back of my head that helped me get through this very, very hard decade.

'10s

Life Goes On

As 2010 ROLLED IN, even as I speak and try to remember it, my life was foggy and hazy. Much of what I did in my alone time, I don't even remember. I know in my outer life I was very distracted with relationships with people on a very mundane level. I was doing a lot of horse playing. I was eating poorly. I didn't really have a handle on direction or purpose. But in the beginning of 2010, my sister-in-law Sheila had already for some time, even before Sharon passed, been diagnosed with cancer. She had called Sharon when she was first diagnosed and asked Sharon's opinion. Sharon and I talked to her a lot about holistic methods and natural healing. Sheila was a very important figure in the AMA. Sheila had pioneered in Chicago, a program to bring alternative healing methods into Children's Memorial Hospital, one of the major children's hospitals in the United States. Sheila was the force behind bringing various healing methods, forms, and concepts into an AMA facility. These kids were very sick, most of them with HIV and other incurable diseases. Sheila was very much involved with the AMA and had vast knowledge of all the cancer treatments, but from the very beginning of her diagnosis, she decided to go the route of alternative healing.

In 2010, we began talking by phone quite a bit and whenever we were together in each other's presence, we became cohorts in an attempt to help her win her fight. We also talked deeply and strongly about spirituality on the planet. Sheila was very much interested in broadening spiritual healing ideas and techniques and methods into mainstream medical consciousness. Sheila and I became closer and closer and talked a lot on the phone about her situation and about healing in general and spirituality as well. She was a very, very spiritual woman. She had many of her father's Taoist traits. Of all the Wang kids, I always had felt she had taken more of his natural Taoist tendencies. That is, of being correct inside and then vibrating that out into the world. Sheila and I became very close partners in healing.

At the end of 2010, at the advice of a friend of mine, who knew I was renting peoples' houses, said, "Why don't you think of a mobile home?"

I had never thought of living in a mobile home for my entire life. But I started looking around the Springs. I went to every mobile home park and didn't think I could possibly live in any of them. Then my next-door neighbor, from where Sharon and I had lived, suggested that I go to this seniors' mobile home park that advertised themselves as a 5-star seniors' park. I went in there and looked. I liked everything immediately; it felt right. In December 2010, I bought a home there. And for the next 3 to 5 months I had to clean up and fix up and change everything.

Then I basically had my cave. For the first time since I had moved out of the house that Sharon and I lived in, I had a comfort zone. I had gotten all my possessions out of storage, I had all my books and my artwork and my spiritual toys and tools, and I made myself a comfort zone. In 2011, I relived in my head a lot of the original Carlos Castaneda books. I had read most of them back in the '70s. I started reading them again, and I actually read the entire set. I became very deeply connected to the Toltec stuff. Of course, my experience with Miguel Ruiz at the Toltec pyramids in 2007 was very powerful for me. It helped pull me out of the darkness of the despair I was in. So I got into studying Toltec literature. I read all the Carlos Castaneda books and then perhaps 10 other books by other students of Castaneda or of Don Juan. Other Toltec people in Mexico. I got very involved. The Toltec work seemed to have really powerfully enveloped me. I often talked with Sheila about it. I had a few friends in town that I had bought Toltec books for. Once they read them, and then we would talk about the different aspects of Toltec spirituality, a very big part of which is lucid dreaming.

Into the spring of 2012, I talked a lot with Sheila about lucid dreaming. I had begun trying to manifest lucid dreaming abilities in my own world. I traveled at least once or twice a year back to the Midwest. One of the trips to Ann Arbor, I was in a metaphysical bookstore with Sheila. She came down the aisle and said, "I think you'll want to read this," and handed me a book written by Robert Waggoner called *Lucid Dreaming*.

I handed it back to her and said, "I don't think I need this. I've read all the Toltec lucid dreaming stuff."

She literally, as she had done only once before, literally smacked me in the chest with this book and said, "No, you need to read this."

It was very unlike Sheila to act like that, so I grabbed the book, took it, and went back to the Springs. And I read the book. It opened up all manner of different avenues into how to access lucid dreaming. It talked about how to actually manipulate the energies during a lucid dream. I called Sheila about the book, told her how incredible it was. She told me that she had just made a trip down to Brazil with a group from Ann Arbor. She had met a man in their group named Robert Waggoner, the author of the book that she had insisted that I read. She told me, "I just got back from Brazil and found out that Robert Waggoner, in the spring of 2012, was going to be doing some speeches, workshop stuff, about lucid dreaming, in Ann Arbor." I immediately said that I was coming for that. I got myself together and drove back to Ann Arbor.

In Ann Arbor, I met with this lucid dreaming guy. There were certain synchronicities in the book that were related to me directly. It was as though he had written them to capture my attention specifically. So we met with Robert Waggoner. Sheila, John, May Lin (2 of Sheila's kids), and I spent a lot of time with this man. Sheila arranged for him to meet a clairvoyant friend of hers. A woman named Barbara. The synchronicity of the meetings and the people and the timing all led me to believe that perhaps Robert Waggoner and his team of lucid dreamers (which stretched around the world) or myself, and Sheila's kids, or some combination possibly could, through lucid dreaming, might possibly bring about the healing of her cancer—which was progressing over the last year or two much faster than it had over the previous 9 years. So by the time I left Ann Arbor, Sheila and her kids and I had all agreed to form a lucid dreaming team where we would attempt to do certain procedures, wake up into a lucid state, go to where Sheila was, and put our hands on her and heal her. We had a little group, and I also enlisted Robert Waggoner. He had agreed on some level. I couldn't get him to personally say that he would do what I was outlining, but he agreed to start working with her through e-mails.

All of this was very exciting to me because I believed that as a combined group or individually, we could have one dream that could heal her cancer situation. So much of 2012 for me was focused daily on attempting to rally our dreaming group and through my own daily meditations, I attempted to manifest some lucid dream healing for Sheila. Sheila herself almost had a healing in one profound dream that she had where she was looking at herself in the mirror. She saw herself with long hair. In the dream she realized that she didn't have long hair; she had lost most of her hair with her treatments. That woke her up inside of the dream. She had a moment of feeling the energy in her hands, and then the dream disintegrated, or fell apart.

I had 2 similar dreams at that time. Both times I saw my hands in dreams; I woke up in one dream and saw my hands glowing. In another, I was moving from where I was in dream state into Sheila's bedroom. One time I got very close to her. She had her back to me; she was close to the wall in her bedroom. I had a moment of uncertainty with exactly what to do with my hands, and in that moment of uncertainty, the dream unraveled. Both times I felt close to completion of intent.

So it enveloped so much of my consciousness from the springtime, all the way through the end of the year. I talked with Sheila, 3 or 4 times a week at least. Her symptomology was getting worse. Her son John had been living with her to take care of her. Paul and May Lin also did everything they could to help and support. Sheila was sadly losing her fight. She made a second trip back to Brazil to be healed down there, but it didn't manifest any results.

In the meantime, Sheila was creating an incredible project that she worked on in 2012 through the beginning of 2013. She had conceived and created a project that was unlike anything that has ever been done in modern science. Sheila wanted to assess a mental health treatment that was widely used in Brazil. It was a treatment in the philosophy of spiritism, which contends that people with mental illnesses are, in fact, possessed or entangled with evil spirits. A spiritist treatment includes the use of mediums and healers and has a ceremonial element to it. Sheila wanted to assess these treatments by setting up a double-blind study in which the patients who were assessed and the doctors who were giving the assessments would not know which patients were treated by the spiritist healers. She was setting up a way to have treatments be done from Brazil to the United States, as well as in reverse, and then also within the United States. This project was an incredible piece of work that had the potential to make a complete paradigm shift in the Western mental health treatments and modalities.

Sheila already had a long history of trying to heal people who had limited success in conventional medicine. She had quite an involvement and history helping and researching interventions with PTSD, HIV and cancer. Now she was writing grants and putting together teams. I remember we would talk for hours on end. The team that she had recruited for this project was unbelievable. World-renowned scientists, psychiatrists, doctors, and researchers who specialized in experimental design assembled to work with Sheila on this project. They were all very willing to further and bring this dream of Sheila's into reality to widen the potential for spiritual healing being done in this country in medical facilities.

It was extremely powerful stuff. It was terribly exciting just to brainstorm with her on the phone. I had quite a background myself of knowing what spiritism was, going back to my days in the Philippines, because all the Philippines healers were spiritism people. In Brazil, South America, and the Philippines, there was a common thread of belief in spiritism, which has its history into the late 1800s in England.

As Sheila fought off her physical challenges, in the same fashion as her father, thought of healing others. She conceived and tried to manifest a paradigm-shifting project to try to bring about humanitarian spiritual relief for people with mental afflictions in this country. She submitted her grant for the Paradigm Shift Award in early 2013.

In early 2013, Sheila's symptomology became very challenging. Her cancer had metastasized from her breast into her lymph nodes, brain, and lungs. She had a most amazing doctor outside of Chicago, who had an incredible new technology, which used cobalt radiation with stereotactic lasers to scramble the DNA of brain tumors. She had had the tumors treated for over 3 years, and over 30 were removed with no cognitive degradation of any kind.

I took her from Ann Arbor once myself to meet with this doctor. He went over with Sheila her whole case history. It was an amazing thing. It was a one-in-a-million chance that she could meet someone with this man's skill and abilities. He did profound and incredible work with her.

In early 2013, she started having more serious symptomology. She had trouble breathing, and she had trouble with her heart. And at the same time, she was desperately trying to fulfill the grant work that she was doing.

Then it just came to an end. John called me up in late February and essentially told me, "If you want to say goodbye to my mom, you better get on a plane right now."

So the next day I got on a plane and flew to Detroit. Sheila had been hospitalized; she was surrounded with her kids and friends and loved ones. She had been in a coma. She had come out of the coma the morning I had arrived. But she was on a respirator, and the doctors were all very clear that she had limited time. That if they took out the breathing tubes, she would probably pass.

We did a ceremony in her room. The tubes were taken out; there were 5 or 6 doctors in the room and her kids and a few friends. When they took the tubes out, it was obvious that the medical people thought she would have only minutes to live. She shocked them. I don't think she shocked the kids or herself. She had a little bit of trouble breathing for a couple minutes, and then she got control over it, and then she was breathing okay. She couldn't talk because her throat had been ravaged by the tubes going down her throat. But she could do sign language, finger spelling the whole time. So she would sign to her kids anything that she needed.

By late afternoon on the day they took her tubes out, her room was filled with joy. The medical staff was shocked. It was such a celebration that at one point I was outside in the hall, and everybody that walked by the room was just amazed at the commotion. It sounded like it was a New Year's Eve party. I thought, "My God, they're going to throw us all out of here." Sheila looked to be on the road to recovery. That day I had the highest hope, I thought, "We're gonna get her out of here. We're gonna get her home." In the coming few days, some of these days the kids would stay overnight with her. In the end, she sort of relapsed. It became clear to me that she was going to leave.

I decided to go back to Colorado Springs. One part of me didn't want to be there and go through the same feelings I went through when my wife passed. So in the moments when I could be alone with her, I said my good-byes to her. She whispered to me certain things, requests that she made of me. We cried together. I got on a plane and went back to the Springs.

We were hoping that she might have an NDE (Near Death Experience) where she could have a last choice, where her guides would give her all the information about staying or leaving the planet. A couple nights later I was home. Her sister Susie, who was like a sentinel, staying by Sheila's side as much as possible, gave me a call.

I was sleeping. I woke up, and Susie said, "Sheila just woke up and wants to talk to you."

Susie acted as the go-between. It sounded to me like Sheila had woken up from some meeting with her spiritual guides and was asking me through Susie what I thought she should do. I had Susie put the phone to Sheila's ear, and I said, "Go back into the meeting and ask them if you can stay. If you can stay, if your body can be completely healed."

Susie said that Sheila understood what I was saying, and Susie hung up the phone. And the next day I found out that Sheila had passed later that night.

It was incredibly hard on everybody. Her friends—she had such good friends who loved her so much. It was especially hard on her kids.

After Sheila passed, the family planned a memorial a couple months later. I went to the memorial. There were so many people there, so many people who testified, who took the microphone and talked about what Sheila was to them in their lives. It was obvious that day that Sheila had almost the same kind of effect, an incredibly profound effect, on virtually everybody's life that she touched.

For me it was bittersweet because in certain ways it felt to me that some strange unknown karmic pattern had played out the same with my wife's passing, as with Sheila's. I felt a deep sense of loss of a spiritual friend and partner. I could only imagine what her kids felt.

It seemed to me that a light had gone out of the planet Earth that the people of the planet had desperately needed to keep shining.

In that same month, March 2013, maybe only days or a week after Sheila's passing, I had a dream. In the dream I was told that I should get canvasses and paints and start painting. The next day I went to a Michael's store. I didn't know what I was doing. I didn't know anything about painting. But I bought acrylic paints and brushes and canvasses. At the end of March, I painted my first picture, provoked by the dreams. I didn't know what I was doing with this picture. I was just throwing colors on. When it finished and dried, a couple days later I looked at it; it was just sort of a blotch of colors, but I had a feeling that it was me emerging from some state of effluvium. Some mudhole or dark place. As soon as I finished that canvas, I had another dream where I was clearly shown a picture to paint with a heart with various colors around it. The very next day I started painting it, and in a matter of a few days, I had duplicated what I saw in the dream. Then they started coming to me one after another. As soon as I finished one painting, I would have another dream within a night or two of painting another. They became more spiritually oriented, a lot of them with images of Christ or Mother Mary or Mary Magdalene. I had been reading for some months all of the Gnostic information that had recently been published about the early Gnostics, the early Christians, the ones who actually lived around and with Christ, and their early attempts to spread Christianity.

These readings were very different from the Bible. Most of the New Testament bible stuff was written between 200 and 600 years, after Christ died. I was reading information that had been passed on century to century, right from the people that were around Christ. So that seemed to play into motivating this series of 6 or 8 dreams which I then put on canvas exactly what I saw in the dreams. That was much of 2013. I was studying and reading a lot of Gnostic literature and having these incredible dreams. In the dreams I was shown the end result and literally given the information of how to do this or how to do that. It was something that literally had never played out in my consciousness. I had never in my whole life thought of myself as having any creative abilities whatsoever. I couldn't sing, I didn't play music, I couldn't write well, I couldn't write poetry, and I didn't know how to make artwork of any form. And all of a sudden, these dreams were coming, and I was putting them on canvas.

At the same time, I remember that, even though I was deeply involved with these spiritual activities, readings, I would write a lot in my journals. I would have various insights into various pieces and parts of my life. I meditated. I never had a sense that I was connected to the work I was doing. I didn't feel spiritual impulse. I thought spiritual thoughts, I did spiritual practices, but unlike most of my life, I didn't feel connected to it. It was a very strange time in my life. It was like the hangover from the time of Sharon's passing, where I had become vacant inside. I was doing all these things, and at the same time I saw out in my world, there was a very subtle disintegration going on of my moral fabric.

I was involved with negative thinking in a way that was foreign to me for most of my life. I was deeply involved with condemnation and blaming. I was blaming the government for wars, I was blaming the bankers for manipulating society, and I was blaming the billionaires. I was so entrenched in negative thinking, it played over into my life, into relationships that I had with innocent people who were always my friends. All of a sudden, I was changing. Almost like Jekyll and Hyde. I was suddenly into condemnation and criticism of people. I was creating trouble and I wasn't even aware I was doing. I was sort of sliding down a slippery slope without even knowing it, while at the same time reading voluminous amounts of spiritual books. It was a strange period that I can hardly even make sense of at this time.

As 2013 came to a close, I felt disconnected from my own spiritual realities while spending hours every day in reading and writing and contemplating spiritual truths, but I didn't feel them. It was like I was robotically doing the spiritual work I had done most of my adult life; only, I didn't feel the rewards. On the other side of the coin, I watched myself just involved with negativity that I couldn't seem to pull myself out of. I didn't pull myself out, because I didn't fully realize I was in.

A New Challenge

In January 2014, I went to a football party. I ate too much food. It didn't agree with me, and I had trouble for several days with very obvious digestive intestinal issues. I didn't think much of it; normally in these situations, I would go on a fast and try to clear my system out. I did go on about a 20-day water fast. But into February, my body wasn't functioning right. I was having trouble that I had never experienced. I started having difficulty breathing. Breathing had at various times in my life been an issue. For example, when I moved to Colorado Springs and moved to the higher altitude, it took me a couple months to get used to the thinner air there.

But in February, I had a dream. In the dream I was essentially told, "Physician, heal thyself." I was into the fasting period at that time, and I thought I was essentially doing that. 2 nights later I was in the middle of another dream, and the voice again said, "Physician, heal thyself." I really made note of it because every time I've had a repetitive dream they have always turned out to be important and not something to be ignored.

Into March, these breathing difficulties became more pronounced. I actually thought that maybe something was wrong with my lungs. I essentially hadn't seen or hadn't sought out a doctor in 50 years. I hadn't had a medical examination in 50 years. I had virtually nothing to do with doctors or the AMA since I was in my early 20s. So I didn't have a doctor to go to. The breathing became really problematic at night when I was trying to go to sleep. I would have shortness of breath that would wake me up just minutes after dropping off to sleep. I would be sometimes gasping for breath. As this continued on through March, I realized that I was in some serious trouble. I began to think for the first time in my adult life that I was up against something that my fasting hadn't taken care of and that all the little tricks that I knew, all the little methods of supplements and correct food, none of it was blunting this increased difficulty of breathing.

Finally in the beginning of April, I called my sister Judy in Michigan. She had been a nurse for over 20 years. Some of that time, she was a supervising nurse for the ICU and in cardiac care. So I thought she could maybe give me a diagnosis. I called her up and told her I thought I had COPD problems, some breathing problems. She said, "Tell me your symptomology."

She listened patiently. She said, "You don't have COPD. You are in congestive heart failure. Your lungs are filling with fluid." She said, "I want you to hang up the phone and go to an ER room."

I said, "No, I'm not going to do anything like that."

She said, "Then go to a cardiologist as fast as you can." In the next couple days, my breathing became so challenged that I could only sleep if I were sitting up. I had never been able to sleep sitting up in my life. So the next several nights I had almost no sleep whatsoever, maybe an hour each night. My symptomology was swallowing me up.

With a referral from a friend in town, I went and saw a female cardiologist. Within minutes of walking into her office, she quickly did an EKG and said to me, "You're in congestive heart failure. Your lungs are filling with fluid." Just as my sister had said. Then she dropped the bombshell on me and said, "You have a very bad heart murmur, which manifests in a leaking mitral valve. And you're in very bad A-fib (atrial fibrillation)." I had already, in the prior month, felt my heart beating out of rhythm, and I didn't think too much of it. I thought that it was just because of my lungs.

I was sort of in a daze at that point. I wasn't ready for this information. She mentioned open heart surgery. I could see on her face that she was quite concerned. Then she said, "Let's try to get everything under control with meds."

She put me on a blood thinner and heart medication, a water pill, and some other medications. That was the first week in April. From that point on, things got very bad for me. My body did not take to the medications at all. The side effects by the day became harder and harder to deal with. After a couple of weeks, the side effects were outweighing the problems I had going in there. The medicines were hitting me hard. At one point, near the end of April, I had an experience in the middle of the night where I sort of woke up in a hypnogogic state. I was in a half-asleep state. The medications had gotten me to the point that I could sleep, but I would be very groggy. I woke up in this state. I think rather than trying to explain it all, I'll read it out of the journal that I wrote the next morning:

I saw these things last night. It all started maybe 3:00 a.m. Waking up into this nether-land between awake and dreaming. It all started with a need to talk to my heavenly Father-Mother God. I needed to ask why my heart was so troubled with physical malfunction and problems. I asked if I was the cause of these months'-long issues. I asked if I could be helped to understand, just to understand. I'm not certain of the exact order or sequence of the events that I will now describe, but just the overall content. First there was a realization of a need of forgiveness between my father and myself. There was a rapid-fire series of pictures and realization of the hatred that brewed between him and me from my conception and the damage that that caused to my heart from before birth. Then I saw the flashing of pictures and memories of the added-on accumulation of damaging actions and events that had combined and harmed my precious physical heart all my life. I saw the abuse of sub-stances, which caused unnatural stimulation and damage to my heart. I saw the negative acts, thoughts, and feelings that harmed and assaulted my vulnerable, innocent, precious heart. I saw streams of harmful, mostly unconscious, negative behaviors and programs, all which caused hardship to myself and my heart. Then in a flash I again saw, sometimes in great detail, the negativity from my father to me, from the very beginning of my mother's announcement of her pregnancy with me. I saw the immensity of the hatred he bore for me; his unborn and unnamed son. I saw more than I can write here now about the hatred that grew in him for me. After birth the eventual hatred that grew in me for him. I saw the culmination of this most bizarre tragedy at his deathbed and my baptizing him in his comatose state at the clear direc-tion at both of our high selves. And then I saw for the first time since that event, the powerful need for forgiveness—not just forgiveness, but unconditional forgiveness. And then in a flood, a virtual tsunami, I saw myself orchestrate and choreograph exactly that forgiveness. Forgiveness back and forth between the lost soul of my father until in a here-and–now-type moment, I saw us embrace in loving holding for the very first time ever. Then I saw us both asking and receiving forgiveness from my mother, whom we had both used as a battlefield for our sad karma. Then everything switched back suddenly to my body. In rapid-fire, I again saw the hate-filled damage to my heart. But these visions quickly spread to the damage I had inflicted, both consciously and unconsciously, not only to my heart, but also to my lungs, my liver, my stomach, my intestines, all my organs, my brain, everything. All the damage that was done over my lifetime with substances, poisons, foods, and negative thoughts and beliefs. I saw myself engage in very powerful sorrow and appeal to my body for forgiveness for all the ignorance, stupidity, and conscious and unconscious harm that I had inflicted upon myself in this lifetime. There was so much more, but it ended this way, with a powerful, overwhelming desire and need to manifest unconditional love, unconditional forgiveness, and unconditional freedom. May it be so, may it be so.

That's how this experience, this visionary experience exploding in my consciousness played out in such clarity, it was like watching a moving picture, the memories of a whole lifetime.

Going into early May, I sort of got down to a pattern of trying during the day to recapitulate much of my life, trying to review and release—let go of the past, let go of memories, let go of experiences. I was trying to clean my slate somewhat as my body went into deeper and deeper malfunctioning. This was all related to my heart condition and it was affecting the rest of my organs and nervous system, and then the side effects of the medications.

In early May, Sheila's son John called out of nowhere and wanted to come and visit me. I think I sort of tried to deflect him, but he seemed somewhat insistent. I told him, "Sure. I'm not in very good shape. I won't be very presentable, but you can come."

He came close to the middle of May and only stayed 3 or 4 days. I was not even able to welcome him into my home. He stayed at a hotel/motel down the road. But in one of the conversations he had with me, just out of the clear blue, he said, "You know, you should get your life story into a book." Sharon had wanted me to do that at the beginning of our marriage. She had wanted me to write a book. Then over the years, I probably had 10 or 20 people tell me, "You've gotta put your life story into a book." I had thought about it for 20 or 30 years but not very seriously.

But one day John took me to a Best Buy, and he had a plan. He said, "We'll get a recorder and you just tell your stories. I'll plug it into my computer, and then I'll transcribe it into the computer." I didn't understand how he could do that. He told me, "I can type as fast as you can talk."

So we actually began with recording just a sketchy introduction and explanation of what the book would be about. He had to leave the next day, but we had started this book. John was going to, in the fall of 2014, take a trip overseas to Europe, India, Thailand, and New Zealand. He expected to be back in early 2015 and said that we would continue the book then.

Well, during that time in late May, I began faltering. During that time, from early January to late May, I had lost almost 50 pounds, and I felt I was losing this battle. At that point, my cardiologist sent me to another cardiologist. She had advised the new cardiologist that I have an ablation or open-heart surgery. He asked me, "What do you want?"

I said, "I want a cardioversion. I want the least-invasive procedure to get my heart out of A-fib and get my heart beating normally." I had done extensive Internet study on my condition. I felt that would turn everything around.

So in the 2nd week of June, I went into the hospital, feeling truthfully that I was within a week to 10 days of leaving the planet. I had no vital energy. I had no strength and was losing weight rapidly. This man did a cardioversion on me, which worked immediately. That night I felt better than I had for months. Then in the ensuing weeks after, I started getting stronger. I insisted to my first cardiologist that I get off some of these meds, which were producing ever-increasing terrible side effects.

By the middle of July, I was off of all the meds, except one heart med. I told her and the cardiologist who did the cardioversion that I was going to go out and try to find other ways to put my body back in shape. So in August, September, and into October, I sought out different holistic doctors, not really with any success. They did a lot of testing and a lot of blood work. They told me a lot of things in my body were wrong. They put me on thyroid medication and inundated me with supplements. I felt I got better more from getting off of the prescription drugs than from the help I was being given by holistic doctors.

In November, after a couple days of one synchronicity after another, I was led to a woman named Dr. Karen Bates, who was an NAET practitioner. That was a new system of treating body problems and allergies. This woman started working on me in November, and by January I was in the best condition since my problems began. My heart was beating better. I was stronger. I was feeling so good that I sort of went a little bit haywire. Instead of having my good friend Dave come over to shovel my walk when it snowed, I would go out and shovel my walk and then my neighbors' on each side of me. I had had 6 to 9 months of being very careful to not exert my body, to stay out of tension and trauma. In those days, I wouldn't even watch the news because it would weigh heavily on my heart. Now that I felt stronger, I sort of threw all of my discipline and all my careful behavior out the window. I had had months and months of a very careful diet. No sugars, mostly just live fruits and vegetables. All of a sudden, I started eating everything that was no good for my body; processed foods, junk foods, candy, cakes. I don't even know what happened to me; it was like I lost my sense of reality. Dr. Bates had gotten me to such a high point, and then I just threw caution to the wind. In February, I started going downhill again. She had gotten my weight up from 138 to 158. I was on such a high thinking that all my problems were ended that I had gotten extremely careless, and everything started going bad again.

In this time, John had made his way around the world; his tour of a few months had turned into a longer, stretched-out trip of about 9 months. Then I sent him an e-mail in April 2015. In the e-mail I just sort of haphazardly, not intentionally, mentioned that we may not be able to finish the book. Because again I was cascading down into breathing issues.

Previously he had told me that he would probably return maybe 3 weeks from then. What actually happened was that he sent me an e-mail and said, "I'm cutting my trip short. I'm going to be back Sunday night. I'll fly from New Zealand right to Colorado Springs."

That sort of shocked me. It was weeks earlier than I had expected him. But on Sunday night, at about midnight, I picked him up at the Colorado Springs airport. Then on Monday we just sort of talked about his trip. For 2 nights prior, I hadn't been able to breathe. I was going back into the shape that I was that had sent me to the cardiologist a year earlier. On Monday night, John slept, jet-lagged from the long trip; he slept long and deep. That night I didn't sleep for 1 minute for the 3rd night in a row. On Tuesday morning, I actually felt that I might have a day or two to live unless there was some intervention. So, Tuesday morning when John woke up, I had already dressed, and I told him, "I think you better get me to an ER room." I called my friend Dave, and John and Dave took me on Tuesday afternoon to Memorial Hospital. In the ER room, they quickly informed me that my lungs were full of fluid again. They treated me. It took hours, but they injected Lasix into me. In 2 hours, I peed out about a gallon of fluid that the nurses told me was straight from my lungs. Late that night they put me to bed.

The next morning the cardiologist who had done the cardioversion on me the year before came in and told me that I was in very bad shape and that my heart was much weaker than the year before. He said if they could, they would give me open-heart surgery right then. But I was too weak. He said, "No surgeons would ever put you on the table. You'd never get off."

So I spent 3 or 4 days in the hospital. I felt a lot better. They put me back on all the heart meds. As soon as I got back home, John navigated and guided me into the book work. For 3 weeks he stayed, and we worked on the book every day. Then he had to leave for a while to meet up with friends and family. He came back and again we went back to work on the book, which is at this moment, bringing us to June 2015.

I don't know what's in front of me. I see the options. I am now committed very strongly to a correct diet and following doctor's orders. Doing the meds right, the supplementation, and exercise. During the worst part of this whole period, in the early part of 2014 leading up to my cardioversion, I had continued during the day to read, study, and paint the pictures that were shown to me in dream state. During the day I didn't have a lot of trouble. I was doing the work that was being shown to me from the inside. I was doing the spiritual practices that I had essentially done my entire adult life. I never really felt connected to it. I mentioned previously, I was doing things robotically sort of, but I didn't really feel the way I normally did. Then in those nights, the first 6 months of 2014, at night I would go into the breathing difficulty. In those nights leading up to the cardioversion in June, I had darkness and fear engulf me every single night. I had never encountered anything like that in my entire life. I had known darkness and fear but maybe for hours, not for days, weeks, or months on end. So I worked diligently during the day to try to clean my slate, clean out my memory, to work with my low self to release everything that I was shown to be old negative patterns and experiences. But at night I would still be engulfed by fear and anxiety. At the point I had the cardioversion, all of that started turning around. By this time, June 2015, 1 year after the cardioversion, I no longer have any of that darkness. In the middle of the 3 weeks when John came from New Zealand and started working on the book, I had 2 nights of waking up each night at 3:00 a.m. with tremendous, tremendous influx of realizations and feelings that I can only say must have come directly from my high self. In which I was shown very, very clearly and told in no uncertain terms that my life had been well lived. That I had no reason for any recrimination or fear of condemnation or judgment against me. That I had lived a very good life, and each of these nights, when I had these realizations pour through me, it left me with an incredible sense and peace of mind that no matter what the future held, no matter if my days are numbered or if I lived 20 more years, my life had been well used and that I could be at peace for the rest of my days. I hold that now very closely as a treasure in my consciousness and in my heart. And I can, from this point on, proceed in hopes of healing this heart and living out a long life of more service to the light. And if it were to not be that way, I can leave this plane at peace with myself and with the world.

Thank you, readers, for your patience.

Special Recognition for Special Souls

I WOULD LIKE TO GIVE SPECIAL RECOGNITION to a number of people. These are people whom I may or may not have mentioned during the book. But these were people who were powerfully influential in my life in positive ways. These were people who one way or another helped me to be a better man and better human being.

Grandma

THE FIRST ONE I'D LIKE TO MENTION IS MY GRANDMOTHER, my mother's mother. She was born in 1891 in May in New Point, Indiana. Her name was Mabel Bennett. Her parents, if I remember right, came from Scotland and Ireland. My grandma, as I grew up, was a very tough, very stern, grandmother. She had five sons and two daughters. My mother had five daughters and two sons. But Grandma, from my early memories on, was a no-nonsense woman. Always busy. She knew how to do everything. Every type of cooking and clothes making and quilt making and canning foods. She could do everything. She was a very good example of a true matriarch. She married Frank O'Neil, my mother's father, early on in her life. She lived with him for 35 years, had all of her children with him. After he passed, she married another man, Matthew Schaffer, who was the grandfather I knew from the time that I was a little boy. Matthew Schaffer was a very stoic, very strong-willed German man who was very powerful in the outer world, but with my Grandma he was very compliant and very well behaved. He was a very quiet and very non-communicative grandfather. He talked little and shared little. My grandma on the other hand was always informative and direct about rearing kids and grandkids. When she laid down rules, we all knew not to cross her, not to get her angry. She was a very strong and wonderful woman. As I grew up, we lived not too far from her and my grandfather. My grandmother had amazing compassion for my mother's plight, my mother's difficulty. But in the very beginning when my mother met my father, my grandmother was dead-set against their marriage. My grandmother didn't like their marriage in any way, shape or form. After they were married, my grandmother pretty much distanced herself from their life and their reality. When she would come and visit, she would try to bring something- loaves of bread or food- something to help my mother out. But she wouldn't overtly be involved in my mother and my father's business. I don't remember ever seeing her in the same room with my father. She would always meet my mother when my father was working or have my mother come to her house.

She was always present, always looming in the background, but she respected the privacy and the life that my mother and father had chosen. She was somewhat helpless to really intervene, to help my mother out in very tangible ways. So as I grew up, grandma was always this powerful woman in the background. She didn't laugh and play a lot. She didn't play with us kids. She was always more of a director of our behavior. If she saw us in any kind of bad behavior, she would correct us immediately, tell us why we shouldn't do that kind of behavior. So that's how I grew up with grandma. In later years, in my teens, I would often go over to where her and my grandfather lived and do little chores for them. As my grandfather got older, I would do yardwork and things like that. I always had a deep respect, even tinged with a slight fear of her. But I never saw her speak badly or treat anybody badly. I understood where my mother got her saintly qualities. She got them from her mother who was a pillar or honesty and goodness. Grandma lived a hard life and understood that her daughter had a hard life and helped in any way she could. In later years, my grandma and I got closer. My grandmother had at one point, I'm not sure if I mentioned this already, but in her 70s, she had a very bad gallbladder issue that after a couple years got worse and worse. It worried my mother terribly. My grandmother didn't want to hear about surgeries or doctors too much and her situation got very bad at one point. I remember my mother got very, very worried. I knew that grandma was having a hard time, she had gone to the hospital and they had sent her home. I came home from work one day and my mother told me. She said, "Son eat your dinner and then get cleaned up, change your shirt and then go over to grandma's house, she wants to talk to you about something."

My mother seemed to be very relieved from the worry that had troubled her for weeks. When I asked my mother what was going on, she said, "Grandma wants to talk to you about it. You go over there as quick as you can."

I drove over to my grandma's house and I went in and she asked me to come into her living room and sat me down on her couch, sat next to me. I knew something big was up because she didn't look bad at all and the last couple of times I had seen her, she was pretty miserable in pain. She sat me down and said, "I want to tell you what happened yesterday evening. They essentially sent me home from the hospital to die. They told me there was nothing they could do for me. So they sent me home and I was laying here on this couch yesterday afternoon as the sun was setting."

She had her couch by her front window and the sun would set right through the front window onto her couch. She said, "I was laying here and Matthew was trying to make himself something to eat. In 35 years, Matthew has never cooked a pot of water. He knew nothing whatsoever about cooking, I cook every meal. I laid here and he was clattering around with pots, dropping things. All of a sudden I became very, very angry and out loud I said to God, 'I'm supposed to be taking care of that man and I can't do it. I want you to either help me take care of him or I want you to take me out of here.'

She said she then closed her eyes for a minute and in no longer than one minute, there was a brilliant flash of light in the room that through her closed eyes, was very bright. She said, she opened her eyes and standing next to the couch, looking down at her abdomen was Christ.

Now my grandma had never talked religious talk in all the years I knew her. I never heard her mention Christ or God. She was born and raised Catholic, as were all her kids, but I never heard her talk or read the bible. No spiritual talk whatsoever out of her. She said Christ looked down at her abdomen and sat down on the edge of the couch, right next to her. She felt the couch depress when he sat next to her. She said he never looked at her, but she stared at him and marveled at his youth and the vitality and the deep complexion and the redness of his hair and beard. She said he only looked at her abdomen and at one point, reached over with both of his hands, and put them down inside of her abdomen. She said at that time she felt a tremendous surge of heat, and closed her eyes and felt her whole body fill up with strength and energy and love (my grandma never talked love talk either). She said that went on for some short period of time, 15-30 seconds, and then she felt his hands coming out and he stood up and without ever looking in her eyes or making any gesture towards her, he just disappeared. One second to the next, he was gone. She said she was so full of energy and strength and vitality that she immediately sat up on the couch, went into the kitchen. Her husband was shocked by her walking in the kitchen and she told me, "I said, 'Matthew go turn your television on and watch your news. I'll make your dinner.'"

He was stammering saying, "You can't stand or walk…"

She said, "You just hush." My grandma never said shut up to anybody, she always said "hush." She said, "Just hush, go in and turn on your news." Then she made him dinner without telling him anything of this event. She told me then that she wanted to tell me about this because she understood that I knew spiritual things. She then went on to tell me that, after dinner, after she had cleaned up, she walked down two blocks to the local church. She occasionally went there on Easter or Christmas. She talked to the priest who ran the church who knew her a little bit. She sat down with him and told him of the entire experience that had happened just hours earlier. He was befuddled, he didn't know what to do or what to say. He thought she was wanting the church to proclaim some sort of miracle and started telling her it is a very hard process to prove this to Rome. She said, "I don't want any of that, I don't need to prove this to anybody. I just felt that I should tell you. I felt that you should know that this just happened to me."

Then she told him that she didn't have to ever talk to him about it again. He didn't have to report it to anybody and then she left. Then she told me, that earlier the same morning that we were talking, around six, she heard her garden gate creaking and she was upstairs in her bedroom; she was already up and around. She looked through her window and saw the priest sort of sneaking into her yard. He came into her yard and got in the middle of the grass right in front of her house. She said she watched, almost humorously, she watched the priest kneel down. He had a black bag, and he took out his vestments and he started making signs of the cross. He was blessing the house. He did that for about 10 minutes. Then he put everything away. Then he crept back out through the yard and then he was gone. When she told me about it, she was laughing, she thought that was very funny.

From that time on, I was in late teens, she and I had a different relationship. She would confide in me certain things that I think she only talked to my mother about. But she would reveal little parts of what was always, to the whole family, secret about her.

Years later she moved out to San Diego to be near a couple of her sons. Grandma had always said from her early 70's on, she wanted to live to be 90 and have a big birthday party. It was a couple months before her 90th birthday and I was out in California, so I drove down to see her in San Diego.

She lived in a mobile park then, two of her sons were close by and they looked in on her. But she was still totally independent, never had any health problems that I'm aware of from that day that she was healed by Christ. So she was getting near 90 and I decided that I really wanted to try to find out the depth of her spiritual understanding and experiences. So I went to her house and spent an afternoon with her. I had a little cassette tape recorder and I asked her if I could record our conversation and she said, "Of course."

I asked her if I could talk to her about her spirituality about her spiritual life. And to my surprise she said, "Yes. I've never told any of you kids anything about what I know about spiritual things. So I'd be glad to tell you. What would you like to know?"

I said, "Let me ask you from the beginning, can you remember how old you were when you had your first spiritual experience of any kind."

She said, "Oh yea I clearly remember I was three years old and we lived on the farm in Indiana, my parents were farmers."

She said, "On the neighboring farm, there was another young girl about my age and we would play with each other. One of us would walk over to the other's house and we would visit each other and we'd spend our time playing during the day. This was my only friend, my only playmate."

She said, "One day I saw my friend by our fence along our property and I waved for her to come over, but my friend didn't move. So I ran over to her and through the fence I said, 'Come on let's play!' My friend said, 'No I can't play anymore. I just came to say goodbye to you.' I was taken aback, and I was very unhappy to hear those words and I said, 'Are you moving? Are you going away?' And without answering my friend just turned and walked away down the road."

So she said that she spent a lot of time by herself thinking about that. Then she went home. Her mother and father were there and were getting dinner ready. My grandma said they were both unhappy, she could tell when they weren't happy and her mother sat her down on her lap and said, "Mabel I have some bad news to tell you."

My grandma said, "What is it?"

Her mother said, "Your playmate, your friend, won't be seeing you anymore, she's passed away."

My grandma told her mother, "Yea I know already."

Her mother said, "How could you know? It just happened this afternoon. Someone just came over to tell us a little while ago."

My grandma said, "She told me. She came to our fence and she told me."

Her mother said, "No that couldn't have happened. She died in her bed."

My grandma said, "No she came and said goodbye to me. And that was the end of that."

Then after that a couple years later there was a black man who worked on a neighboring farm and he would often see her through the fields and wave. Then my grandma would go by him and they would talk. She said he was a very old man. They were talking once and he told her, "You have the gift."

She said, "What kind of gift?"

He said, "You have the gift of seeing people who have passed on. You have the gift of knowing that things will happen before they happen. You have to protect yourself and your gift."

She said they were sitting on a stone wall and he very carefully for hours talked to her about how she had to not tell people about the things she saw. How, if she told people, they would make trouble for her and make trouble for her parents. He said, "You have to always not be afraid of what you see. Nothing will ever hurt you because you're protected by God." So this man tutored her in how to handle her clairvoyant or psychic abilities.

She said, "I won't tell you all the things that happened as I grew up. I would commonly see relatives that had passed on or friends. Sometimes I'd talk with them and sometimes not. When my husband Frank died, the very next night I saw his spirit standing out in front of our house. There was an old gas light outside and it was someone's job to come and turn it on at night and off in the morning. Frank was standing by the light, looking up at the house. I would just look out the window and every night as soon as it turned dark, he would be there and he would stand there all night." She said, "Finally I got annoyed with it and I put on my robe in the middle of the night and I went out through the gate, I approached him and I told him, 'Frank you're not supposed to hang around here, you're supposed to move on. You're supposed to go to heaven. Don't hang around here just because you miss me or don't want to be away from me. You move on, you've got another life.'" Very dutifully, as he always was, he turned and walked into the darkness and she never saw him again.

She had very clairvoyant and psychic abilities that she apparently shared with no one. She didn't tell her husbands, didn't tell her kids. I know when I told this later to my mom, my mom was just amazed to hear that grandma had told me these things. Once, grandma was just washing the dishes (my mother and my brother and sister and I, the little ones, lived upstairs from her at this point), looking out the window into the back porch and all of a sudden she saw my sister running down the stairs and a rope falling around her neck and my sister swinging out off the porch hanging by her neck. She immediately ran out the kitchen and as my sister came running down the stairs and turned to go down the next landing into the yard, my grandma snatched her by the back of the neck, pulled her to her body and a rope came down and dangled right in front of them. My brother had tied a rope up to the railing and had tied a noose in it and had just thrown it down. She told me that that kind of experience had happened to her many times. She scolded my sister for running down the stairs, she went upstairs and scolded my brother and untied the rope and said don't ever do anything like that again. So I sat and recorded all that. I heard these stories from her. There were more that I won't go into, some that I don't remember. She had this ability but kept it to herself most of her life, shared it rarely with anybody. When she told my mom about Christ manifesting in her front room and healing her, I went home and my mom and I talked about it for several hours and that was the first of any type of visionary or miraculous event that my mother knew that my grandmother was involved in. Apparently, my grandmother lived as a psychic clairvoyant through her entire life but just never told anybody.

My grandma was a pretty amazing woman. After my visit to her, I had to go back to Chicago. I missed her birthday party, and shortly after that, she left the planet. There was only one time that I ever saw her emotionally distraught or emotionally overwhelmed. That was at my mother's funeral. My grandma at that time was living in San Diego and when my mother passed, her two sons flew with her from San Diego to Chicago and it was in the evening during the last day of the wake, the funeral home was full. Every night of the wake, people who I never saw, who I never knew anything about, never even heard of them, would come in and pay their respects to my mom. Just talk about my mother with the most powerful reverence and love. My mother seemed to have touched so many lives that I wasn't even aware of. Anyways, my two uncles brought my grandma in and she goes up to the casket and she just came apart at the seams. I had never seen her cry or be emotionally distraught. She would show her anger at any time, but I had never seen her breakdown emotionally. The uncles took her from the casket and sat her down in the front row. One of my uncles told one of my sisters that he thought 911 should be called. No one had ever seen grandma like this. She was sobbing and crying. Then one of my other uncles, he grabbed me and pulled me over and said, "You know how to talk to her, you talk to her."

I got on my knees in front of her, she had her head buried in her hands. I pulled her hands away and made her look at me and I said, "Grandma, everything is going to be okay."

They were afraid she was going to have a heart attack. That's what everyone was concerned about, that she was having a nervous breakdown and might have a heart attack. I said, "Grandma, I know this isn't easy on you, but don't let it trouble your heart. My mom wouldn't want you to be so sad."

She quieted down and she motioned for me to sit next to her. We sort of wrapped our arms around each other. And she said something that I never forgot. I've always had a greater empathy and compassion for mothers in this position since then. She looked at me with tears running down her face and looked me in the eyes and she said, "Son, you'll never understand the depth of sadness and the hurt that a mother feels when she has to bury a child. And now this is the fourth of my children that I have to bury."

It struck me so deeply how wounded she was by this repeated pattern of having her children die. Everybody who heard it was very deeply affected, even to the point that a year later, my uncle John died and the other brothers said, "We shouldn't even tell her because she won't be able to handle it."

So they never even told my grandmother that another one of her kids had died. My grandmother was an amazing woman that, as I grew up, was this very strict and very strong matriarchal figure. She wasn't mean or hurtful to anyone. She loved animals, she loved her gardens and her flowers. And as I grew up, I had no idea of the strength and power and the spiritual nature of this woman until the events I just described. So my wonderful grandma, Mabel Bennett (later O'Neill and then Schaffer) was a rare, powerful woman. I got to be around her and I got to feel the benefits of her goodness and her good big heart.

Billy Dehart

NOW TO MY GOOD FRIEND BILLY DEHART. Dr. W. W. DeHart Jr. I met him when I was a bartender on Rush St. at 21, and he was in podiatry med school. We became very close friends in those years. He was the first person to influence me to begin searching for information about self-awareness and self-improvement. He directed me to Earl Nightingale, who was a famous positive thinker and self-help motivator. He influenced me to take the Dale Carnegie public speaking course. His father was a teacher of that course in Michigan.

Billy and I stayed very, very close. I was the best man when he got married. He then went to Michigan and became a noted podiatry surgeon and doctor. Later he became a minister and spent many years in China, Russia, Mozambique, and Haiti, doing ministry work, giving out Bibles and preaching. When he came back to the United States after many years overseas, we reconnected and reunited our friendship.

Billy was a man who was a natural healer. He had tremendous empathic qualities. He was incredibly sensitive to the suffering and the downtrodden, to the underdogs, to people that were in any kind of physical, mental, or spiritual difficulties. He preached for many years in Michigan. We lost contact for a long period of time, and then we reconnected. I found out he had married and had a family, and his health was not very good. I reached out and made a number of journeys up to Flint, Michigan, to see him and spend time with him. He, at that point in his life, was perhaps the first person that I had interacted with, who I felt had the Christ-like qualities of absolute unrequited, unconditional love. He loved all people. He had enemies, he loved them. He loved all life, all animals, and all creatures of nature. He exemplified an ability to not succumb to any form of reactionary attitudes or behavior or thinking or feeling related to any of the negativity that he saw in the world or that came at him. The last 10 to 12 years of his life, I communicated with him as much as possible; we talked by phone often. Every time I took a trip to the Midwest, I would always go up and spend time with him. His ability to vibrate and exemplify this idea of unconditional love just became more powerful, more palpable. The last several times I was up there, he walked with a walker, and he had some difficulty getting around. But I would go with him to different churches that he was preaching at, different men's groups, sometimes to see violent parolees; he taught prayer groups. He was a prolific prayer. I never knew anybody who could pray like him. Wherever I went with him, every person I saw was taken by him and touched by him. He had a smile on his face virtually every minute. He exuded enthusiasm, and he never complained about any of his hardships or difficulties in his life. He would give everything to other people. He was the type of person who would literally give the shirt off his back to a homeless person.

I'll repeat the one quality that he had, which in the last years, especially the last 10 years or so, so powerfully influenced me; it was his ability at what I believe was unconditionally loving every person he came into contact with and loving every form of life. Billy passed away just after Christmas 2013. We had talked a few weeks before that. He was overjoyed that Christmas was coming. It was his favorite time of the year, Christmas and Easter. I met many powerful positive thinkers in my life. Many teachers and gurus and spiritual beings who were powerful forces of light and love. But this man was more locked into it. He lived by Christ's principles; he exuded the highest form of what Christianity could possibly mean. He was, as I've repeated, the cleanest, clearest, unconditionally loving man that I've ever been in the presence of.

That was my good friend Billy DeHart. He was also the man who supplied me with the means and the money when I had to get to the Philippines to have my brain tumors removed when I was broke, and I had nothing. He immediately the next day had specially delivered to me the funds to get on an airplane to get to the Philippines. He was one of the truly great friends a man could ever have, and I'm proud to have been so close to him for so long.

Three Families

IN THIS PART OF GIVING SPECIAL MENTION TO SPECIAL PEOPLE, I've named only a few. It would take another part of a book to give full credit to those who have influenced my life in very positive and powerful ways. I would like to make a brief mention of my 3 families. I've talked about some of them through the book, but I'd like to make it clear that in this lifetime, I've been blessed by 3 families.

Of course, I have the family I was born into, my blood family. My twin sisters—my oldest sisters Jean and Joan—who have both passed on. Then my sister Joyce and my sister Judy and then my brother Mike, whom I have mentioned, has passed on, and then my younger sister, the youngest of the bunch, Carol. We came up in such hard times and depravation and difficulty, we never had a chance to learn to be a normal, regular family. There was so much dysfunctionality, it's truly an amazing credit to my mother for raising the 7 of us and have us all turn out to be essentially good people with good hearts.

I then, as previously mentioned, became somewhat adopted when I was 19 years old by what I call my Puerto Rican family. This started with meeting Joe and Nancy Martins. Both played such an incredibly important role in my life. Joe became, from 19 years old on until his passing, my best friend. He was my brother on every level; he was my spiritual partner. From those early years on, we searched for a spiritual meaning in life, even when we didn't know what we were doing, when we had no understanding of our path. We worked together, and we played together, and I watched Joe's children, Adrianna and Joe, grow up. Nancy took me into her heart and into her family with so much passion and so much love. She accepted me in such a way that I had never felt from my own sisters. She embraced me; she thought I was wonderful. Nancy was very psychic, very clairvoyant, although she never spoke of those things or of her gifts. But she watched over Joe and me and many times warned us before we were about to make errors in our lives that would have been very bad for us. Joe and Nancy took me to New York, to the Bronx, to Spanish Harlem, when I was just 20 years old. They introduced me to their relatives—Joe's relatives, his family, Nancy's relatives, her family, their friends, and the people they grew up with on the streets of the Bronx. It was such an amazing time for me because I was welcomed. I was obviously a stranger and an outsider. I know some of them even wondered, "Who is this white boy suddenly in our homes and in our lives." But because I was under Joe and Nancy's umbrella, I was accepted by a tremendous group of loving, caring people.

My Puerto Rican family were the opposite of my blood family, in regard to their incredible loving, passion, their joy, and their happiness. They showed their emotions in ways that, when I walked into that world, I was overwhelmed with the sincerity and honesty of all their expressions. There seemed to be pure joy among these people. None of them had anything. They were all hardworking people, but they just exuded happiness and joy. It was an incredible thing for me to be a part of at that early stage in my life. It continued to grow, and it continued to go down this path of me becoming part of a family of friends and relatives that stretched from New York City down to Florida. I met down there Slim Padro, Joe's cousin, and his wife Lulu, with whom to this day, I stay in close contact. We've been very close for 50 years now. Slim, Lulu and their sons, Raymond and Anthony—I became part of their family. It was just an incredible thing. I spent most of my Christmases and holidays with my Puerto Rican family. For the next 20 to 30 years, I lived with them, played with them, did spiritual work with them. They were all open to spirituality. They were all Christian-based, but there were so many of them who had had experiences, spiritual experiences over and above anything that would come out of normal Christian lifestyles.

This family became my foundation, and they became my happiness and joy all the way until I married, and to this day!

When I married my wonderful little wifey, she brought me into her family, the Wang family. That was another tremendous experience for me because when Sharon first came to Chicago, when I proposed to her, she introduced me to her brother Woody. We had an immediate good relationship and friendship. Later at the various gatherings of the Wang clan, the family vacations, etc., I was to meet Susie, Sheila, and Sandy. I was again blessed because Dr. Wang— was a true patriarch, not in a domineering, controlling way, but by his very beingness, he was the leader of the clan— and he accepted me so graciously. When I met Sharon's mother, she and I had a very interesting tug-of-war for all the rest of her days. She was an incredible woman in her own right, but she was a self-proclaimed atheist and thought that the paths of Sharon and I and what we believed and espoused were sort of goofy. And eventually I was to meet all of the nieces and nephews. I met Brian and David and later the twins from Susie's family.

Eventually, I became very close to Sheila and took a tremendous liking to her kids—Paul and May Lin and John John. When I first met them, John John was just a little boy. He was, I don't know, 6 or 7. I saw so much of myself in him, in my very early years; he was so happy and joyous. In my early years, pre-school, when I was with my mother all the time, I was also very happy and joyous. I was so well received by the Wang family. They were not as demonstrative as my Puerto Rican family with their love and their passion. But they were much more demonstrative than my blood family. So I had sort of a balance between my 3 families.

Not many people have gotten to have the type of experience that I had. It has been a true blessing to me and a joy. There are family members of my blood family, my many nieces and nephews who have gone unmentioned, same with my Puerto Rican Family, the extended Wang family—I'm so grateful to those that I've mentioned and those that I haven't mentioned because between the 3 families, I saw and experienced many different levels of camaraderie and love and caring and sharing. I am a very blessed man for the wonderful, wonderful experiences that I've had.

Additional Salutations

I GIVE A FINAL SALUTE AND HUMBLE GESTURE to all my dear friends and loved ones not mentioned in this book. My love and light to you all from my heart and soul. You know who you are, and if our lives and loves ever intertwined, then please, in this moment, know that I love and adore you for what you have contributed to my life. And I hope that in some way I have contributed to yours. Dear blessed ones, dear friends, thank you for being part of my journey and blessings to all of you.

Prologue: The Last 4 Years

I**N THE SUMMER OF 2015,** John Kessenich, my dear friend and relative, finished writing *CORKY*, the book of my life. At least we were both pretty certain we were finished. Now, more than 4 years later, I am going to bring the book up to date and finish the decade of the 2010s.

When we stopped writing, I was facing very serious health and heart challenges. I had many doctors and healers working with me, and it was time for John to get on with his life. So he left for California, with the task of transcribing all my stories into written form and into his computer, and I continued my work to stay alive.

As summer turned into fall, my condition slowly deteriorated despite the attempts of many doctors and healers, as well as medical procedures, to reverse my condition. I will not go into all the details of what was being done for me or by whom. I will only say that I had a team of dedicated people trying in every way to help me.

Also, during that time, I had a rock, an old friend and lover who, though living in Chicago, spent time every single day and night on the phone with me, sometimes for hours, to keep me grounded in hope. Her name is Nancy Anda, friend for over 35 years, and my dear friend and love.

Nancy flew out to Colorado Springs twice for procedures to shock my heart back in rhythm from severe atrial fibrillation—just one of my many problems. But the best way I can describe her help was that on many nights I felt I was falling down a deep, dark well, and she would call at bedtime and reach down and find my hand in the darkness and pull me up and out. Her love, concern, and DAILY connection to my mind and heart was a blessing I cannot easily explain.

Now Nancy was not the only person who kept me on the planet. My dear friend Dave and his wife Mary hovered over me and helped me every day in every way that I asked of them. Then friends, loved ones, and spiritual family, from all over the country and world, through calls, e-mails, prayers, and inner connections kept me going daily.

But in the fall, I was getting worse, and doctors were telling me to go for open-heart surgery as time was running out. John returned and moved into my mobile home. He had printed rough copies of *CORKY*, and we were pretty certain that was it for the book. We had gotten some of my life stories in print as a record, with no intent of really publishing or anything like that; after all, I was dying.

John and Dave went with me to meet a heart surgeon who was recommended to us. We were unanimous in our distrust of him, and after several people, including my nurse sister Judi, suggested Cleveland Clinic in Ohio, I began the process of contacting them and finally having them tell me to come to Cleveland ASAP, which was the very beginning of December.

Again, I will spare the reader the mostly difficult experiences I went through there but will give this short account.

Dave Cartee and I flew into Cleveland. John loaded my minivan with supplies and drove it to Cleveland. My niece Anama and my beloved Nancy joined us in Cleveland, Nancy from Chicago, Anama from California. The day before the surgery, we all met with the surgeon who went over the planned procedures. He was very relaxed and cool about what would happen. It was to be a 3 ½-hour surgery at most, no problems, no complications. Wrong!!

Now a personal note that I really did not share or hardly mention. But from well before heading for Cleveland, I had strong feelings that I would not survive the surgery. I had no fear whatsoever and was ready to leave the planet if that came to pass. I had, just before leaving home, spoken with and old man I had known for many years—who was a clairvoyant and medical intuitive—by phone. After a short catch-up, he asked why I was calling. I told him of my departure for Cleveland and what was in the making. He was silent for a long while and then quietly said, "If you go to Cleveland Clinic, you will die on the operating table." I thanked him and hung up. So, on the morning of the surgery, as we drove to the hospital, my dear friends were full of hope and encouragement, while I was silent with a certainty that I would probably never see them after this day.

I awoke after a nearly 9-hour surgery. I was first surprised and then shocked by the condition of my body. I will not drag this out but will report that I was in terrible shape. I learned in the coming days that many things had gone wrong, and though the surgeon had promised to come as soon as I awoke, I never saw him or got straight, honest answers. But apparently, I flatlined at least twice (Anama later told me the surgeon, after he was finished, told her 3 times). I also had what my nurse told me was the "worst case" of "pump head" syndrome she had seen in 16 years at Cleveland Clinic. But for me, despite terrible pain and complications, I was alive, and very grateful!!

On the 5th day after surgery, at the insistence of the hospital, John loaded me into the back of my minivan and drove me to the Self Help rehab home in Chicago. Much could be written here about how poorly I was taken care of in Cleveland, and much more could be written about that absolutely amazing job that the team at Self Help did in the next 6 weeks. From their initial shock of seeing the condition I was in upon arrival, to their honest assessment of what bad shape I was in and their candid explanation that they were not set up to handle such a case as mine, but were willing to try to get my crippled body back to walking—if I was willing to try. I quickly told them I felt I was in the right place, and they quickly went to work. 6 weeks later, I slowly walked out of there in deep gratitude for their incredible care and healing. As soon as John made certain I was okay, he returned to his home. Nancy, who lived not very far from the rehab, began visiting me and continuing her incredible commitment to my healing.

When I left Self Help, I moved into Nancy's condo on the lakefront. She took care of me in my very feeble condition for several months. In that time our love and mutual respect deepened by the day. In early April, I packed my van and left for home.

During my stay at Nancy's and continued recovery, I had bodywork done by a rolfer who had worked on Nan. She did great work in several sessions to rebalance and help my body begin to normalize. When I went for the last session, she said she wanted to do something different; she wanted to work with my energy body. I agreed, and she sat behind the table and put her hands on either side of my head and, for the next hour, neither spoke nor moved. I had 2 foggy but obvious recalls during that time. Both times, I saw myself floating above the operating table and watched the surgery team frantically working on me. Each vision was a little different, with people in different places and doing different things, but always with a sense of urgency. When she finished, I asked her what she saw. She said, "You tell me first." I did so, and she said, "You did flatline, but not twice, I think more than 3 or 4 times." Then she laughed and said, "But who's counting."

By June, all my doctors were not only amazed to see me still alive, but were in total agreement that the high altitude of Colorado Springs would not be conducive to my recovery, and would eventually be my downfall. So, Nancy told me to come back to Chicago and find out if we could live together permanently. Nancy had lived alone since her husband had passed many years earlier and was certain she would never want another man in her life. After my wife Sharon had passed 10 years earlier, I was also certain I would be alone for the duration, but we agreed to a 1-year trial to see if we, both self-proclaimed "staunch individualists" could live together.

I went to work on the very difficult task of getting rid of an enormous amount of goods, furniture etc., etc. With the help of Dave and others, I got things packed and stored; I sold my mobile home, and the first week of September, I drove back to Chicago with my van loaded and moved in with my precious rock—my loving friend Nancy—and her precious black Lab Buzz.

Nancy was a very private and busy, busy person. So, I knew she was sacrificing a lot to have me there. Nan was the hub of many social gatherings and activities. She did water aerobics, several yoga classes, exercise classes, as well as long walks with different girlfriends. She did morning yoga in the living room to a DVD tape, five mornings a week. She was part of a woman's group that she had started as well as many family gatherings and social functions. I tried not to get in the way of any of that. She also loved meeting with many of her girlfriends for breakfast or lunch. I mostly stayed home and rested, read, and did daily walking or treadmill in the building gym. Things went pretty smoothly. We would venture out together for movies, concerts, or live performances by people we had both been fans of. At Thanksgiving and Christmas, I joined in with her family gatherings, which were great. As the New Year rolled in, life was good. We had a very few moments of brief troubles when I overstepped my bounds, but they were quickly talked out and put behind us. But 1 thing was growing very clear to us both; we were very happy and deeply in love.

By the end of the year, I was recovered and feeling better than I ever believed possible when I left Cleveland. Nan and I settled into great routines. We both gave each other all the space and privacy that we were accustomed to and enjoyed everything that we did together. We had a lot of private time during the winter and spring and just got closer and closer. We flew to Florida and visited friends of mine and hers. It was a great trip. Then she asked if I would go with her to upper Michigan in August for a family vacation with her distant relatives. I agreed, and we drove up and stopped off at my sister Judi's house and spent several nice days with her and her husband Bill. They were married over 50 years. Then we went on to the family reunion. While staying at a cozy little B&B, we went to dinner in a converted courthouse, now a great restaurant. After ordering, I went around the table, got down on one knee, pulled out a ring, and proposed. She was absolutely surprised and delighted. Later she told me it was her greatest hope that I would ask her to marry, but she did not know if I felt that way. We were so happy.

As 2017 approached the holidays, I asked her to pick a date for our union. She did not hesitate. She said, "The universal day of love, St. Valentine's Day." I agreed and said, "Let me pick the place." I made a call to an old ashram friend who married people in Lake Tahoe and made all the arrangements. She was delighted. The rest of the year was a whirlwind of activities and plans for our wedding. Life was soooo good!!!

The Heights and the Depths

THE BEGINNING OF 2018 was wonderful. John and Jasmin came and spent New Year's with us, it was so perfect. Nan just gushed about what a perfect couple they were. Great holidays, followed by a wonderful birthday for Nan. We had dinner on the 95th floor of the Hancock Building, watching a beautiful sunset, then seeing the city light up at night. A perfect day.

Then the next weeks of preparing for our wedding. Nan busy with her daughter and granddaughter, getting her clothes and all her needs for the wedding ready. Her girlfriends were all so helpful and happy for us. My friends and family were overjoyed that I was in love and ready to spend my life with a good, loving woman.

On about February 10, we flew into Reno, rented a vehicle, and drove to Lake Tahoe. James McIntyre, my old friend, had gifted us with a honeymoon suite for a week at a lodge he worked for. It was really nice, and we spent several days exploring the area, taking long walks by the lake, and eating great food.

On our wedding day, as per our desire, we had a small chapel located in the lodge to ourselves. Sherry McIntyre, James's sweet wife, took many pictures and helped Nan get ready. James did a fantastic job and even cried as he said, "I am so happy to be uniting Corky, my friend for over 50 years, and his lovely bride." We were treated like royalty and were both amazed at how loving and caring Sherry and James were to us. Later we had a most romantic dinner, and the high energy never let up all night. We were walking on clouds. It was perfect!!!

2 days later, we flew home, still riding a wave of happiness that was magical. When we got home, there was much celebration and congrats from so many folks. We decided to have a wedding party, and 2 weeks later we were joined by her dearest friends and family and a few of my old friends. It was so good, I can hardly put words to it. Nan and I were inundated with so much love that we could hardly believe how blessed we were. Everyone had a great time, and the party was such a success. We were elated.

It continued on for weeks. We would even talk about it and wondered what we could have done for the universe to give us such happiness and joy. Nan told me several times it was the happiest she had ever been. I felt the same. We were so lucky, so grateful, so appreciative, and not ready in any way for what was in front of us.

On April 28, the day after we went to a Chicago Cubs game, we spent a quiet day at home, had a wonderful dinner, did the dishes together, and sat down to watch some TV. Nan got up and said, "I am going to make a cup of tea. Would you like one?" I said no thanks, and she went into the kitchen. Several minutes later I got up and headed for the kitchen and saw her legs on the floor. I ran in. She was lying on her side on the floor. I got down by her and knew instantly that she had a stroke. I talked to her and said I was getting help. She protested and said she was alright and just wanted me to put her in bed. I put 2 of my fingers in each of her hands and told her if she could squeeze both fingers, I would put her to bed. She nearly broke the finger in her right hand, and nothing from her left. I called 911 immediately. As I held her head in my lap until the paramedics arrived, only minutes later, I knew our lives would never be the same and could only begin asking for spiritual help for her to stay alive.

The paramedics quickly took her to a local hospital. After initial treatment, they told me they were not equipped to handle the severity of her stroke and needed to transfer her to Northwestern, where the best doctors to help her were at. Many hours later I was told by a neurosurgeon who tried to remove the blood clot from her brain that she would live. Then, he took out his phone and, with tears in his eyes, showed me the picture of the damage and told me that the clot had hit right on the area that controlled her left arm and not to expect to ever see movement there, and that the whole left side was severely damaged.

Even as we waited for the paramedics and in the ER rooms of both hospitals, Nan kept saying to me, "Don't worry, I will be okay. We will get through this." From these moments on, it was her mantra, her belief, and the only thing she would say to everyone. I will not go into the details of the coming few days, the hardest of both of our lives. But the initial tests showed she had complete and total paralysis in her left arm and leg and had extensive damage to her memory, cognition, and perception. But through it all, she had an indomitable positive attitude and belief and trust.

Then 9 days after her stroke, she was transferred to the Shirley Ryan Ability Lab, touted as the best stroke rehab facility in the world. 6 weeks later, she showed enough improvement in her leg so that she could stand and slowly walk with assistance of PT folks, but no help with left hand. In all this time, she worked hard, cooperated with all caregivers, and never complained, even though carelessness by staff led to 2 very bad injuries. She spoke only glowingly and lovingly to everyone, at all times. Life was hard for both of us. Harder than we ever imagined it would be.

John came back to help, and against the advice of the Ability staff, John and I took her home on June 6. I had ordered a hospital bed for her and gathered all the supplies we would need to care for her. During her time in rehab, I was there every morning early and stayed till after her dinner and was ready to sleep. So I thought I could handle her being at home. I arranged for home nursing, therapy, and care and thought I could find more good help. Though John and I did fantastic, we were in way over our heads. Nan was delighted to be home and being cared for by 2 men who loved her and she loved. But in 2 weeks we were both burnt out, and John needed to return to California. So I sat with Nan one morning, and as we both cried freely, I explained I had to take her to Self Help for proper rehab and care. She was so loving and gracious and told me not to worry and that she would be fine. The next day John and I took her to Self Help Home, the same place that I was rehabbed at. Many of the staff immediately recognized both of us from my stay and immediately made her feel that she already had a team to help her. I was grateful and relieved, and I took John to the airport to again get on with his life after showing her the best care and love that could be imagined.

I could write volumes about her stay in Self Help. Though I hesitate to compare, she was treated and cared for so much better here. The therapists did more diligent, conscious work with her. The caregivers were so much more sensitive and gentler (with few exceptions), and overall it was much easier for her and I to be separate for the hours I was not with her. Again, she stayed for 6 weeks, and in the meanwhile, I formulated plans to bring her home again. I had a dear old friend Chad Wensel from Colorado Springs agree to come and help me get her home, and on August 18, Chad and I brought her home again.

Again, it would take another book to write all the events after getting home, but I will do so at another time perhaps. What I will report is that she was happier than words can describe at being home and now sleeping together in our king-sized bed with each other. It was really great for us both. I again got professional nursing and physical therapists and found good women caregivers so that we could properly take care of her. There were many ups and downs in the coming months, and in October, after many months of planning and red tape to get her qualified, and really phenomenal help from United Airlines, Chad and I took her to a center in Boca Raton, Florida, where she had a spinal injection of a drug called Etanercept, an anti-inflammatory drug that went directly into her, in the hopes of helping the damaged area of her brain to self-heal. Nan felt help immediately with her speech, memory, and cognition. It was a very taxing trip for all of us, but I was determined from the time I took her home to try every avenue that might help her healing or ease her pain. We also tried many acupuncturists, pain therapists, bodyworkers and PTs. I must mention Jennifer, a trigger-point therapist, who did miraculous work on removing stroke-related pain that I was told would never resolve. This woman was a true miracle for us. Chad went back to Colorado in November, and things got a little harder. By this time, I was leaning on Leticia, a very dedicated and experienced caregiver.

As we headed into the holidays, I was focused on doing everything possible to make Nan's life seem somewhat normal. Though it was difficult on me, and I was truly unconscious as to the amount of pressure I took on and put on myself, still with decorations, Christmas gifts and presents she wanted to give, and all the other stuff, she had a great Holy Day period. As we entered 2019, I was burnt out again, with many outsiders taking me aside and pleading with me to take care of myself. I ignored the many warnings until—

My Fall from Grace

On the morning of February 9, I left Nan with Von, her young Filipino caregiver from Self Help whom I hired to come in every Saturday and bathe her and walk her, etc. I went to do some errands. I parked my car, got out, and fell on my face. For the next 14 days I have no recall of anything, not one moment. My first memory was waking up with John standing at the end of my bed. I said, "John, what are you doing here, and where am I?"

Again, I will make a long story short and just say what I read in the Northwestern Hospital records when I got them.

76-yr-old male found on sidewalk. No heartbeat, No CPR for 15 minutes. The records then describe 45 minutes of CPR, defibrillation, injections and then heartbeat–

From the hospital Nancy was called and told of my peril and that I may not survive. Von loaded her and her wheelchair into his small car and drove to the hospital. Nan was told I might not make it through the night and that I might have severe brain damage from no oxygen for about an hour. So now, I woke up in Self Help for the 2nd time, crippled and in serious pain. John tried to bring me up to date, but I did not remember any of the events of those days. He assured me that Nan was taken care of and would be okay until I got home again. I was devastated to hear what I had been through in this blackout period but more crushed at the realization of what she must have been going through and more to come. A woman cardiologist from Northwestern came to Self Help and told me that it was miraculous I was still alive. I asked her to explain what happened, and she said, "Your electrical system of your heart stopped from one beat to the next, and you went unconscious instantly. Essentially, you were dead when you hit the sidewalk." I had many thoughts in rehab of "On Borrowed Time" again!!! My mental distress in rehab was great. I was mostly worried about Nan and would I ever be able to care for her again. After 6 more very hard weeks, I left the rehab with a walker and to the absolute delight and relief of both Nan and I—returned home.

I spent our 1st wedding anniversary unaware and fighting for life. After a surgery and pacemaker, I then spent my birthday in rehab, struggling to take steps again. But now I was home and quickly put aside the walker and started the same routines I did when I left there after Cleveland. Nan had had a very rough 2 months without me. She told me much of it, and Leticia, who stepped up from day 1 to spend 24/7 with Nan until I returned home, later told me Nan would cry every night I was gone and she would have to go in and comfort and console Nan and assure her I would return. I needed to give Leticia time off and began her with taking a day a week off, then 2 days until Leticia was also burnt out in the summer. I very luckily found Olga, who was Von's aunt, and she took over. Leticia would work 24 hours for 5 days. Olga worked 6 hours for 6 days. So again, I needed to get back to normal to handle the extra care. But Nan and I were back together and could not help but count our blessings. Things were looking up again.

Shock and Disbelief

THE SUMMER WAS GREAT FOR HER. She dearly loved Olga, who was so tender, loving, and the perfect companion for Nan. Her walking was getting so good that she could walk 200 to 400 feet with just her cane and someone next to her. Her arm and shoulder pain were gone, and after the treatment in Florida, there was slow but steady progress and improvement with her arm and fingers. She could do things that we were told would never happen. Her primary doctor and her cardiologist were both very pleased with her condition. Then I got an e-mail from John from Germany. He had been on a trip around the world and was soon coming back. I was surprised because, even though his love and fiancée Jasmin was 6 or 7 months pregnant, he told me he was going to fly right to Chicago to visit Nan and I. We were happy to see him, and in mid-August he arrived at our door. For several days he helped me take Nan to appointments, fixed various problems in our house, and just hung with us. Things were really moving along nicely.

On the morning of August 19, Olga dressed Nan in a new outfit she loved. Olga fixed her hair and helped her with makeup and jewelry, and

Nan was so very, very pleased. We were going downtown to get her teeth cleaned. Before we left, Nan went on the Internet and found 2 wonderful brother cats who were at a nearby shelter and asked if we could adopt them. I said of course. At the dentist, everyone was glad to see her and remarked how wonderful she looked. She was beaming. When we got home, she went into the animal shelter website again and then called them. Nan was concerned someone might claim them. They were still there, and she arranged to go the very next day and we would claim them. Nan was beyond happy; she was picking names, which would be hers or mine, and where they would sleep on our bed. I had not seen her this happy since the stroke.

After a wonderful dinner that Olga prepared, John suggested a short period of thanks and voicing our gratitude. We did this and were interrupted by a phone call from one of Nan's friends. When she hung up, she said, "I do not feel well. I think you better put me to bed."

John and I did so, and then I tucked her in, and she wanted to sleep. A while later I went in, and she said, "I think I am going to be sick. Get my pan."

I did so and raised the bed, and in a moment, she vomited forcefully. I was not too alarmed as she had twice before gotten sick in bed. Nan said she wanted to lie back down and sleep. I said okay and tucked her in and went to the kitchen. A while later she rang her bell for me to come in. I went in quickly and was scared right away. She was wet with sweat and did not look good. I said, "Nan, since you came home, I have never suggested this, but do you want me to call for help?"

Very quickly she said, "NOOOO—but I am going to be sick again."

I got her pan and yelled for John to come in. As soon as he entered the room, he took one look and said, "SHOULD I CALL?" I said, "Yes, right now." He ran out and I got her bed up and she vomited again. John came back in and helped me hold her upright, and she continued to vomit. Then as soon as she stopped, she let out a long moan, went stiff in our arms, and had a massive heart attack. She was gone almost immediately, while we both held her in our arms.

John said, "Let's do CPR." So we laid her flat, and he climbed on the bed and began pumping her chest and counting, and I would breathe air in her lungs when he stopped. We continued in rhythm until the paramedics burst through the door and pushed us aside, and the 6 of them went to work. John put his arms around me and held me for the 30 or 40 minutes they worked on her. Then they said they were taking her to the nearest hospital and keep trying. 2 hours later they told us she was gone. We already knew that. The terrible calls to Soleil and Chris that I had to make to tell them their mom was gone were met with shock and disbelief. In the coming days and weeks of informing everyone about her passing, it was the common denominator—shock and disbelief. Then crying and gnashing of the teeth from so, so many people.

Nan wanted her body donated to the Gift of Hope group to hopefully help others. I did that. Then her wish as stated in her will was to be cremated. John took over the next day and made those arrangements. Then because I was pretty useless, he began making all the phone calls to government agencies, legal people, banks, utilities, etc. If he were not there, I have no idea what would have happened. Nan also wanted "no funerals, sad gatherings, or anything like that." She wanted a party where everyone would "come together, share good stories, eat good food, and be happy." I asked Soleil to help with that. She took control, and 2 weeks later we had a grand party.

Nancy C. Anda Celebration of Life

O**N S**EPTEMBER **7,** at Calo's Restaurant, between 75 and 100 people showed up to celebrate her life. It was the most perfect day imaginable. Bright sunshine and warm weather. Soleil did a perfect job setting up an altar with candles, flowers, pictures, and a great banner. I was so proud of Soleil and Chris for making this day work so well. Her beloved granddaughter Sarah flew in from New York, and Nan's grandsons and their mom all helped. Women from Nans "women's group" came, as well as all her "Honey Girls," her most treasured friends. People she had worked with 50 years ago, neighbors from our building, and so many others whom I had never even met. My closest friends also came, and my friend Dave from Colorado came after John left a week earlier. Mixed in the inevitable sadness that everyone felt was just what Nan wanted, a true celebration of a dear soul no longer with us. I am certain that, from above, Nancy C. Anda was beaming with light and happiness.

Putting the Pieces Together

A**FTER THE "**ASCENSION PARTY**"** as I prefer to call it, I found myself with much more work to do. With John and Dave gone, returning to their lives, I felt a strong need to understand to the best of my ability, what had just happened to Nan and I. So I started to put the pieces together.

From her stroke on, we each seemed to quickly enter into "coping mechanisms" to help our very survival. The 2nd day after her collapse, she told me, while still totally paralyzed on her left side, "I manifested this. The universe did not do this, God did not do this, no one is to blame for my stroke but me." She was adamant and repeated this several times in the coming months. Her way of coping was, it seemed to me, to disconnect from all negativity and fall back on her greatest strengths, which were her positive attitude and unending belief in goodness in all life. She became a bright, shining star in a rehab center, which was full of depressed and angry stroke patients. Her way of dealing with all the strangers caring for her and handling her body was to be so grateful, so appreciative, and so thankful for ALL help given her that she amazed everyone. Never for one minute after her stroke did I ever see her complain or blame. She shined light and love on everyone!

For me, I fell back into my lifelong comfort zone. I became a "workaholic" again. I was faced with a gigantic challenge to take over all the work that Nan did and my own offerings. I dove into it and took care of all the many challenges that I now faced to keep her supported and cared for and do all the outside tasks. It was my way of surviving.

Upon taking Nan home after 3 months of hospital and rehabs, I morphed into another way of coping. I began making things lighter by allowing myself to push aside hardship with joking, laughing, making up songs for her, and in general becoming a sort of "fool" or "jester," which most often would elicit laughs and happiness from her. I was in essence letting my inner child come out and play, and we both warmly embraced it.

With the help of caregivers, visiting therapists, nurses, and her family and friends stopping by, we settled into a pattern of home rehab and peaceful survival, until my fall, surgery, and rehab. At the end of my rehab, I had a very bad night. A caring, loving nurse from Self Help, named Chorda, came in my room after a long bout of crying freely and depression. She spent an hour with me and talked me through it. When she left, I lay there and asked my spirit, "What should I do?" Shortly, it came into my head like a teletype machine: "To make her as happy as possible—to make her feel as

LOVED as possible." It was perfectly clear: "To make someone happy, one special someone happy!" The love part was easy.

After getting home I did just that. Without telling her or any fanfare, I did that. One day, after her beloved granddaughter Sarah visited us and set up Netflix, we watched *The Secret*, and both of us had incredible realizations at the same time. We both saw how we had manifested our health issues. Her stroke and my heart failure, and from that day on we were both totally on the same page about how to continue on our paths. We both saw at least some of the lessons each of us needed to learn from our downfalls.

The Toltecs (Don Juan, Carlos Castaneda, Ken Roberts, etc.) would say that after a person reached their 70s, they needed to recapitulate their lives. Needed to examine their entire lives and correct errors as best they could, especially related to forgiveness. Nancy began doing exactly that, without coaching or direction from me.

Every afternoon she would nap for several hours in our bedroom with the curtains closed. She loved this routine and her quiet time. It was beautiful for me to watch what began unfolding. I would go in to wake her from her naps, and she often would excitedly tell me of remembering situations with people from childhood on, where the need for resolution involved forgiveness. Sometimes it was her need to forgive someone or them to forgive her, and often the biggest need was for her to forgive herself. I would then coach her through the ways suggested by the Toltec teachers, and she would experience great relief. This was incredibly rewarding for her.

Then in these same nap periods, she had 3 or 4 more dreams with Jesus. In 1 dream he told her to "collect all the love you ever felt for anyone or anything, and hold it in your heart." She would do that often for the rest of her days and always seemed incredibly happy after. In another dream he told her he would take away her burden. These dreams always lifted her up and eased her plight.

In these nap times she also had several dreams with her old teacher, Louise Hays. Louise would talk to her about the stroke and encourage her to persist in her recovery and stay positive. It became for me an honor, privilege, and duty to serve her. Our love kept getting stronger and deeper!!

At this point Nan stated that her lessons were about humility and compassion. Though I felt she already possessed those qualities, she said, "I knew the meaning of those words in my head, but until now I never felt them through my whole being."

In certain ways her stroke had slowed her down from her rapid pace and lifestyle of activities and social interactions. It allowed certain wonderful things to emerge and happen. It made her "smell the roses" so to speak. Her light and love shined brightly to her last day.

For me, I also learned certain lessons, not the least of which was to appreciate life as I had never done, every day, every breath, every heartbeat. It has been incredibly difficult to again lose a loving wife, friend, and soul mate. Now, as before, I will do as I know they both wanted me to do—continue on with life and be the best man I can be. Truly, each of these loving women have made me be a better man. In the end, I feel that Nan's great gift to me has been in helping me to accept love from another, more deeply and truly than I had been able to during my entire life. Thank you for that, dear soul, and for all the happiness, joy, love, and intimate, tender moments you shared with me.

Final Words

IT IS NOW DECEMBER 2019, and John and I shall soon turn this manuscript over to the publishers. As the end of this story and perhaps my time here on Earth approaches, I want to record my final words, thoughts, feelings, ideas, observations, and suggestions, again inspired from within and without.

First, I will speak of love, self-love. For I have learned in my life that if self-love is not part of the equation, then its power is limited. Then love of life, all life, all God's creation. Including the love of family, friends, neighbors, countrymen, etc. Love of God is love of all God's creations. But to me love of self is crucial!

Along with love, hand in hand comes forgiveness. As with love, it should be unconditional and total for all life; and most important is forgiveness of self. These things I have learned though not yet mastered, perhaps before my time is gone? Does this spiritual work ever end?

I have collected the following suggestions and affirmations. Each one stands on its own merit, and might not work for everyone, but they might be helpful if contemplated and experimented with personally.

To do with the army of planetary healers:

◊ There are students, people young and old, all over the planet screaming out, "It is time to stop the rape of Mother Nature. It is time to heal this planet."

◊ Many of these children are indigos, rainbows, and they feel they have come here at this time to do this healing work. Honor and respect them!

◊ Either support and aid the young healers, or step aside.

◊ Discernment is the ability to judge well. Greta and her followers have discernment in spades. Bless them!

Finally, these words to do with heart and love:

◊ Show your love and light. Do not keep them under a bushel, or hidden inside.

◊ Love tempers emotions and negativity and supports self-mastery!

◊ Try as soon as you hear of violence out in the world, go into your heart, surround that place or situation with love and light, image it, feel it—love is immensely powerful!!

◊ Every moment you hold love in your heart, it helps those who are downtrodden and suffering to hold on to their hopes and dreams!

◊ Meet evil with peace and love. Speak to power with truth and conviction!

◊ Ask yourself daily, "Do I think act and speak from love? Or do I allow negativity to pull me out of love?"

◊ Connect with your heart, listen with your heart, live from your heart!

Peace Be Unto You

AND SO, THIS DECADE NOW APPROACHES THE END. The Holy Days soon and then, well, who knows. My wonderful nephew (by my first marriage) and "ANGEL" John and I will soon put this book into cyberspace. Hopefully, it will be of some service or value to someone. My last hopes are for a renewed sense of love and peace to befall this entire planet and all beings and all life. Peace Be Unto You.